Engaging in Community Music

Engaging in Community Music: An Introduction focuses on the processes involved in designing, initiating, executing and evaluating community music practices. Designed for both undergraduate and graduate students in community music programmes and related fields of study alike, this co-authored textbook provides explanations, case examples and 'how-to' activities supported by a rich research base.

The authors have also interviewed key practitioners in this distinctive field, encouraging interviewees to reflect on aspects of their work in order to illuminate best practices within their specialisations and thereby establishing a comprehensive narrative of case study illustrations.

Features:

- a thorough exploration and description of the emerging field of community music;
- succinctly and accessibly written, in a way in which students can relate;
- interviews with 26 practitioners in the US, UK, Australia, Europe, Canada, Scandinavia and South Africa, where non-formal education settings with a music leader, or facilitator, have experienced success;
- case studies from many cultural groups of all ages and abilities;
- research on life-long learning, music in prisons, music and ritual, community music therapy, popular musics, leisure and recreation, business and marketing strategies, online communities – all components of community music.

Lee Higgins is the Director of the International Centre of Community Music in York St John University, UK, and is the current President of the International Society of Music Education (2016–18).

Lee Willingham is Associate Professor in music and directs the Laurier Centre for Music in the Community at Wilfrid Laurier University in Waterloo, Ontario, Canada.

Engaging in Community Music

An Introduction

LEE HIGGINS AND LEE WILLINGHAM

NEW YORK AND LONDON

First published 2017
by Routledge
711 Third Avenue, New York, NY 10017

and by Routledge
2 Park Square, Milton Park, Abingdon, Oxon OX14 4RN

Routledge is an imprint of the Taylor & Francis Group, an informa business

© 2017 Taylor & Francis

The right of Lee Higgins and Lee Willingham to be identified as the authors of this work has been asserted by them in accordance with sections 77 and 78 of the Copyright, Designs and Patents Act 1988.

All rights reserved. No part of this book may be reprinted or reproduced or utilised in any form or by any electronic, mechanical, or other means, now known or hereafter invented, including photocopying and recording, or in any information storage or retrieval system, without permission in writing from the publishers.

Trademark notice: Product or corporate names may be trademarks or registered trademarks, and are used only for identification and explanation without intent to infringe.

Library of Congress Cataloging in Publication Data
Names: Higgins, Lee, 1964– author. Willingham, Lee, author.
Title: Engaging in community music: an introduction /
Lee Higgins and Lee Willingham.
Description: New York; London: Routledge, 2017. Includes bibliographical references and index.
Identifiers: LCCN 2016037949 ISBN 9781138638167 (hardback)
ISBN 9781138638174 (paperback)
Subjects: LCSH: Community music—Instruction and study.
Music—Instruction and study. Music—Social aspects. Community arts projects.
Classification: LCC MT87 .H54 2017 DDC 780.71—dc23
LC record available at https://lccn.loc.gov/2016037949

ISBN: 978-1-138-63816-7 (hbk)
ISBN: 978-1-138-63817-4 (pbk)
ISBN: 978-1-315-63795-2 (ebk)

Typeset in Minion Pro and Helvetica Neue
by Florence Production Ltd, Stoodleigh, Devon, UK

Visit the eResource at www.routledge.com/9781138638174

Contents

List of Figures ix

Foreword xi

Preface xiii

Acknowledgements xvi

Introduction 1
Why Was This Book Written? 2
What Do We Mean by Community Music? 3
Organisation 4
Key Features 6

1 Music And Meaning in Community Contexts 9
A Musical Society; How Meaning Is Constructed 9
Authentic Self-Identity within the Music Community
    Collective 11
Music Meaning, Perception and Mediation 12
Gerard Yun: Meaning Making with Music in Cross-Cultural
    Contexts 14
Patricia Shehan Campbell: Facilitation and Education in Diverse
    Cultural Settings through Applied Ethnomusicology 17
Questions and Topics for Discussion 23
References 24

2 Negotiated Curriculum, Non-Formal and Informal Learning 26

Formal Education as Socialisation 27
Pedagogy for Diverse Community Contexts 27
Gillian Howell: Participatory Music with New Arrivals and
  their Teachers 28
Facilitation as Enabling Music Interactions 31
Informal Learning 32
Non-Formal Learning 33
Brent Rowan: Community Wind Bands – 'Your Best is Good
  Enough!' 34
Intergenerational and Lifelong Learning 36
Andrea Creech: Making Music with Older People 37
Negotiated Curriculum 40
Don Coffman: Building Community through Wind Band 41
Conclusion 44
Questions and Topics for Discussion 45
References 46

3 Inclusive and Empathetic Perspectives 48

Participatory Music as 'Open-Door' Policy 48
Process and Musical Potential 49
Phil Mullen: Community Music Engagement with Children
  and Young People in Challenging Circumstances 50
Culturally Responsive Workshop Characteristics 54
Donald Devito: Engaging with an Adaptive Curriculum for
  Diverse Learning Contexts 56
Inclusive Action in Participatory Music, Personal and Social
  Well-Being 59
Kelly Laurila: Keeper of Song, *Mino Ode Kwewak N'Gamowak*
  (Good Hearted Women Singers) 60
Questions and Topics for Discussion 65
References 66

4 Strategic Leadership and Facilitation 68

Facilitation, Definitions and Applications 68
Rebecca Gross: Finding Voice in the Choir 69
Facilitation, Essential Qualities 72
Chris Bartram: Selecting the Right Tools from a Broad Toolkit
  of Skills and Activities 73
Passion and Building Trusting Relationships (Nikki-Kate Heyes) 76

Dana Monteiro: Building Community through Samba Culture in an Urban High School 77
Multicultural Curriculum and New Kinds of Educational Settings 78
Doug Friesen: Creative Processes with Listening as an Empathetic Act 81
Indicators of Success (Gillian Howell) 83
Conclusion 86
Questions and Topics for Discussion 87
References 88

5 Mindfulness, Activism and Justice 91

Music's Role in Enacting Justice 91
Sing Fires of Justice: Festival of Song and Word 93
Creative Tensions Between Activism and Contemplation 96
Debbie Lou Ludolph: and a Community Choir, Inshallah 97
Action as Risk-taking: Social and Cultural Capital Building 100
Benefits of Civic Engagement 101
Role of Larger Collective in Self-Identity 101
Mary Cohen: Oakdale Prison Choir 102
Questions and Topics for Discussion 104
References 105

6 Wholeness and Well-Being 108

Participatory Music Making as 'Spaces' Promoting Health 108
Multi-Dimensions of Well-Being 109
Nick Rowe: Converge 110
Community Music and Therapy (Community Music Therapy) 112
Phoene Cave: Freedom through Singing and Holistic Practices .. 113
Addressing Mental Health through Musicking (Way Ahead, Simon Procter) 118
The People We Are: The Intergenerational Choir 119
Conclusion 123
Questions and Topics for Discussion 124
References 126

7 Culture of Inquiry 129

Role of Research in Emerging Field of Community Music 129
Examples of Graduate Research Projects 130
Dave Camlin: Informed Practice at the Sage Gateshead 131

Science-Art Dualisms (Elliot Eisner) 136
Examples of Research Processes in Doctoral Programmes 137
Four Hypothetical Research Vignettes 139
Questions and Topics for Discussion 141
References 142

8 Careers and Management **145**

Exploring Relationships Between Music and Business: How Are
   They Mutually Beneficial? 145
Project Building 146
Stephen Preece: Developing a Systematic Business Plan for a
   Start-Up Project 147
The Grand River Jazz Society 149
Pete Moser: More Music 151
Alicia de Banffy-Hall: Strategic Development of Community
   Music in Munich 155
Nikki-Kate Heyes: SoundLINCS 159
Partnerships Are Key 160
Conclusion 162
Questions and Topics for Discussion 163
References 164

9 Ways Forward **166**

Engaging in Community Music: Locating Place and Purpose 166
Contextual Chapter Summaries 166
Qualities of Community Music Facilitators 170
Intersections and Future Pathways 171
Community Characteristics of Belonging 174
Questions and Topics for Discussion 175
References 176

Contributor Biographies **177**

Index **187**

Figures

I.1	Foundational Principles of Community Music Diagram	5
1.1	Gerard Yun, Shakuhachi	14
1.2	Patricia Shehan Campbell and Wagogo Musician	21
2.1	Gillian Howell Music Making with ELS Students	29
2.2	New Horizons, Guelph, Canada	35
3.1	*Mino Ode Kwewak N'Gamowak*	60
3.2	Good Hearted Women Singers Benefit Concert	64
4.1	Dana Monteiro and Samba School	78
4.2	Samba School	80
4.3	Doug Friesen Workshop	82
5.1	Sing Fires of Justice	94
5.2	Debbie Lou Ludolph and Inshallah	98
5.3	Mary Cohen, Oakdale Prison Choir	102
6.1	Communitas Choir	111
6.2	Phoene Cave	114
6.3	Intergenerational Choir	119
7.1	Dave Camlin, Human Music Project, Sage Gateshead	132
7.2	Dave Camlin, Sing 4 Water Project	135
8.1	Stephen Preece – Jazz Room	149
8.2	Jazz Room	151
8.3	Pete Moser – More Music	152
8.4	More Music Hothouse	153
8.5	More Music Lantern Festival	154
8.6	Munich Philharmonic Community Music, Photo by Andrea Huber	157
8.7	Munich Philharmonic Community Music, Photo by Andrea Huber	158
8.8	Insert Group Star, soundLINCS	160

8.9 Business Model Canvas 163
9.1 Networking and Partnerships 169
9.2 Facilitator Qualities 170
9.3 Intersections 172

Foreword

Few would argue that there is a palpable groundswell in community music worldwide. Those of us who have been immersed in the field's recent developments have certainly observed a substantial increase and deepening of projects, courses, programmes and scholarship within a diverse range of cultural contexts. These tangible developments have fuelled a growing appetite for new and dynamic resources that both respond to and propel these international developments. *Engaging in Community Music: An Introduction* quenches that appetite in abundance. It promises to satisfy those readers seeking to develop new perspectives and insights, those seeking inspiration and frameworks and, above all, those looking to further their knowledge and practice in this growing field of community music.

If I were to draw up a wish list of the community music leaders from around the world – whose diverse perspectives are needed in order for the field to continue on this growth trajectory – the names that appear in this book would be on it. Insights from these world leaders have been skilfully woven into a compelling narrative that invites readers on a dynamic journey. This ambitious undertaking has been carefully crafted by two of the world's leading community music practitioners, thinkers and educators. The different experiences and cultural insights that Lee Higgins and Lee Willingham bring to this resource, coupled with their leading roles as community music educators, position them perfectly for this task. As such, the co-authors are able to articulate the values and processes, outcomes and impact of community music with an evocative and authentic voice.

As the field continues to mature, and as this groundswell generates momentum to further growth worldwide, new learnings will emerge from the interfaces of practice and research, process and outcome, and the places where community music collides with other fields and cultural contexts. At such interfaces, there are likely to be healthy tensions that challenge the field to move in new and uncharted directions. This book embraces these complexities and possibilities, featuring a dynamic interplay between these different perspectives in a way we have rarely seen in other community music resources.

The core themes explored in this textbook acknowledge the realities and diverse contexts in which community musicians are now working across the globe, paying particular attention to issues of social justice, cultural activism and well-being. Of significance is the text's discussion of the real-world practicalities of building careers in this field. Those of us working in community music – and those in higher education in particular – have detected in the next generation of community musicians a real thirst for such advice and resources to help navigate the rapidly changing landscape in which they will soon be working.

Engaging in Community Music will undoubtedly become a must-have resource and necessary companion for many community music leaders, educators, students and workers in the field. As more and more community music programmes and courses develop in higher education across the world, this book will provide students with a source they can return to for inspiration time and time again, a tool for reflection on practice and scholarship. Not only will readers take away from this book inspiration and ideas of current best practices, but they will also garner a strong sense of the possibilities and potential of what is emerging on the horizon of community music.

Brydie-Leigh Bartleet

Queensland Conservatorium Research Centre
Griffith University (Australia)

Former Chair of the ISME Community
Music Activity (CMA) Commission

Founding Member of the Asia Pacific
Community Music Network

Preface

We observe on a daily basis the phenomenon of people engaged with music making. Whether it be a teacher working in a public school classroom setting, a music facilitator sharing songs and stories with seniors, a church choir or a rock band organised by a group of enthusiastic youth, people are participating in music as part of their everyday lives. Both authors of this book have adult-aged children who are engaged in creating and performing music in a variety of genres. We experience the pride of having parented those, such as Esme Brydie, singer-songwriter, or Geoff Willingham, guitarist, songwriter and producer, who exemplify in their own lives the richness of living with music as a core component of who they are and what they value. Their engagement in music is not just for observation or contemplation, it is active, participatory music and vital to the very identity of the person submerged in the action. We firmly believe that there is an appetite for the study of music that is intentionally participant-centred, inclusive and diverse, and in this book we explore these practices and values that ultimately add cultural and social capital to both individuals and their communities.

Community music has evolved from a grassroots practice into a discipline within the larger domain of music education – a field of study that is coming of age as it is finding place in higher education programmes and arts policy. The ascendency of community music in the academy is a result of a number of factors, including the widening of perspectives to address broader societal issues, cultural diversity and sustainability along with the role of music as an activist force and contributor to the health and well-being of its participants. There is considerable irony in this newfound interest in community music where universities and conservatoires, once bastions of privilege, seek common philosophical, moral and pedagogical ground with community music, initially a grassroots movement in resistance to those institutions that insisted on a particular version of formalised music education.

It is our intention that what we have termed 'community music practice' be illustrated in such a way that creative, cross-cultural and inter generational engagement be emblematic of the contexts in which the reader identifies. It is therefore important that these practices be firmly grounded in community music foundational principles as exampled from the wide tapestry of projects taking place across our planet daily. *Engaging in Community Music: An Introduction* provides the framework to become actively involved in facilitating the community music practice.

Organisation and Features

As collaborative authors, bearing in mind that we each live and work on different continents in very different contexts, we have set out with a single purpose to present a focused, consistent narrative in *Engaging in Community Music: An Introduction* that supports courses of study, scholarship and research in a wide range of music settings. Each chapter features the work and philosophies of professional practitioners whose wisdom, skills and strategies are deeply valued within their own communities and beyond. Music leaders, whether in schools, community settings or other locales will glean practical and applicable tools for enhancing their own practice.

Each chapter is based upon a foundational principle and within each theoretical frame are links to the action and application of the broader idea. For example, in addressing making music with older people, case studies are provided of effective practice, such as group music making in wind bands and choirs. Through the concept of inclusivity and hospitality, we present examples of culturally responsive engagement with children and youth as well as those who find themselves in disadvantaged situations. In the careers and management chapter, we provide a business canvas model to help mobilise ideas into action using processes we have observed to be effective. While not offering a 'how-to' manual in every situation, the reader is encouraged to extract applicable ideas to move forward in developing their own music engagement and leadership.

Each chapter includes topics for discussion that serve both to deepen the ideas presented and extend discussions to more closely reflect the contexts readers either currently work in or aspire to do so. Illustrations enhance the narrative text, and information about each of our contributors includes a biography and contact information. A useful reference list and practical index help sort through sources and topics as the reader finds their own narrative through the various themes.

As a textbook, *Engaging in Community Music: An Introduction* is a resource that instructors may find valuable as the spine of a course outline. Themes and issues addressed open pathways and connections to a myriad of related topics and issues and lay out a set of guiding principles for the study of music and music leadership from within a host of contemporary contexts. Valuable as a primary text, or as supplemental material in virtually any area of study that engages people with music, this book provides an interconnected web of people, ideas and networks.

Undergraduate and graduate students will develop a working familiarity with those professionals currently leading community music practice in the world today. Through exposure to their approaches to practice, readers become acquainted with real-world music leadership. The writing is intentionally accessible and not excessively lengthy, and is ultimately intended to stimulate thinking and action as musicians face the changing world of professional practice.

Engaging in Community Music: An Introduction is a resource that encompasses wide and diverse perspectives on community music practice for the twenty-first century. Yet as its boundaries are wide, it demands of the reader a personal engagement that brings a robust depth to the understanding.

The authors appreciate your feedback and especially welcome examples of how *Engaging in Community Music: An Introduction* has found a place within your community of practice. As a continuation of this project, collecting other examples of effective practice will help enhance the work about which so many of us feel passionate.

Acknowledgements

The kernel of this book begun when I met Constance Ditzel at a College Music Society meeting in Cambridge, Massachusetts in 2013. I'd like to thank Constance for the encouragement to make this project happen and her flexibility in the occasional change of direction. I would especially like to thank my co-collaborator, Lee Willingham, without whom, of course, this book would not exist. A great working partnership on both sides of the Atlantic and a growing friendship fuelled by good IPAs.

I would like to sincerely thank those that have lent their voices to this project, in order of appearance: Gerard Yun, Patricia Shehan Campbell, Gillian Howell, Brent Rowan, Andrea Creech, Don Coffman, Phil Mullen, Donald DeVito, Kelly Laurila Rebecca Gross, Chris Bartram, Dana Monteiro, Doug Friesen, Debbie Lou Ludolph, Mary Cohen, Nick Rowe, Phoene Cave, Dave Camlin, Pete Moser, Alicia de Banffy-Hall and Nikki-Kate Heyes.

I would like to acknowledge Chole Queen, a student researcher from York St John University who did some preliminary interviewing early in the project. To my family, Michelle, Holly, Esme and George, who are continually supportive of my endeavours. Finally, a shout-out to the Download crew, Tom, Gary and Phil – a certain type of community music engagement.

Lee Higgins
York, England
9 July 2016

I am indebted to a vast host of those who have contributed to my own understanding and practice as a music educator and scholar. Teachers, mentors and professors, too many to name, have shaped and guided my journey to the present, and continue to inspire and open up pathways to the ever-changing present.

To my colleagues at Wilfrid Laurier University, and especially to the Dean of the Faculty of Music, Glen Carruthers, I am deeply grateful for the encouragement and support as community music has found a solid home under his vision and leadership. I acknowledge especially two colleagues and dear friends, Debbie Lou Ludolph and Gerard Yun, who have been tireless advocates of community music and have shown the way in their own eclectic practices of facilitating participatory music making. Thank you for encouragement, advice and loyal support.

Over almost four decades of teaching, I have encountered the best students one could hope for. Their honesty, creativity and courage have created conditions for my own growth and development. I am grateful to those for whom I have had the privilege to teach.

It has been a sheer pleasure to collaborate with Lee Higgins, whose sharp intellect and focus are matched with an abundant well of energy and confidence. This project has been truly one of sharing, discovering and developing new ways of thinking, reimagining and creating, and I am indebted deeply to Lee for his generosity of spirit and his commitment to scholarship and quality.

This book presents the voices of the most respected leaders and practitioners of community music in the world. We have become better acquainted and the result of these connections has deepened my personal admiration for the incredible work that is being done to enhance the communities of music makers globally.

Most importantly, I am grateful for my family . . . the community of music makers that I name as my parents, children and partner. To Ted and Ruth who still take pride in their son's musical enterprises, to the most interesting musicians I know, Geoff, Jessica, Leah and Nora – thank you for always acting as though you have interest in my work! And to my wonderful partner, Eva Mezo, whose often challenging but always inspiring responses to my ideas continue to propel me forward. As family, we are community and to you I owe a great deal.

Lee Willingham
Waterloo, Ontario
9 July 2016

Introduction

Community music as a field of practice and research has been gaining steady momentum over the last decade. During this time, a large increase in practices, courses, programmes and research as well as publications in forms of books, chapters and journal articles has become evident. This growth in practice and scholarship has also been reflected in organizations for community music, such as the International Society for Music Education's Community Music Activities commission as well as the development of new networks such as the Asia Pacific Community Music Network. Within this context, new debates about the intersections of practice, pedagogy, research and ethics have been emerging and new voices have begun broadening the agenda to consider settings where community music is engaging in social justice, political activism, peace-making, health and well-being and online engagement, amongst other fields (Bartleet & Higgins, 2017). The interest in this subject has meant an increase of scholarship and academic courses and consequently significantly expanded the amount of people engaging in community music. These new voices, agendas and contexts indicate that the field is continuing to grow, diversify and mature.

Set within a broad notion of music education, community musicians place emphasis on inclusive musical participation and as an expression of cultural democracy. As a conceptual idea and a mode of empowerment, a sharing of values among the many cultural groups, musicians who work within the framework of cultural democracy are focused upon the practical concerns of making and creating music and musical opportunities for people of all ages and abilities. As an example of non-formal education and learning, community music reflects a bottom-up or negotiated curriculum formation that involves a music leader, or facilitator, in continue dialogue with the people they work with.

Why Was This Book Written?

This book has been written because we believe there is now a strong appetite for music making that is consciously inclusive, participatory and culturally diverse. With around 40 years of professional activity, there is a wide range of exemplars illustrating worldwide community music practice and it is our intention to bring the key elements together in a series of outlining frameworks and individual case studies. This, we hope, will provide a much needed resource into perspectives and processes of what is now a growing music education practice globally. We have not set out to produce an academic book, in the sense of creating an argument backed up by prior scholarship, but rather, our challenge has been to write something with a broader appeal. What we mean by this is that the purpose of this book is to contribute to community music's growth and development through the expanding education and training opportunities on offer throughout institutions worldwide. As a text book, *Engaging in Community Music: An Introduction* supports the academic literature and in return the research and scholarship support the material in this book.

Engaging in Community Music is, then, a single narrative co-authored effort. This means that the book has a focused through line and a consistent narrative essential for a textbook. We do, however, recognise that our experience in community music is limited to the particular contexts in which we have worked, and importantly, our cultural, social, political and economic encounters. This is why we provide space for professional community musicians to offer their 'voices' and thus their wisdom, experience and expertise. This strategy has enabled us to develop a book that gathers expertise from those currently working as practitioners in a variety of environments while maintaining a clear narrative positioned upon an uncluttered perspective of community music. As a text for community music leaders, educators, students and current professionals, our target audiences are those who provide leadership in community music programmes and courses in higher education, students who are engaged in such learning at universities, colleges and conservatoires, current professionals working in the field as well as those working in overlapping practices such as music therapy and music education.

What Do We Mean by Community Music?

The question 'What exactly is community music?' is a complex one. Community music, by its very nature, defies tightly constructed definitions. As a human practice, making music is as diverse and colourful as the food we eat, the clothes we wear or the languages we speak. Community music is fluid, dynamic and its approaches to practice are designed for moving targets and flexible purposing. Community music practice embraces all types of learning, including informal learning and non-formal education as well as formal instructional strategies:

> Indeed, it might be argued that one of the most common and enduring features of the different definitions of CM [community music] put forth over the years has been a certain ambiguity, characteristic of the term's effort to speak to and encompass a broad array of activities, processes and practices.
> (Brown, Higham, & Rimmer, 2014, p. 10)

Often, it is easier to describe the characteristics and domains of community music or to describe its practices, than to confine it to a concise definition. Lee Higgins (2012) addresses the challenge of attempting to situate a set of practices by concluding that community music is 'a musical practice that is an active intervention between a music leader or facilitator and participants' (p. 21). In the broadest of strokes, this quasi-definition serves well as a starting point to define our roles in community music; we facilitate or intervene through the practices and processes of music with our participants, and in turn, participants are encouraged to contribute to the creative music process with their whole self, body, mind and heart.

With this in mind, what we mean by community music within this book is as follows.

Community musicians intentionally set out to create spaces for inclusive and participatory musical doing. This impulse comes from a belief that music making is a fundamental aspect of the human experience and is therefore an intrinsic and foundational part of human culture and society. As a perspective, those that work this way do so with a commitment to musical expression as a crucible for social transformation, emancipation, empowerment and cultural capital. As a broad approach to music education, community musicians place emphasis on conversation, negotiation, collaboration and cultural democracy. Community music is, therefore, an interventionist approach between a music leader or facilitator and those participants who wish to be involved.

As a supplement to this statement, the following five keywords will help as orientation.

People: Music is one of the distinctive aspects of being human. Placing participants alongside community musicians as co-authors and collaborators encourages journeying together towards transformative musical experiences.

Places: The context is paramount and becomes a pivot for music making, critical inquiry and conversation.

Participation: Creating opportunities for active music participation forms the heart of community music. This means those that work in these ways seek ways to increase accessible pathways that lead towards meaningful musical engagement.

Inclusion: Community music emphasises the importance of making connections among people, across issues and over time. By encouraging expansive and ongoing frameworks for interaction, community musicians seek to create engaged populations and communities of practice.

Diversity: Integral to community music is the celebration of difference that can only take place in a safe, positive and nurturing environment.

These five words, people, places, participation, inclusion and diversity, have provided us with some secure footing from which to develop this text. To some extent, these are our foundation stones helping us select the illustrations of practice and offering a guide to the plethora of work often described using the words music and community.

Organisation

The organisation of *Engaging in Community Music* captures the sentiments outlined above by presenting a framework or 'spine' upon which the musician is invited to think through how the ideas might effectively be woven into the context they work in. Rather than a 'manual' or 'how-to' instruction book, *Engaging in Community Music* provides insights and examples taken directly from the field. Metaphorically we have set out to provide some skeletal frames as an invitation for the community music reader to add flesh whilst the sinew and muscle of facilitation and the context of non-formal education provides shared common principles that cut across most community music practice. The following figure (I.1), first produced for the

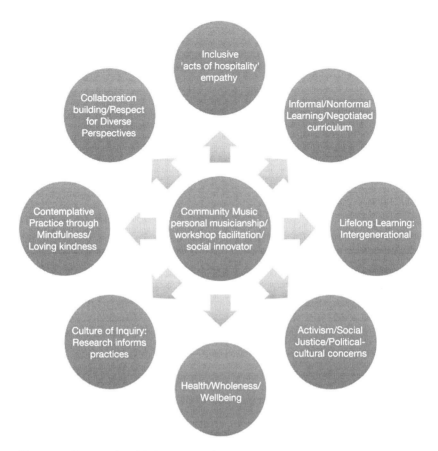

Figure I.1 Foundational Principles of Community Music Diagram

development of a Master programme in community music, has acted as a guide for structuring this book.

Here you can see that radiating from the central point, community music is understood to reflect eight domains. These areas have informed our chapter headings and thus the way we have gone about both organizing this book and structuring the conversations we have had with those musicians we interviewed. In the final chapter we revisit this, refining the ideas and reimagining the figure, by drawing upon the narratives of those who contributed their story and experiences through the case studies.

Key Features

As a text book, we designed the chapters to be flexible, responsive and dynamic. Conceptual considerations such as working within and through issues of social justice, cultural activism and well-being are explored as important issues of the day and the realpolitik pertaining to careers and management and the growing culture of scholarship amplify what it means to be a working professional. Supporting our narrative and enhancing the text throughout, each chapter is enriched by contributors who are active in both the international discourse and the practice of community music. Chosen for their contribution to the development of cutting-edge techniques and scholarship, these contributors are representative of the international community music field.

Outlined below are the key features that provide entry points into each chapter. We have conceived these features as portals, ways of moving in and out, over and above, up and down the material pathways through which community music can be experienced.

- The through-line **frame** adds the connective tissue between the individual case studies and serves to contextualise the thoughts, practical ideas and reflections of those that spoke to us.
- The **activity** examples provided by some of our community musicians are there to stimulate the development and growth of participatory music making. These are not fixed instructional strategies, but rather, suggestions or stems from which the facilitator may personalise and contextualise according to the needs and goals of the local community musicians.
- **Reflection, mindfulness and contemplation** are intentionally infused in the practice of community music. Empathy and generosity of spirit encourage risk-taking in a safe environment. The facilitator is reminded that in all things, respect for the individual is paramount. The default position of 'yes' can result in challenges for the community, yet community music as 'an act of hospitality' is reflected in the claims that this book makes, and the practices that it provides.
- **Lessons from community music** can be applied to other educational contexts. For example: How can the school classroom reflect the principles and characteristics of community music? How can the studio teacher build relationships that enrich the music experiences of the students by incorporating community music values? How can non-formal and informal pedagogies enhance the educational worth of music

participation? And, how can community music principles be applied to intergenerational and life-long learning?
- **Inquiry and research** are integral to ongoing practice. Overarching interests in a variety of 'what if?' and 'how might?' questions spawn investigations that provide new insights, deepen processes and advance personal musicianship. A 'culture of inquiry' is one where curiosity is mobilised into action, where complex concepts are honoured and pursued.
- **Activism and justice** are at the core of community music. In each facilitation experience, how can peace and justice values be reflected? Social concerns are oft best expressed and clarified through human music participation. How can this be so in the reader's perspectives?
- **Health, wholeness and well-being** are top-of-mind in today's communities. Music is vital for many in maintaining a network of friends and in providing an expressive outlet for all sorts of life conditions. Community music addresses the whole being, head, heart and hand. Not only are there neuro-cognitive benefits, we know from prior research and personal experience that music making in community brings many socio-physical benefits. How does this frame the practice?
- **Questions and topics for discussion** are provided to evoke discourse and critical thinking. Framing topics that guide the more specific ones include but are not limited to such thinking as who is my community? What does community music sound like/look like in my context? What are some cultural resources available to a community music facilitator? And, what do I need to know/understand/do to move forward?

In conclusion, *Engaging in Community Music* provides readers with a wide range of ideas and practical examples located within a breadth of contexts and differing environments. As community music activities are enhanced, both at the local grassroots level and in a global, international context, cultural capital is being built. Communities are enriched and individuals' creative potentials are developed. In fact, it might be said that in practice, community music is a form of social innovation to the extent that its activities provide a catalyst for 'an initiative, product, process, or programme that profoundly changes the basic routines, resource and authority flows or beliefs of any social system'.[1] Or further, community music in practice may be considered as 'an idea that works for the public good . . . progressive-minded . . . willing to make systemic change'.[2] Whatever community music means to you the reader, it is the authors' wish that this resource will advance your own understanding, skills and confidence as a community musician and in some way strengthen your practice as you journey through this important work.

Notes

1 http://sig.uwaterloo.ca/about-the-waterloo-institute-for-social-innovation-and-resilience-wisir
2 Ryerson University roundtable on Social Innovation and Social Justice, Dr. Laura Mae Lindo.

References

Bartleet, B.-L., & Higgins, L. (Eds.). (2017). *The Oxford handbook of community music*. New York: Oxford University Press.

Brown, T., Higham, B., & Rimmer, M. (2014). *Whatever happened to community music?* Swindon: AHRC Research Network Report.

Higgins, L. (2012). *Community music: In theory and in practice*. New York: Oxford University Press.

Chapter 1
Music and Meaning in Community Contexts

[. . .] music can never be a thing in itself, and [that] all music is folk music, in the sense that music cannot be transmitted or have meaning without associations between people.

John Blacking[1]

If everyone is born musical, then everyone's musical experience is valid.

Christopher Small[2]

Perhaps now, more than ever before, we can consider ourselves to be living in a musical society. We can also assert that virtually everyone is, to some degree, musically educated by means of a variety of community-based contributors along with the ever-increasing role that media plays informally in individual musical lives (Willingham & Bartel, 2008). Studies reveal clearly that citizens who claim to have some musical understanding or experience did not become musical primarily in school.[3] We ask then, what is the role of music in peoples' lives, where and how do they derive meaning from those musical experiences and to what degree does meaning with, in and through music making inform self-identity? Most importantly, what is the role of music in community music practice?

A Musical Society; How Meaning Is Constructed

Ethnographic research on the ways humans make sense of musical life experiences provides clues as to how both an individual and social construction of meaning occurs (DeNora, T. 2000, Green, L. 2002, Finnegan, R., 2007).

There are many shades to the concept of meaning, and especially when that concept is contextualised within the dimensions of community music engagement and practice. Some have defined meaning as construing or interpreting experience or 'to give it coherence' (Mezirow, 1991, p. 4). Music and its relationship to memory is the focus of much neuroscience research with studies on how music influences memory, the hypothesis being that the very act of listening to and playing music may strengthen one or more of our memory systems (Jensen, 2000; Zatorre, Evans, & Meyer, 1994). Music education philosopher Bennett Reimer (2003) suggests experiences in music offer an alternative reality and an alternative way of being. Music can bring an intuitive and emotional sense of human experiences to a conscious level, opening possibilities to alternative ways of knowing (Brookfield, 2002).

Constructivist theorists support the notion that individuals construct meaning as the result of prior experiences, interests, social connections and where they are situated. The social and cultural experiences contribute to the construction of meaning where it is not necessarily inherently found in the music itself (Froehlich, 2007). From a constructivist perspective, music leadership is viewed as a shared process between facilitators and musicians. The organizational structure is flattened and integrated, and participants share common values and purposes. The interactive nature of a community promotes continuous improvement, built on the theoretical constructs of human relations and systems theory and ecological thought (Lambert et al., 2002). It is assumed that knowledge, or in this case innate musicianship, exists within the participant and in emphasizing the social nature of learning in a community music setting, multiple outcomes are encouraged and human growth is an imperative. Constructivist theory is touched on briefly in Chapter 2 where connections to informal and non-formal learning practices are made.

Among the various perspectives in the discussion of music and meaning is the notion that musical works and musical participation have the capacity to 'engage people's beliefs about deeply important matters: about culturally shared expressions of emotion, culture-specific traditions of artistry, community values, or musical characterizations of socially shared events, personalities, or issues' (Elliott, 1995, p. 205). Further, it is suggested that while such experiences are unique to each individual, there is a 'kind of magnetic field that brings people or different musical understanding [. . .] together' (Elliott, 1995, p. 205). This leads to the concept of music and meaning in a socially inclusive community context.

Psychologist Mihaly Csikszentmihalyi (1990) reminds us that

> we have conceived of individual human beings as separate from one another. We have invented abstraction and analysis- . . . it is this differen-

tiation that has produced science, technology and the unprecedented power of mankind [sic] to build up and to destroy its environment (p. 240).

However, the integration into accepting a cooperative role, rather than a competitive individualised one, is to realise that community-based societies are built with systems dependent upon shared values and guidelines. It is in this context that we are reminded that 'the problem of meaning will then be resolved as the individual's purpose merges with the universal flow' (Csikszentmihalyi, 1990, p. 240). Community music, then, offers a space where ideas and practices may grow from the bottom up, where there is a democratic and inclusive culture that listens, respects and acts on the individual voices of those who make up that community.

Authentic Self-Identity within the Music Community Collective

Community music practice is built on the premise that everybody has the right and inherent ability to create and participate in music. There is an emphasis on a variety of musical genres and cultural practices that reflect the uniqueness and/or diversity of the community makeup. People are inexorably linked to their music. Lee Willingham's (2001) ethnographic study of a community of singers revealed that personal identity is a large part of personal meaning making and is often linked to a musical practice. The nature of the relationship and identifying with the music must be an authentic one, one that is true to self (Trilling, 1972).

There is no space here to delve deeply into the various forms of authenticity as addressed by scholars, however philosopher Søren Kierkegaard's three levels of aesthetic, ethical and religious ethics, where he derives from these the concept of the universal rule of ethics (Miller, 1993), are germane to this discussion. In this perspective, an authentic existence involves looking directly at one's life while not evading the universal rules of ethical practice, that is, community expectations and norms. One who is holistically authentic (Emerson, 1965) is one who acknowledges the link between the inner life and other beings.

The larger discussion around authenticity and self, then, considers the group and how one is authentically true to self while adhering to the values and expected norms of the society or community (Taylor, 1991). Based on he influential thinking of philosopher Jean-Jacques Rousseau, this notion of authenticity can be thought of as listening to one's inner voice. Taylor goes on to describe the idea of authentic self according to Charles Rousseau as the inner voice or an inner virtue that speaks to us in the language of nature; a voice of reason that emerges to one who understands their identity within society. The voice can be drowned out by all sorts of interferences, especially when influenced and dominated by the opinions of others.[4] True authenticity calls on us to be true to ourselves, our very special and original selves, an aspect that is interwoven and connected to our creative aesthetic life, and that would include our relationship with music (Taylor, 1991). And it is here, within the shared values of community in a music context, that individuals can find common ground.

The focus of this book is on community music engagement, on developing a practice that is true to one's authentic self and grounded in foundational principles. Educator and activist Parker Palmer (2007) suggests that a true sign that one is following an authentic vocational call is deep gladness. When one devotes one's self to something that does not flow from within, from the person's very nature, it is not integral or true. It does not enhance the community or build social cohesion. This does not exclude the challenges or the difficult days, but to be true to self is to be in a place where even the challenges will gladden, since they pose the kinds of problems that bring personal growth and deepen understanding. In fact, the only means by which we can wholly participate in community is to work from the voice within, the voice that 'invites me to honour the nature of my true self' (Palmer, 2007, p. 30).

Music Meaning, Perception and Mediation

As we embark on this journey of community music engagement, it is useful in the interest of meaning making to address how we perceive music and its value. In western (often referred to as 'classical') traditions, the practice is to honour what is transportable with notation providing a storage and retrieval system. What is not readily transportable is the context. Previously composed music can be retrieved and presented without contextual aspects, creating an arbitrated or mediated meaning.

Classical music is highly mediated. Consider this: In 1835, Chopin plays an idea on the piano (unmediated other than by the technology of the piano itself), he notates his idea with pencil and paper (storage system), the notated idea is re-created (score serves as retrieval system) by a young pianist in Canada in 2015, now mediated by 180 years of time, by historical study of performance practice, by more advanced piano technology and by interpretation through the human expression of a person influenced by twenty-first century culture. Our modern understanding of the context in which the idea was germinated and developed can only be inferred through historical writings and more recently various interpretations through recorded performances. There is a further mediation, that of the listener. Composers are the creators, musician performers and the audience listeners. (Of course, composers and performers are also intentional listeners, but for different reasons than audiences). From the idea pouring out of Chopin through his fingers on the piano, to the re-enacting of these ideas in modern time, the ideas themselves are exposed to a myriad of other influences and distractions. The sound in and of itself is not the whole package, and without the cultural context, the meaning is obfuscated or possibly even lost (Takemitsu, 1995). Perhaps this is one of the keys to the endurance of significant composed musical works where, to a great extent, the meaning of the music is often determined by complexities of formal structures and internal references rather than the one-to-one relationship between creator and listener.

By contrast, community music practice often takes place with a single person (facilitator) intervening with a group where the active music making includes shared listening, shared improvising and performing where leadership roles are semi-mediated, rather than autocratically directed. The facilitator evokes, engages, provides ideas and imagines with the musicians. In this context, roles become fluid, and the sharing is deeply personal rather than ritualised.

Unmediated music is embodied within the music makers and transmitted or shared directly with co-music makers or listeners. For example, an improvised piece is essentially untransportable. It is created in and for the place, the time, the individuals involved and the precise venue where it is shared. Even in recording an improvised event the direct meaning that is derived by those present can be considered diluted or without the original impact. In oral music traditions, as in Canadian Aboriginal communities, musicians seek to engage in unmediated practice where songkeepers share songs of tradition and meaning exactly as they were taught by elders. (See Kelly Laurila, Good Hearted Women Singers, Chapter 6). Music that is meaningful within its own culture or place (e.g. South African freedom songs, Irish folk music, Quebec fiddle music, Brazilian sambas) loses aspects of its context when performed, for example, in a concert hall by ensembles not connected to the culture. Witness Celtic music, or African-American spirituals arranged by composers and performed by ensembles in formal concert settings, ignoring the festive atmosphere of a *celidh* (kitchen party) or an oppressive work setting where the spiritual provided respite and hope for the slave labourers.

Gerard Yun
Meaning Making with Music in Cross-Cultural Contexts

Gerard facilitates participants in creating elaborate pieces of sonic art in cross-cultural settings such as workshops, schools, choirs and in multi-faith and social justice events. Although the forms of music he works with may seem highly diverse or even incompatible (e.g. First Nations drumming and chanting combined with a pipe organ and Christian hymn), he works to facilitate their collaboration through finding and exploiting similarities, commonalities and musical parallels.

In this work, Gerard believes that he must be in an open, meditative state. This is the opposite of a type 'A' personality that inhabits the typical ensemble podium. The sense he experiences is less of leading and more of mediating. In the process, Gerard believes that he is engaged in healing the musical textures by connecting or reconnecting them together. This is a process of facilitating the connection and moving towards the expression of the commonality through the music, rather than maintaining the musical differences.[5]

The goal in Gerard's work is connectedness. How can the music be connected without altering the distinctiveness of various practices of musical production or form? The challenge is in maintaining that cultural distinctive-

Figure 1.1 Gerard Yun, Shakuhachi

ness while making musical structures adequately permeable to provide connection to a variety of sonic systems.

He uses the shakuhachi (Japanese bamboo flute) or the voice because of the flexibility with regard to timbre, pitch and intensity. The sound becomes a bridge or missing puzzle piece to the linkage between the various musics or groups. This type of leadership requires openness and a process of deep listening.[6] The success of working with diverse groups is dependent upon Gerard's ability to connect personally, creatively in a deep, open form of musical empathy. There is a huge meditative and spiritual component – the opposite of his normal teaching state. Rather than standing in front and pulling, or behind and pushing, Gerard feels he is in the middle and is creating a relationship as the mediator between music and participants.

As he steps back from the normal focused perspective, the view widens in such a way that the space becomes larger than the sum of the participating groups. This space is needed to hold and contain the work being revealed through the process of creative participation. This process is based on the facilitator's internal workings where inward sight and intra-personal responses are leading the process. There is nothing external happening for much of it. Gerard states that there 'is a need to be extremely attentive, requiring interaction and movement'.

Spontaneous creativity derives from tremendous openness to elements, sounds, mood changes all at an instant's notice. These are the raw materials to create connection.

An example of the various sequential stages of a workshop is as follows:

1. An event with more than one group or musical practice starts by listening to each other. Each group sings or plays an excerpt of their musical genre.
2. Seek to find one common aspect of the music. It might even be humming or singing one note together, filling that space in unison and unity. This common moment provides a start for building a musical relationship.
3. 'Play' begins as if mixing and matching . . . play with sounds and musics, working them back and forth in a musical jam session.
4. Eventually collaborative ideas emerge that the participants find compelling. This is demonstrated by body language, interaction and visible levels of engagement. At this stage, participants begin to offer encouragement to each other to sing, play and listen. A decentralised form of facilitation, the participants begin to take the lead.
5. Voluntarily, using musical empathy, the participants begin to adjust their musicking. This adjusting must come from the participants, not from the facilitator. (Gerard comments that if he asks them to change something

about their musical style he gets compliance and it might even instantly sound better. However, the level of collaborative engagement may be lost; they become engaged with the leader more than with each other.)
6. By using the shakuhachi or the voice, a sonic bridge is created between two or more forms of music, usually in the form of some sort of long note.[7] The bridging of forms may be framed in ambiguous or even more specific harmonious or heterophonic relationships, such as pentatonics or a rhythmic pattern.
7. Gerard uses silence intentionally to create attentive listening spaces. This is different than asking them to be quiet. Rather, it is more like playing silence as part of the creative texture.
8. Up until this point, very little text has been implemented. Adding text, even one word, or a nonsense syllable unifies the sonic shape. Vowels emerge. If participating groups work in different languages, space can be created to accommodate them.
9. The conclusion is the creating of a 'sensible' piece of music that has shape and structure. By drawing upon the various aspects of the creative process, the summative experience is a presentable work that sounds and feels like a piece of music or, at the least, a large musical phrase.

Meaning is constructed, depending upon social, cultural and physical contexts. Common musical experience is a uniting, connecting factor. A connected context is created that is by definition diverse, and multicultural, and it may only exist for that brief time. Historically, societies would build social unity by identifying common enemies. In contrast, this process builds unity through common experience, creating a new socio-musical context that allows for meaning to be freely volunteered and created without it being mediated or dictated.

This participant-constructed meaning is most deeply revealed in post- event comments, conversations, reflective journaling and blogging. For most, this creative facilitation process is unfamiliar in professional training and it borders on the mysterious. As a result, it requires alternative forms of meaning revelation.

The attitude that 'good enough is perfect' must be held, so as not to offer a preconceived or outside perspective on the offering. Gerard feels that much of the success of his work derives from educated artistry. His is a musical brain that has developed with concurrent musical systems, including folk, pop, classical, alternative and especially influenced by Japanese music in addition to other global musical practices. This internalization of systems provides a colourful palette of resources, ingrained to the degree that it is almost automatic.

As humans engage music in all of its forms, meaning is sought in order to help make sense of the experience, to measure its value and to be fully aware of wholeness that music brings to lives, including the cognitive-intellectual, the sensory-emotional, the somatic-physical and the psycho-social aspects. Yet, it is not actually meaning in the sense that direct information is conveyed or that verbal understanding is achieved. Rather, it is more of a 'meaningness' that is derived, an impression, a sensation or a feeling, a holding space that enables a process of negotiating the resulting effect that the experience has upon one's life. For some, music has had the effect of self-transformation, to the degree that aspects of the person's life have been deeply affected, changed or re-ordered (see Phil Mullen, Chapter 3). An experienced facilitator is aware of these processes as participants are fully engaged in the various contexts of community music practices. Here is a second case study exploring the work of a highly skilled and experienced scholar-musician, where sometimes seemingly rather inaccessible areas of study are revealed through application and practice in the fields of music education and applied ethnomusicology.

Patricia Shehan Campbell

Facilitation and Education in Diverse Cultural Settings through Applied Ethnomusicology

Patricia Shehan Campbell is a music educator and ethnomusicologist, involved with preparing students for teaching and facilitating music in settings of considerable diversity. This includes schools, universities and community projects. Pat is committed to providing those she works with experiences in knowing diverse music practices through projects that provoke listening, cultural analysis, performance and participatory experiences both within groups and person-to-person exchanges. At the heart of her work is the study of music in culture and as culture, her focus surrounds the consideration of music as it lives locally and across the globe. In the tertiary setting at the University of Washington, USA, Pat's programmes aim to advance students' under-standing of music and its meaning through work with guest artist-musicians in ethnomusicology, music education and world music perform-ance courses. It is here, at the seams of ethnomusicology and music education, that Pat's work has been important for community music. Her many publications including *Lessons from the World* (Campbell, 1991), *Music in Cultural Context* (Campbell, 1996), *Songs in Their Heads* (Campbell, 2010), *Teaching Music Globally* (Campbell, 2004), *Musician and Teacher* (Campbell, 2008), co-author of *Free to Be Musical* (Higgins & Campbell, 2010), *Music in Childhood* (Campbell & Scott-Kassner, 2014), and co-editor of the Global Music Series (with Bonnie

C. Wade, 2004-continuing) and the *Oxford Handbook on Children's Musical Cultures* (Campbell & Wiggins, 2013), give steady attention to ways in which we can honour cultural diversity, including race, gender, religion and socio-economic status, allowing music to be the gateway to a developing cultural understanding of people close and far from 'home'. This has meant that those studying with Pat to become both certified music teachers and/or ethno-musicologists find jobs as diverse as education, the media, museums, concert management and community schools while the aim for those working toward a PhD will, hopefully, be open to, engaged in, receptive and supportive of a great diversity of musical cultures, expressions and practices of the world's peoples. This is important because landing a job within higher education with these accruements can help promote the cen-tral themes through which this book is about. Examples of those that have travelled this journey include: Sarah Bartolome (Northwestern University), Amy Beegle (University of Cincinnati College-Conservatory of Music), Ann Clements (Penn State University), Sheila Feay-Shaw (University of Wisconsin-Milwaukee), David Hebert (Bergen University College, Norway), Karen Howard (St Thomas University), Chee-Hoo Lum (National Institute of Education, Singapore), Christopher Roberts (University of Washington), Amanda Soto (Texas State University), Matt Swanson (University Child Development School) and Sarah Watts (Penn State University).

When asked about the essential personal qualities in enabling effective music-making with young people, Pat replied:

> Enthusiasm and evident energy that are made manifest in a powerful musicianship: These are the top qualities in enabling effective music-making within my university classes. Whether it's me, when I can manage it (in musical matter that I choose very carefully), or an outstanding student, or a visiting artist whom I engage because of these very qualities, the genuine interest and excitement that exudes from a fine musician as s/he sings it, plays it, dances/moves it are the qualities that motivate effective music-making with the students.

Pat's ambition for her students is that they receive, and maybe become, 'this music' with the same drive as the visiting artists and in time are able 'to take it out' to their own clients, whoever they are.

When Pat reflects upon the key skill sets she believes are vital to the work she does, it is very clear that the concept of rhythm stands front and centre. Pat suggests that

> this is central by way of thinking about the music one makes, the pulse that connects the participants, the rhythmic complexity (or redundancy)

of the music that is experienced – not too complex, not too redundant, but just the right 'fit' for the individuals and the collective they become.

In concert with Charlie Keil, a musical collaborator with whom she worked on the Music Grooves project and in setting up the Jubilation Foundation (along with Honk-Fest groove specialist Becky Leibman), rhythm is seen as critical in the pacing and flow of the facilitator, the teacher, and in the fluidity of what is said and gestured through musical doing. Rhythm becomes the key to the musicians' skill set followed by a sense of rhythmically determined sequence. This understanding of what-goes-when is the capacity to allow any thoughts of a predetermined procedure and outcome to be adaptable to the circumstances of the group – key skills for any community music facilitator. Pat certainly feels that it's very useful for a teacher-facilitator to be able to sing and play a few harmonizing instruments such as the piano, keyboard, guitar and ukulele as well as to know how technology can make a marvellous sound source that can interface with live acoustic instruments. It is however with rhythm that her heart lies, she states, 'an affinity to want to move, groove, dance is essential to modelling the music, bringing the pulse into the group, stimulating an ease of the body as central to the group music-making venture'.

As an illustration of Pat's facilitation strategies, she recalls a recent story of how a group of undergraduate students in world music, performance and music education interacted with Native American song and dance in Fresno, California:

> [They] danced, and drummed three powwow songs – two with recordings, one without – coming in with the pulse-keeping immediately, gradually immersing themselves into the vocables ('heys', 'weys', 'yahs' and such), moving in small sideways steps and facing the centre of the circle. Immersive, coming to terms with the music by doing it, the students required little verbal direction and picked up on the model as we performed the phrases, repeatedly, with no breakdown of them, holistically.

This approach based upon many experiences of musics in other cultures can also be understood in how Pat works with the voice. Using the example of Bulgarian song, she brings the students to the music aurally. As a group, they listen to a recording of an eight-bar melody, in this instance in a seven-beat metre, each run through there is a question that challenges to focus and their attention: 'Who's singing?', 'How many parts/singers?', 'Where's the tonic? Hum it', 'Listen for this phrase', 'Keep the 2–2–3 rhythm', 'Sing a part, quietly'. As the facilitator of this session, Pat plays a lead role singing the phrases and melody but is always mindful of bringing in the students at every given opportunity. In this illustration, the group made the piece happen vocally over a five-minute period, extending it through the use of the simplest Lesnoto[2] footwork while singing the song. Following exposure to two different kinds of music making, the students push forward to create new music – music they can own – using Native American or Bulgarian techniques, processes and stylistic nuances as inspiration.

Pulling these ideas together, it is clear that Pat is a firm believer in modelling practice either by visiting artist, by the student-participants in a class or session or by her as the music leader. Working in small groups is understood as an effective way to bring people into the learning circle through peer teaching where all students can feel active in contributing to the whole. From a philosophical standpoint, Pat suggests that cultural diversity is all around us, and everyone has a song to sing or a groove to move and music to share. Within her own context as a university professor, an important first step in working with music majors within the fields of music education and ethnomusicology is recognizing that in every cultural community and in every neighbourhood, music happens. She goes on to say:

> We-the-trained (and educated) musicians are not the musical hub, or source, or 'font' of musical repertoire and skills. We can have our antennae out for music of every style, by musicians and music-fans of every hue. We can listen up, talk with people in public spaces, at cultural festivals, in restaurants of various culinary tastes, in places of worship, in schools, on the street, and learn a lot about communities of musicians. We should, if we hope to own the professional role of a working musician in contemporary society of considerable diversity.

Pat's interaction with community music coincided with her growing awareness of the interstices of music education and ethnomusicology: 'There was a small opening between the fields which, through the rise of community music practice (and theory), is now filled by our music/their music and the processes by which "my music" (or "their music") can become "our music"'.

Pat's work is interesting for community musicians for a number of reasons, not least of which is that she works on the cusp of music education and ethnomusicology. As a field of study that joins the concerns and methods of anthropology with the study of music (Shelemay, 2001), ethnomusicology has followed the anthropological lead in its utilization of the prefix 'applied'

Figure 1.2 Patricia Shehan Campbell and Wagogo Musician

(Ervin, 2004). Applied ethnomusicology, like community music, is best understood through the work that it *does* rather than any attempt to describe what it *is*. One broad definition states that '*Applied ethnomusicology* puts ethnomusicological scholarship, knowledge, and understanding to practice use' (Pettan & Titon, 2015, p.4). More specifically, Titon (2005) suggests that 'applied ethnomusicology is a music-centered intervention in a particular community, whose purpose is to benefit that community – for example, a social improvement, a musical benefit, a cultural good, an economic advantage, or a combination of these and other benefits' (p. 4). Sound familiar? With clear resonance with community music, applied ethnomusicology is based on social responsibility and is intended to function for the beneficial use of communities outside university departments. As an early advocate, Keil (1982) explained that applied ethnomusicology 'can make a difference ... (and) can intersect both the world outside and the university in more challenging and constructive ways' (p. 407). Despite being a professor in American Studies at SUNY-Buffalo for most of his academic life, Keil's career was dominated by an interest in music and music education. His scholarly contributions took many forms, such as ethnographic fieldwork that resulted in wide-ranging books, many essays and papers on music and music education, and efforts in promoting music education in the Buffalo area through his organisation M.U.S.E. (Musicians United for Superior Education) (Mantie & Higgins, 2015).

Resonant with past practices in community music, applied ethnomusicologists have been concerned with the development of projects in the public sphere that involve and enable musicians and various musical cultures to present, represent and affect the dispersion of music (Pettan & Titon, 2015; Titon, 1992). Because of changes in the political, social and economic landscapes, there are now many more ethnomusicologists engaged in applied work with a primary intended output of musical or social benefits, rather than in the increase of original scholarly knowledge. Van Buren (2010), in organizing a World AIDS Day event in Sheffield, UK, illustrates this. Emerging from Van Buren's fieldwork in Nairobi, Kenya, and building upon her experiences of partnerships between African musicians and a host of Kenyan and foreign institutions focused on local, national and international development, Van Buren cemented a partnership of her own back in the UK. Teaming up with the National Health Service (NHS) Centre for HIV and Sexual Health, Van Buren organised a day-long event that combined performances by a variety of local performers with a keynote speech from a health professional (Van Buren, 2011). This type of community engagement points towards another developing field with cross-references to both music therapy and community music, a practice described as medical ethnomusicology. Described as 'a new milieu of consciousness' between researchers and practitioners, medical ethnomusicology explores holistically the roles of music and sound phenomena in any cultural and clinical context of health and healing (Koen, 2008). Van Buren's work may be seen through a medical ethnomusicology perspective and further example the interdisciplinary nature of scholarship in the early twenty-first century.

These illustrations of practice underscore the diversity and range of possibilities within community music practice and engagement. Whether through the highly mediated process of re-enacting previously composed music such as in western classical traditions, or through improvising and composing new music, or finding intercultural connections that deepen mutual understanding and respect, or even the simple act of sharing one's music with another, all serve to enhance our experiences of what music means as it intersects with our lives. This is how music makers construct meaning in their lives from musical experience, and how that meaning leads to a transformation of self. The ways that musical experiences are designed and facilitated flow naturally from this understanding (Dillon, 2007, p. xiii). Community music practice recognises and celebrates the fullness of life that music engagement can provide where people come together to make music. As you make your way through this book, it is our hope that you will find your own meaning and sense of self in the various principles and practice of community music.

Questions and Topics for Discussion

1. What does music mean to you?

2. Explore the concept that humans are innately musical.

3. Community music has developed on the premise that everybody has the right and inherent ability to create and participate in music. Discuss the democratic aspects of this concept. How can it be applied in practice?

4. Discuss mediated vs. unmediated music. How do cultural norms influence humans as they transport it from one context to another?

5. Explore the meanings of 'applied ethnomusicology' and share examples of it from your experiences.

Notes

1. Blacking (1973, p. x).
2. Small (1998, p. 13).
3. In two studies, with *n*=c.980, 12 percent of participants reported that school music experiences were important to them, and less than 10 percent elected to take music in high school (surveys conducted in Waterloo Region, Ontario, Canada, 2006–8). Ninety-four percent reported that they incorporated some sort of music experience in their daily lives, whether it be listening, participating or for some, creating new music.
4. Source: Bertram, Christopher, 'Jean-Jacques Rousseau', *The Stanford Encyclopedia of Philosophy* (Winter 2012 Edition), Edward N. Zalta (ed.), URL http://plato.stanford.edu/entries/rousseau/, accessed 4 May 2016.
5. Takemitsu (1995).
6. This relates to Pauline Oliveros's concept of 'deep listening' from *Sonic Medications* (1974).
7. In shakuhachi meditational practice (suizen [blowing meditation]), long notes are foundational, similar to scales in western music. The shakuhachi practitioner uses the instrument to 'harmonise surroundings'. This includes sounds, the emotional states of listeners and the internal state of the practitioner.

References

Blacking, J. (1973). *How musical is man?* London: Faber and Faber.
Brookfield, S. D. (2002). New directions for adult and continuing education. Retrieved from http://onlinelibrary.wiley.com/doi/10.1002/ace.7502/abstract
Campbell, P. S. (1991). *Lessons from the world.* New York: Schimer Books.
Campbell, P. S. (1996). *Music in cultural context: Eight views on world music education.* Reston, VA: Music Educators National Conference (MENC).
Campbell, P. S. (2004). *Teaching music globally.* Oxford: Oxford University Press.
Campbell, P. S. (2008). *Musician and teacher: An orientation to music education.* New York: W. W. Norton.
Campbell, P. S. (2010). *Songs in their heads: Music and its meaning in children's lives* (2nd ed.). New York: Oxford University Press.
Campbell, P. S., & Scott-Kassner, C. (2014). *Music in childhood: From preschool through the elementary grades* (4th ed.). Boston, MA: Schimer Books.
Campbell, P. S., & Wiggins, T. (Eds.). (2013). *The Oxford handbook of children's musical cultures.* New York: Oxford University Press.
Csikszentmihalyi, M. (1990). *Flow: The psychology of optimal experience.* New York: Harper and Row.
DeNora, T. (2000). *Music in Everyday Life.* Cambridge: Cambridge University Press.
Dillon, S. (2007). *Music, meaning and transformation: Meaningful music making for life.* Newcastle: Cambridge Scholars Publishing.
Elliott, D. J. (1995). *Music matters: A new philosophy of music education.* Oxford: Oxford University Press.
Emerson, R. W. (1965). *Selected writing* (W. H. Gilman Ed.). New York: American Library.
Ervin, A. M. (2004). *Applied anthropology: Tools and perspectives for contemporary practice* (2nd ed.). Upper Saddle River, NJ: Pearson.
Finnegan, R. (2007). *The Hidden Musician – Music-Making in an English Town* (2nd ed.). Middletown, CT: Wesleyan University Press.
Froehlich, H. (2007). *Sociology for music teachers: Perspectives for practice.* Upper Saddle River, NJ: Prentice Hall.
Green, L. (2002). *How Popular Musicians Learn.* Farnham, Surrey: Ashgate Press.
Higgins, L., & Campbell, P. S. (2010). *Free to be musical: Group improvisation in music.* Lanham, MD: Rowman & Littlefield.
Jensen, E. (2000). *Music with the brain in mind.* Thousand Oaks, CA: Corwin Press.
Keil, C. (1982). Applied ethnomusicology and a rebirth of music from the spirit of tragedy. *Ethnomusicology, 26*(3), 407–11.
Koen, B. D. (Ed.). (2008). *The Oxford handbook of medical ethnomusicology.* New York: Oxford University Press.
Lambert, L., Walker, D., Zimmerman, D. P., Cooper, J. E., Lambert, M. D., Gardner, M. E., & Szabo, M. (2002). *The constructivist leader* (2nd ed.). New York: Teachers Collage, Columbia University.

Mantie, R., & Higgins, L. (2015). Paideia con salsa: charles keil, groovology, and the undergraduate music curriculum. *College Music Symposium, 55*. Retrieved from http://symposium.music.org/index.php?option=com_k2&view=itemlist &task=user&id=2577:rogermantieleehiggins&Itemid=126 doi:10.18177/sym. 2015.55.fr.10885

Mezirow, J. (1991). *Transformative dimensions of adult learning*. San Francisco, CA: Jossey-Bass.

Miller, J. P. (1993). *The holistic curriculum*. Toronto: OISE Press.

Palmer, P. J. (2007). *The courage to teach*. San Francisco, CA: John Wiley and Sons.

Pettan, S., & Titon, J. T. (Eds.). (2015). *The Oxford handbook of applied ethnomusicology*. New York: Oxford University Press.

Reimer, B. (2003). *A philosophy of music education: Advancing the vision* (3rd ed.). Upper Saddle River, NJ: Prentice Hall.

Shelemay, K. K. (2001). *Soundscapes: Exploring music in a changing world* (1st ed.). New York: W.W. Norton.

Small, C. (1998). *Musicking: The meanings of performance and listening*. London: Wesleyan University Press.

Takemitsu, T. (1995). *Confronting silence: Selected writings*. Berkeley, CA: Fallen Leaf Press.

Taylor, C. (1991). *The ethics of authenticity*. New York: Harvard University Press.

Titon, J. T. (Ed.). (1992). *Ethnomusicology* (Vol. 36, No. 3). The University of Illinois Press.

Trilling, L. (1972). *Sincerity and authenticity*. Cambridge, MA: Harvard University Press.

Van Buren, K. (2010). Applied ethnomusicology and HIV and AIDS: Responsibility, ability, and action. *Ethnomusicology, 54*(2), 202–23.

Van Buren, K. (2011). Music, HIV/AIDS, and social change in Nairobi, Kenya. In G. Barz & J. M. Cohen (Eds.), *The culture of AIDS of Africa: Hope and healing through music and the arts* (pp. 70–85). New York: Oxford University Press.

Willingham, L. (2001). A Community of voices: A qualitative study of the effects of being a member of the Bell'Arte Singers (PhD), University of Toronto, Toronto.

Willingham, L., & Bartel, L. (2008). *Redefining the education of a musical society*. Paper presented at the Redefining the Education of a Musical Society, Bologna: Spoken Research Paper, ISME, Bologna.

Zatorre, R., Evans, A., & Meyer, E. (1994). Neural mechanisms underlying melodic perception and memory for pitch. *Journal of Neuroscience, 14*(4), 1908–19.

Chapter 2
Negotiated Curriculum, Non-Formal and Informal Learning

No one is born fully-formed: it is through self-experience in the world that we become what we are.

Paulo Freire[1]

Humans continue to explore the ways in which we learn. The development of skills and knowledge and the ability to apply and adapt them into practice is the subject of much inquiry and interest. Cyclical trends in public education have ranged from the free-discovery pedagogies to the more rigid, standardised exam preparation emphases where measurement and test results are considered to be the primary evidence of quality learning. Even in innovative initiatives that focus on learner-centred strategies, such approaches as the guided discovery method (Mosston, 1973) to the constructivist approaches spawned from the works of psychologists Piaget and Vygotsky (Moll, 1990) depend upon the teacher as central to the process of learning. This is reflected in a contemporary study from Durham University in England that supports the traditional didactic method of teacher-centred instruction stating that 'the best research suggests that teachers with a command of their subject, allied with high-quality instruction techniques such as effective questioning and assessment, are the most likely to impart the best learning to their pupils' (Coe et al., 2014). There are voices within community music circles who resist the teacher role, due to the notion of the 'expert' and conventional education models of music transmission.

> What has been exciting to many of us is the way that the practice of community music seeks to move away from the expert teacher [...] to a more dynamic and interactive community of participants.
>
> (Mullen, 2002)

Formal Education as Socialisation

Within formal education through schooling, the development of literacy in a number of valued disciplines is the goal. Development, 'in literacy terms, comes from supplying the deficits through inputs (training)' (Rogers, 2004, p. 31). The viewpoint that education through schooling is a process of incorporating younger generations into society through socialisation, with an aim to reproduce the dominant culture, permits change to occur within a limited framework of institutional processes. Other perspectives, such as those from Paulo Freire (2002), Brazilian educator and founder of the movement often termed Critical Pedagogy, views literacy in terms of power. Non-literates in this context are considered to be oppressed by the literate and thus the purpose of literacy development is to gain power in order to change the system.

Pedagogy for Diverse Community Contexts

Community music, historically, has found itself in concert with Freire's ideas resisting the hegemonic trends of orthodox education and embracing the existence of multiple perspectives, what educator Rolland Paulston, known for his work in developing social cartography, understands as 'consisting of disputatious yet complementary knowledge communities, that have come to recognise, tolerate and even appreciate the *difference*' (Paulston, 1996, pp. 32–33). It is within these diverse community contexts that various pedagogical approaches emerge as necessary ways to engage participants in the development of musical literacy. The role of the expert teacher is the focal point in literacy development in the school setting. As Phil Mullen remarks earlier, community music sees leadership from a somewhat different viewpoint. Community music practitioners demonstrate a diverse range of pedagogical approaches but share the aim of creating a community without hierarchical or oppressive structures. Gillian Howell's work with new arrival youth in Australia illustrates a profoundly interesting approach, in that she begins by exploring the personal stories of the individual.

Gillian Howell
Participatory Music with New Arrivals and their Teachers

Gillian Howell is an Australian musician, facilitator and educator with an interest in music making and the ways that participating in ensemble music making can assist people to feel strong, positive and valued in their lives, and as members of a community. One of the projects that she has been involved in revolves around working with recently arrived children and teenagers (often called 'new arrivals') in Australia. Some of the participants are refugees and asylum seekers that have had severely interrupted prior schooling and in some cases no prior schooling at all. Others are recent immigrants that have had age-consistent schooling in their country of origin. Using her skills as a community musician, Gillian engages them in music to help the young people share stories of their life experiences including themes of journey, transition, loss and new possibilities. One of the key aims is to connect the new arrivals with others in the hope that they might feel more settled and as a consequence increase their positive feelings about their new lives in Australia. The context where this work takes place varies, but has frequently taken place in English Language Schools (ELS). ELSs are a particular feature of the south-eastern part of Australia's education system and are government schools that are focused on providing newly arrived young people of school age with a school environment through which they can build English language proficiency before transitioning to a mainstream school. They are therefore transitional environments, making them very different to international schools that accept students from around the world.

Gillian's work is mainly with young people, but she feels that it is vital that their teachers are involved, stating, 'I support generalist teachers to incorporate music and creative activities into their daily work with students, and I help schools to develop curriculum plans in which music is included as an important vehicle for student wellbeing and school engagement.' Even though the site through which Gillian's work takes place is within the formal education system, the pedagogical style that she employs has its roots in approaches commonly employed by community musicians. For example her music leadership is non-formal, participatory and collaborative. Musical ideas and expertise come from the participants as often as from the leader.

One of the key words Gillian uses to describe the personal qualities vital in working with this client group is 'patience'. For example, the students' language ability in English may range from total beginners, to fairly fluent; some may have excellent spoken language but struggle with both reading and writing;

Figure 2.1 Gillian Howell Music Making with ELS Students

some may have excellent receptive language (understanding what is said), but have only basic expressive language (ability to speak), and there are occasions where interpreters are employed to assist in translation. This can mean that there are increased opportunities for misunderstandings and confusion, and it can take time for concepts, ideas and even instructions to be understood. It is because of this that 'humour' is another important personal quality. Trying to cope and succeed in learning when working with the unfamiliar can be very stressful and frustrating for students, and Gillian has found that it is always valuable to show readiness to smile and laugh – in short, keeping things light in spirit and helping to keep students' stress and frustration levels as low as possible.

The ability to respond to a wide range of communicative expressions is also paramount. Gillian notes that as a music facilitator working in this environment, you need to be alert to the students' wide range of signals and cues. Understanding these gestures helps Gillian understand whether the students are comfortable in the activities she is presenting. Some students, in particular those coming from traumatic backgrounds, struggle with group participation, particularly a shared focus towards a single activity. Sustaining work over any length of time can be very difficult and Gillian has found that the students work better when the music making is structured and organised in increments, for example, mouthing words rather than singing aloud, or simply watching rather than joining in.

One child crawled under a table in the middle of an activity once, but then I noticed she was still mouthing the words to the song we were singing. For her, on that day, participating from under the table was the safest way for her to participate and even though it was unexpected, there was no real reason to reprimand her for leaving the group. As it was, she returned to the group when she felt ready, later in the same lesson.

This example highlights that there needs to be a willingness to adapt and vary communication style to suit the needs of the group. In Gillian's work, this might include speaking very slowly with simplified language, miming or acting things out, drawing sketches, modelling and demonstrating, and repeating musical material many times over to give the group time to catch on. Quick thinking and quick responses are essential as this work is student-centric, and the facilitator should be ready for things to turn in an instant, taking on a new direction or course. Communication and interpersonal skills build trust and a sense of emotional safety within the group, so that those involved can relax and are able to contribute ideas. Many will have experienced quite stern and authoritarian schooling where corporal punishment is the norm and where offering ideas to the teacher is a sign of disrespect. A music leader among this cohort needs to be able to support students to gradually disarm their learned defences and emotional armour.

In terms of skill sets, Gillian emphasises the importance of musical skills, noting that these need to be sufficient to explore concepts in experiential ways, without a reliance on music-specific terminology. This also extends to aural skills and musical memory: 'An extremely powerful strategy is to work with musical knowledge and ideas that students bring with them from their home countries, and the music they listen to for leisure.' Having the ability to adapt these musical ideas to instruments available in the school relies on the musician's flexibility and capacity to improvise, and she notes that working with students' personal stories and musical ideas means being ready to respond musically in the moment. In these situations, musical ideas are often tentatively volunteered and require the facilitator to respond with enthusiasm in an effort to gain the group's trust. Understanding that process and performance are on a continuum, Gillian places arranging skills as a critical part of the community musician's toolkit. Preparing the group's work for performance, recording or sharing means developing musically effective ways of showcasing the work that uses each individual's skills, and the range of available instruments. In Gillian's experience, playing instruments is one of the most important things that students get from the music sessions, so it is important that this is part of each and every project and/or workshop. Supporting groups to create their own compositions – such as group-composed original songs – as a platform for exploring and expressing their experiences is a vital part of this work. While there is much that is beneficial for students in learning music that someone else has composed, creating their own work is a very affirming experience that validates their experiences and contributions and as a consequence helps build confidence in the skills and experiences they have to offer in their new country.[2]

Facilitation as Enabling Music Interactions

Community music practice honours the role of a leader, or facilitator – one who creates the conditions whereby participants may grow and apply their skills and knowledge. A facilitator sets out to 'enable music interactions' (Higgins, 2012, p. 16) in authentic music doing. These interactions are typically part of a workshop, an event where members of community engage together within this facilitated, low-risk environment. The workshop itself may revolve around a variety of learning modalities, including formal transmission, non-formal structured and purposeful practices and the often casual, unregulated practices of the informal (Veblen, 2012). Further, these musical interactions are built upon a constant framework of welcome and empathy, a blanket of hospitality that permeates the experience.

While not discounting more formal and institutional learning contexts, community music takes somewhat different approaches to the experiences of learning. Rather than a formulaic set of curriculum expectations outcomes that are to be evidential and observable by the end of a set period, community music encourages an organic process of participation and reflection that engages the musician in a procedural thinking action (Schön, 1991). This takes on a variety of forms, which have been categorised within a range of approaches as informal and non-formal learning.

> [T]eaching-learning modes in CM [community music] situations often include a rich mixture of oral, notational, experimental, conservative, experiential, spiritual and/or analytical elements. Moreover, it is usually the case (usually, but not always) that CM [community music] leaders and students are not bound by written curriculum 'plans' organised in terms of verbal statements of objectives, rubrics, concepts, evaluation criteria, 'standards' and so forth.
>
> (Veblen, 2008, p. 7)

Informal Learning

The mode of learning that is often called *informal* can occur anywhere, in any order, with or without sequence, agency or guidance. This type of learning exists in all communities and to some degree within all individual practices. This learning occurs without formal guidance, without direct teacher intervention and without the normal assessment and evaluation processes normally associated with education. Informal education, then, might be considered as

> [. . .] the lifelong process by which every person acquires and accumulates knowledge, skills, attitudes and insights from daily experiences and exposure to the environment- at home, at work, at play; from the example and attitudes of family and friends; from travel, reading newspapers and books; or by listening to the radio or viewing films or television. Generally, informal education is unorganised and often unsystematic; yet it accounts for the great bulk of any person's total lifetime learning- including that of even a highly 'schooled' person.
>
> (Coombs & Ahmed, 1974, p. 8)

Referred to as a set of practices rather than a methodology, informal learning leaves open the possibilities of unconscious learning, unsought consequences and may include self-taught concepts (Green, 2008). This is often exemplified where people learn from listening to a recording, share musical ideas, songs, riffs, chords or other information. Drum circles and singer-songwriting circles often invite situations where people join in and learn by observing, playing or singing along, thereby expanding their own knowledge and skills. Oral musical traditions are passed from one generation to the next in settings such as folk festivals, pubs and family gatherings. These examples are forms of situated learning, learning that is embedded within activity and context (Lave & Wenger, 1991). Often, this form of learning is unintentional rather than objective or outcome based. Informal learning naturally occurs in authentic contexts, settings and situations that immediately embrace the knowledge or skills being learned into applied practice. Informal learning is frequently social in nature, engaged collaboratively between people or within groups. Social interaction is an essential ingredient for situated learning, and in a community music context, for music engagement.

Non-Formal Learning

Non-formal learning may be considered to have taken place within organised or semi-organised educational activities outside the established formal system (Paulston, 1972). This position, of course, infers the primacy of formal systems: i.e., *formal is normal*. Community music practice claims otherwise: non-formal education leads to the empowerment of the participants by enabling them to take control over their own learning, operating in both the pedagogical and developmental processes. The 'pedagogy' or practice of teaching engages the learner in a self-generated development of literacies within the disciplines of study. A community music non-formal process includes support and facilitation from a leader, that is, the pedagogue, and the initiative and self-management from the learner as she develops facility and understanding in her musical practice. This is often most realised within a community.

Theories of learning support the notion of social interaction as a key part of cognitive development (Vygotsky, 1978) where individuals move from a known base of knowledge to new material. The range and quality of teaching and learning within that social milieu can depend on the skills of a tutor or leader. As noted earlier, non-formal learning may include any organised, systematic, educational activity that occurs in any learning contexts (Coombs & Ahmed, 1974). This approach, as distinct from informal learning, is as a form of education usually voluntary rather than mandatory, yet most often there is an intention to work towards a pre-planned goal. While the ranges of ways people learn music defy concise compartmentalization, Annie Mok On Nei has offered the following as a working definition of non-formal learning in a music context.

> Non-formal learning is relatively systematic and (but not necessarily) pre-planned with an explicit intention on the part of both learner and mentor to accomplish a/some specific learning task(s). It is clear that non-formal learning involves some kind of guidance from a mentor.
> (Mok, 2011, p. 14)

Throughout the twentieth century, changing understandings of education and learning emerged. A major influence was the increasing feeling that knowledge was not transferable, rather constructed individually through life experiences. Non-formal learning is symbiotic with the constructivist approach, depending upon student-centred learning, where learning is always 'an act of self-search and discovery. One cannot be "taught" . . .' (Rahman, 1993, p. 222)

Non-formal education, and the learning that emulates from its structures, is evident in a variety of forms in virtually every culture. For example, children may begin learning musical forms and instruments aurally from a master musician, without ever taking formal instruction. This mentor-student relationship that begins unintentionally may develop into a formal, structured situation. On the other hand, the learner may find the non-formal environment satisfactory for continued lifelong personal improvement. While the focus is on learning, the student has ultimate control over the choices within the learning processes (Veblen, 2012).

Online tutorials, such as those that have proliferated on YouTube, provide instruction for voluntary learners through a variety of pedagogical approaches (Waldron, 2017). Non-formal practices, then, frequently include social interaction within a range of settings that welcomes intergenerational participation.

Brent Rowan
Community Wind Bands: 'Your Best Is Good Enough!'

On Thursday mornings, approximately 70 seniors arrive for band practice. Divided into beginner, intermediate and advanced, they sign up for a 12-week programme, although most stay all year long. Brent Rowan manages the extensive programme, which includes large ensembles, flute choir, clarinet choir, brass ensemble, jazz ensemble and jazz improvisation. He, along with five other leaders, provides a rich community music experience for people in his Guelph, Ontario, Canada region who want to play traditional wind orchestra instruments.

Affiliated with New Horizons International, these programmes provide entry points to music making for adults, including those with no musical experience at all and those who were active in school music programmes but have been inactive for a long time. Many adults would like an opportunity to learn music in a group setting similar to that offered in schools, but the last entry point in most cases was elementary school. By being connected to the larger organisation, information and programme sharing, a music lending library, camps and workshops are available. The resources are bountiful. Questions can be answered and musical or organisational challenges dealt with through the connection with the international organisation.

The membership is a diverse group and marketed directly towards novices. These mostly retired people have never played music before and want to learn. Some have had school experience, but have not maintained their musical practice. Brent relates that some who were quite experienced

Figure 2.2 New Horizons, Guelph, Canada

but out of practice 'get up and ride their bike again immediately'. There is also a group of advanced musicians who just do not want to do evening rehearsals, and want the opportunity to play a lead part and they form the basis of the advanced ensemble.

Brent uses humour and keeps the mood light and fun. 'This is super important,' he states, and acknowledges that people are there by choice. They do not want to be yelled at. They think that participating in music is very worthwhile and healthy and in this light it is important to be positive and encouraging. In this climate, the constructive criticism is received better and not taken personally.

Working with ageing adults requires considerations such as speaking more slowly and giving instructions clearly and repeatedly. Processing time is needed and patience is required. Brent works at being his authentic self in his leadership practice, and in so doing, develops relationships that are deep.

His main skill set in working with older musicians is deep listening. He includes along with hearing wrong notes and seeing incorrect fingers that ability to read the emotion in the room and watching the physical reaction. Brent listens to what they say. He relies on the maturity of the adult learner to identify and self-correct many of the mistakes and find ways to fix the problems. He employs what he terms as instructional reflexivity and says it is really quite parallel to musical improvisation. Brent remarks, 'Patience is a necessity, not a virtue!' Adults must feel that it is safe to ask questions. He states that if they do not understand something, it is because he has not explained it well enough. His participants want to master something, to accomplish a skill or idea that he facilitates through a complex and yet empathetic leadership practice.

Of course, Brent has a basic knowledge of all the instruments, but admits that it is not 100 percent necessary to know everything. His facilitation strategy includes encouraging the participants to listen around them and respond to what they hear. He does exercises off the page with them, such as rhythmic patterns, finding pulse and changing pulse, sharing leadership in these activities with the players. He uses musical games to improve something and will invent such an activity on the spot. He frequently asks them what they feel or what they would like to express as they work through their selections.

It is important to know the soundtrack of the participants' lives. All kinds of music is important, from 12th St Rag, to Aquarius from Hair, to the New World Symphony, and the greatest hits of Michael Jackson. Brent draws upon his vast performing experience as a saxophonist to create a place where many genres, backgrounds, abilities and personal tastes are respected and included.

Brent is committed to developing young musical leaders and also leads a youth jazz ensemble. These teenagers can act as apprentices, not only as musical performers, but also in facilitation roles. The youth play similar repertoire to the seniors and the youth combos work together with the seniors under the mantra of 'talk-listen-understand', creating a respect energy between the generations. The seniors support the youth financially, and by being in the audience for their performances.

Brent notes that when his participants were in their careers they were known as accountants, professors, doctors, electricians and so on. As retirees, they have lost that identity and seek to find something that they can self-define as part of their personhood. As one commented, 'I have so much fun here. I like how you do things. You are teaching without us knowing that we are learning.' Brent responds with his means of determining success: 'I know I've been successful when I've worked myself out of a job!'

Intergenerational and Lifelong Learning

A unique aspect of community music in non-formal education and learning contexts is the frequency of multi-age participants in the same group; for example, we can recount a community music workshop in which among the 40 or so participants was an 8-year-old girl, a 75-year-old grandmother and a range of ages in between. Of course this is not the case within formal instruction in schools that demands that the administrators sort students in batches based upon date of birth. This reflects compulsory schooling practices whereas community music activities tend to rely on participants volunteering to be engaged, often due to common interests. As an increasingly healthy, ageing population seeks to add meaning and value to their lives, post-career and retired participants may find themselves in community music ensembles or activities with much younger musicians: 'Ongoing professional and career learning as well as leisure, health, and self-help learning are now recognised as important dimensions of a positive and productive adulthood' (Myers, Bowles, & Dabback, 2013, p. 134). Case studies of intergenerational music learning reveal that the awareness of age differences tend to disappear in the engagement of music participation: 'Many [. . .] expressed the belief that their age and the age of the adolescents is somehow less visible and less important when they frequently interact with each other' (Beynon & Alfano, 2013, p. 128). The common belief in formal education that music instruction must begin within a window of early age is contradicted as adults engage in intentional, non-formal and semi-structured learning experiences with great success. Further, the notion that music learning should be limited to those with inherent talent is shown to be false. Music is for everyone. Music is for life. Music is for participants of all ages and abilities.

Andrea Creech
Making Music with Older People

Andrea became interested in creating community music programmes for young people as part of the Royal Liverpool Philharmonic Orchestra's community outreach work in the 1980s, and extended and developed that work in Ireland while exploring both classical music and Irish traditional music synergies in that context. She investigated ways in which classically trained orchestral musicians could connect with the youth in communities. As she worked with prospective teachers in developing leadership skills and programmes, she became aware of the increasing number of older people in her life. It gave cause for her to think about music and community and what that might mean for all of us as we grow older, as the demographic projections suggest a growing number of seniors.

Andrea highlights that too often, the idea of music education or music making with older people is limited to a sing-song or a feel good session. The thought of musical growth of personal progression musically has typically been reserved for children and youth, as evidenced for example by 'Youth Music' initiatives in the UK. Andrea uses the term 'musical possible selves' in describing our 'hoped for', 'reclaimed' or 'lost' musical selves that we develop through exploration.

In 2009, the United Kingdom Research Council supported a study, The Music for Life Project (part of the New Dynamics of Ageing Programme),[3] and in partnership with the Guildhall School of Music & Drama, Andrea and her colleagues at the University College London Institute of Education specifically began looking at how music might be used with older people in community contexts. A key question addressed the processes and principles that could support positive social-emotional outcomes, at that time an under-researched area.

The Music for Life Project team, supported by the Guildhall Connect Programme, through community outreach set up groups within sheltered housing in East London where older people participated in a variety of music programming.

Another project partner site was the Sage Gateshead 'Silver Programme'[4] involving 1,000 participants over the age of 55 who access all sorts of music making – everything from gospel singing, rock groups, choirs, instrumental groups and more on a weekly basis. Andrea's research also extended to the Westminster Adult Education Centre,[5] a continuing education college where 500 older people participated in a project involving music making in various settings.

The Music for Life Project opened up connections to many other communities throughout the country where, in some cases, local city councils would provide start-up grants to hire music facilitators who created space for older people to engage in music activities. As the nature of this practice was studied, it was apparent that this demographic had specific needs that presented potential challenges for facilitators. The music had to be of good quality. There were age-related issues that need addressing in leadership and teacher training and preparation. It was reported that some facilitators felt intimidated by working with people the age of their grandparents! Out of this came a funded research project (funded again by the UK Research Councils) that focused on facilitation issues. Professional development workshops were held, resources developed and local networks created to generate support in these communities.

As a music psychologist, Andrea provides a foundational framework of psychological perspectives and with that lens is able to focus on the wider benefits of music making, of musical social networks and connections to health and well-being. She supports the premise that there is something extra special about music benefits; in music people can be seen 'firing' on multi levels including cognitive, emotional-affective, physical and social and participation of this type results in a fully engaged stage of life through music and the arts.

It is important for music facilitators to make the point that in dealing with older people, they are not dealing with a homogenous group. Those labelled as 'older' are as diverse as any other group in society. Older is also intergenerational. People often make the leap to 'older equals dementia'. While not wanting to diminish the enormous importance of acknowledging the challenges of dementia, it is also important to recognise that dementia is not proxy for ageing. Studies show that about 20 percent may show signs of dementia, but an equally significant problem among older people is isolation and loneliness. The overarching quality required to work with this sector of community is flexibility – to be aware of who is in the group and what their particular needs are. Andrea identifies four aspects of leadership in engaging older people in music.

Integrity: Older people need quality experiences with integrity, leaders with qualifications, skills and professionalism. Too often, older people get palmed off with experiences that are not good enough for other kinds of groups. For example, bringing in plastic toy rhythm instruments and 'dumbing down' the quality of the music offered is not acceptable. They want the authentic materials and challenges.

Ethics: There is a duty of ethical care around working with older people. Myths of ageing are perpetuated in how we relate to older people. The soundtrack of their lives is important. Andrea recalls colleagues finding it comical when she recounted doing rock 'n roll with seniors. There is a myth that older people cannot learn anything new. Andrea says they can! Older people have musical possible selves to continually develop throughout their lives and can do so at any age. Another myth is that they do not want to learn new things. While people often cherish the music that they experienced between ages 18 and 30, it is also important to push boundaries to open up space where there can be exploration and new awareness. Research shows that singing-songwriting in care homes is very successful, and is comprised of people of full spectrum to severe dementia. New music is created that become artefacts and cultural contributions to the community in which they live.

Reflexivity: It is important to be self-reflective and aware of one's own attitudes towards ageing. One of the biggest barriers among participation with older people is their reluctance to do something, which may contradict their own stereotypes about what is possible for older people. Responses such as 'not for me, I'm too old' can be met with finding their comfort zone and bridging the familiar to the new in safe and supportive contexts.

Excellent facilitation skills: The leader must have a well-developed sense of group dynamics, someone who can manage situations with materials and structure, but can also navigate the space between working alongside people as a fellow traveller and providing pathways for the participant to discover music making for themselves. It is important that the work has the challenge and sense of achieving something important. The members of the group must feel that they are contributing as much as they are taking. There is a sense of loss as people retire and lose their professional identity. That loss can be redeemed within a group where the greatest value is that you can give back, that music is a place where one can protest against the narrative of decline and decrepitude.

Key dimensions of a successful project include: engagement and flow in the moment, social affirmation through giving and receiving, opportunities for collaboration, joy in the music making and evidence of learning. Older people can develop musically. 'I've never done music. I can't sing. I don't know a thing about music' can evolve into amazing musical outcomes. People learn to sing, play instruments, write songs, join in group music making and grow into their musical possible selves.

As we get older we become adept at compensating for areas that become difficult. We get slower. This does not mean that intelligence diminishes. We might not be good at speed tests but we might experience life more profoundly. It is important for facilitators to adapt and realise that reflecting and thinking deeply are key (e.g. quick call-response games used with children often fail with older people). Along with compensating, older people learn to optimise, to become more selective at what we spend time doing. There is no reason or room to waste time.

Older people may decline in their ability to utilise fluid intelligence, such as abstract fast problem solving measured by timed tests or problems divorced from the real world. However, there is some evidence that crystallised intelligence does not decline. The ability to apply prior knowledge and experience is measured in real-world problem solving through reflection and drawing on capacities developed earlier in life. Creative music making provides a rich context where older people can use this type of crystallised intelligence, engaging in musical exploration and experimenting with musical possible selves.[6]

Negotiated Curriculum

Underlying the discussion of *how* we learn is the matter of *what* is to be learned. The curriculum is the set of learning expectations that learners are to demonstrate as evidence of mastery. Typically, a list of general and specific learning outcomes are listed, and instructors engage the learners in a variety of skill and knowledge-building tasks that can be assessed, evaluated and reported as part of formal learning accountability. Community music practice invests in a fluid process of *currere*, the root Latin word for curriculum, which by definition means to run the course. Rather than a fixed set of learning tasks, the facilitator along with the participants determine the path for the community as goals are identified, challenges arise and successes enable movement towards growth. Much the way that ancient athletes were trained for unforeseen obstacles in their epic races, the facilitator is equipped to deal with any encounter that may arise, whether it be a social matter, musical roadblock, emotional challenge or other. The curriculum, then, is actually negotiated until the identified needs are addressed and met, sometimes referred to as a 'bottom-up' process. Elliot Eisner, who was a professor of Art and Education at the Stanford Graduate School of Education, refers to this as flexible purposing. As the journey progresses, the targets move. If the initial course plan is rigidly adhered to, the goals are wildly missed and the learners are now 'off course' (Eisner, 2002).

The curriculum is therefore negotiated by participants and facilitators when:

- The facilitator negotiates with participants regarding the learning experiences;
- Workshops and events offer participants choice in forms of tasks, topics, coverage of knowledge and skills and pacing;
- Participants are invited to respond to learning activities in a variety of genre, modes and media;
- Participants' suggestions are accepted and used in planning;
- Content and processes are introduced by the facilitator in response to individual needs.

Don Coffman
Building Community through Wind Band

We cannot teach another person directly: we can only facilitate learning.
Carl Rogers[7]

In North America, community music frequently presents itself in the form of a concert band or choir that is supported by its members or through other forms of funding. Don Coffman is building a community band programme as part of the New Horizons International Music Association at the University of Miami where he has been since 2011. Prior to that he spent 24 years working with a New Horizons community band at the University of Iowa. This case study explores contrasts in the two locations and reveals some of Don's strategic work in finding ways to make music accessible to people from diverse backgrounds and ages. This 'tale of two cities' begins like this: imagine 65–100 people from a highly educated university town population made up of retired professors and community leaders who met regularly twice weekly to practice music in a band setting. Retirement life enabled scheduling flexibility, so this group could find time to meet on weekday mornings without feeling rushed. Iowa City's New Horizon's Band programme thrived by a word-of-mouth network that recruited interested participants, and the majority of these musicians had considerable prior musical experience. The playing level, Don recalls, was at about a Grade 3.5–4 and sometimes a 5 (band literature rating) level.

By contrast, the Miami group attracts 25–30 players who do not have the same level of music background and the only workable time in the schedule to meet is Saturday mornings. Most of the players are working in various careers and represent a younger demographic than the Iowa group. Traffic in the Miami area is constantly busy and people have many family and other obligations, but after exploring the options, this was the only feasible time to meet. This results in staggered arrival times and unpredictable attendance. In short, the Miami situation requires a different approach and an innovative set of leadership skills.

As Don meets the challenges of the Miami group, he embraces some essential leadership qualities. One must enjoy people more than perfection. The product is important, but how one gets there is more important. Patience is critical. One must be more concerned about the person behind the instrument that what comes out the end of the horn! Don's goal is to ensure that everyone has a satisfying time in each rehearsal. Individuals can become frustrated at specific musical challenges, but if the rehearsal is generally a downer, then it is a failure. While mastery of the physical aspects of playing an instrument is essential, Don never exposes an individual who is having difficulty. He senses that they are already somewhat apologetic about their abilities, so his strategy is to address the section or the row the individual is seated in. The idea is to provide anonymity yet work at fixing the problem.

Having realistic expectations is another quality a leader must have. If a person begins to play trumpet at age 50, the expectation of achieving a great range within a few months is a false one. It is important to accept the realities of the limitations with ageing players, the physical demands on muscles or arthritic fingers on the clarinet or flute. The limitations of ageing on the individual also translates to the ensemble as a whole. The progress journey is really up to the players as there are no tests or assessment pieces. If someone never practices outside of band rehearsal and never gets better there is still a place for that person. Some may find this irritating, that someone never improves, yet there is an understanding that this is a family, a community and not everyone is a star.

A typical rehearsal follows a model like this. The group starts with a non-concert material warm-up, such as a scale or line from a method book that brings focus and a common purpose to the group, soon after they arrive. The warm-up is where technique is addressed as well as foundational music theory. Developing facility on the instrument by playing in multiple keys, rhythm patters, sight reading and chorale work takes up anywhere from 10 to 30 minutes of an hour and a half rehearsal.

Following the warm-up, suitable literature is introduced. Usually, Don will lead them through the new piece from the beginning to see what they can handle. This, of course, is particular to the piece; sometimes a homophonic section is introduced or a melodic theme that all can play. Using adult learning theory, it is expected that the players will self-correct as they become more familiar with the piece of music. Even so, some players make the same rhythmic mistakes week after week and Don purposes not to stress about wrong notes. Things seem to work themselves out! His strategic plan is to do what gets the piece going quickest. For some, it is listening to it being played, either live or by recording. For others, repetition and practice work best.

Don observes that in both Iowa City and Miami, the players all wanted to be better. However, the intensity and effort varied greatly, reflecting the amount of time available for the Iowa retirees to get lessons, practice on their own compared with the Miami group who work five days a week, have family needs and many other life distractions. In Iowa, the connection to the university included a graduate teaching assistant and a staff of about six students, mostly undergraduates, who received a modest stipend to coach sections of the band. The players understood that band was a lab setting and they enjoyed working with young, emerging musicians. Understanding that not all of the students were strong, the elder musicians gave a little extra for them, found their youthful energy compelling and most importantly were part of the musical leadership maturing process.

In Miami, the relationship with the university is less developed. He has a graduate teaching assistant and supplements this leadership in spring semesters by requiring that undergraduate music education students participate in the band as players and prepare a few teachings as part of their methods courses. Don comments that his role with student leadership is 'trial by fire'. When things are not going so well, the students will come for feedback. He resists the micromanager role and is more of a 'clockwatcher' in keeping schedules and pacing moving forward. In his experience over the years, some strong student standouts have emerged who have demonstrated the capacity to 'run the show'. Weaker students need support and in the process they either improved, or moved on into other applied capacities for development.

There are those within the ensembles who get involved with leadership. Don notes that a variety of facilitation styles are evident, especially when experienced retirees take over and engage in some old school methods. These occasions provide opportunities for community music principles to be applied. Common agreement around practices of safety, hospitality and self-directed learning combined with good teaching facilitation create a community music culture within a structured wind band setting. This can result in a shift away from 'my way or the highway' style of teaching toward a person-centred approach where teaching becomes facilitation and students take greater responsibility for their learning accomplishments.

Don supports the idea that good teaching and good facilitation are essentially based on the same guiding principles. Earlier writings from the community music practitioners and scholars may have been overstatements of what was really happening in both community music and modern day music education. By arguing the differences between the two practices, we are in fact creating caricatures of both. Community music and music education actually need each other – a marriage of convenience built on a working relationship of mutual respect, whether it is paper music, or improvised, it is still people with music. The key is not how good someone is, but how they get better.

Don explores concepts of andragogy, the study of the theory and practice of the education of older adults, and heutagogy, the practice of self-determined learning. Heutagogy, a term coined by Stewart Hase and Chris Kenyon of Australia,[8] is an approach that a learner should be at the centre of the learning rather than teacher- or curriculum-centric pedagogies. The application of both andragogic and heutagogic principles to the wind band environment provides theoretical frameworks for strategic planning and progress assessment. How do older people learn in this setting? How do they take informal and non-formal approaches and apply them to their own progress? How much progress is based upon self-directed initiatives rather than facilitation interventions? How are short-term and long-term goals met?

Don concludes by re-stating his premise in this work: 'Music is a vehicle rather than an endpoint. It is all about the journey, not the destination.'

Conclusion

This chapter has explored a range of pedagogical approaches that community musicians employ in efforts to include all ages and people from diverse backgrounds into the circle of music engagement. In avoiding ideological and template approaches in facilitation, community music practices seek to adapt to the group of participants. While more formal approaches are the norm in educational institutions, it is acknowledged that informal learning and non-formal education have been a means by which people discover, explore and grow in various areas of interest. We are reminded of the mandate of the ISME Community Music Activities commission: 'We believe that everyone has the right and ability to make, create and enjoy their own music. We believe that active music making should be encouraged and supported at all ages and at all levels of society' (from http://www.isme.org/).

Questions and Topics for Discussion

1. Identify some examples of informal learning in your own life. According to this chapter's definition of non-formal education, how might that occur in a formal learning setting?

2. How does the community music approach contrast from traditional music education practices? Provide some personal examples.

3. Think of some settings where 'situated learning' takes place. In what ways does this learning context provide an authentic experience to the learner? Discuss some areas in your own learning journey where situated learning might have been more helpful than other modes of teaching/learning.

4. Why do you think schools are organised by grades according to date of birth? Are there other possibilities? How might a community music programme be structured, based on criteria other than age?

5. Discuss the role of curriculum in learning. Reflect on the premise that a bottom-up process engages the learner more deeply.

Notes

1. Freire (2002, p. 47).
2. See also Howell (2011).
3. www.newdynamics.group.shef.ac.uk/music-for-life.html
4. www.sagegateshead.com/join-in/music-for-silvers/
5. www.waes.ac.uk/
6. For more information, see the *New Dynamics of Ageing: Music for Life Project* (Hallam et al., 2011), 'Critical geragogy: A framework for facilitating older learners in community music' (Creech & Hallam, 2015), *Active ageing with music* (Creech et al. 2014), *Facilitating music for older people: Facilitator's handbook* (Creech, Hallam, & Varvarigou, 2012) and the websites Creative Aging (www.creativeaging.org/) and Age of Creativity (www.ageofcreativity.co.uk/)
7. C. R. Rogers (1994).

8   Hase and Kenyon of Southern Cross University, Australia, launched the heutagogy theory in 2000. Since then, it has become accepted as a practical approach, especially in online learning environments. [www.psy.gla.ac.uk/~steve/pr/Heutagogy.html]

References

Bartel, L., & C., Linda. (2004). From Dilemmas to Experience: Shaping the Conditions of Learning. In L. Bartel (Ed.), *Questioning the music education paradigm. Volume II of the series 'research to practice: a biennial series.'* Toronto: Canadian Music Educators Association.

Beynon, C., & Alfano, C. J. (2013). Intergenerational music learning in community and school. In K. Veblen, S. J. Messenger, M. Silverman, & D. J. Elliott (Eds.), *Community music today* (pp. 121–31). Lanham, MD: Rowman and Littlefield.

Coe, R., Aloisi, C., Higgins, S., & Major, L. E. (2014). *What makes great teaching? Review of the underpinning research.* Retrieved from www.suttontrust.com/researcharchive/great-teaching/

Coombs, P. H., & Ahmed, M. (1974). *Attacking rural poverty: How nonformal education can help.* Baltimore, MD: John Hopkins University Press.

Creech, A., & Hallam, S. (2015). Critical geragogy: A framework for facilitating older learners in community music. *London Review of Education, 13*(1), 43–57.

Creech, A., Hallam, S., & Varvarigou, M. (2012). *Facilitating music-making for older people: facilitator's handbook.* London: New Dynamics of Ageing.

Creech, A., Hallam, S., Varvarigou, M., & McQueen, H. (2014). *Active ageing with music supporting wellbeing in the third and fourth ages.* London: Institute of Education Press.

Eisner, E. (2002). *What can education learn from the arts about the practice of education? John Dewey Lecture.* Stanford, CA: Stanford University.

Freire, P. (2002). *Pedagogy of the oppressed.* New York: Continuum.

Green, L. (2008). *Music, informal learning and the school: A new classroom pedagogy.* Aldershot: Ashgate.

Hallam, S., Creech, A., Gaunt, H., Pincas, A., Varvarigou, M., & McQueen, H. (2011). Music for Life Project: The role of participation in community music activities in promoting social engagement and well-being in older people. Retrieved from http://www.newdynamics.group.shef.ac.uk/music-for-life.html

Higgins, L. (2012). *Community music: In theory and in practice.* New York: Oxford University Press.

Howell, G. (2011). Do they know they're composing? Music making and understanding among newly arrived immigrant and refugee children. *International Journal of Community Music, 4*(1), 47–58.

Lave, J., & Wenger, E. (1991). *Situated learning: Legitimate peripheral participation.* New York: Cambridge University Press.

Mok, O. N. A. (2011). Non-Formal learning: Clarification of the concept and its application in music learning. *Australian Journal of Music Education*, (1), 11–15.

Moll, L. C. (Ed.) (1990). *Vygotsky and education, instructional implications and applications of sociohistorical psychology.* New York: Cambridge University Press.

Mosston, M. (1973). *Teaching: From command to discovery.* Belmont, CA: Wadsworth.

Mullen, P. (2002). *We don't teach we explore: Aspects of community music delivery.* Paper presented at the Community Music Activities Seminar Rotterdam Conservatoire. Retrieved from www.worldmusiccentre.com/uploads/cma/mullenteachexplore.pdf

Myers, D., Bowles, C., & Dabback, W. M. (2013). Music learning as a lifespan endeavor. In K. Veblen, S. J. Messenger, M. Silverman, & D. J. Elliott (Eds.), *Community music today* (pp. 133–50). Lanham, MD: Rowman and Littlefield.

Paulston, R. G. (1972). *Non-formal education: An annotated international bibliography of the non-school sector.* New York: Praeger.

Paulston, R. G. (Ed.) (1996). *Social cartography: Mapping ways of seeing social and educational change.* New York: Garland.

Rahman, A. (1993). *People's self-development: Perspectives on participatory action research.* London: Zed Books.

Rogers, A. (2004). *Non-formal education: Flexible schooling or participatory education?* Hong Kong: Comparative Education Research Centre, the University of Hong Kong.

Rogers, C. R. (1994). *Freedom to learn* (3rd ed.). New York: Macmillan College Publishing Company.

Schön, D. A. (1991). *The reflective practitioner.* London: Basic Books.

Veblen, K. (2008). The many ways of community music. *International Journal of Community Music, 1*(1), 5–21.

Veblen, K. (2012). Adult music learning in formal, nonformal, and informal contexts. In G. McPherson & G. F. Welch (Eds.), *The Oxford handbook of music education* (Vol. 2, pp. 243–56). New York: Oxford University Press.

Vygotsky, L. (1978). *Mind in society: The development of higher psychological processes.* Cambridge, MA: Harvard University Press.

Waldron, J. (2017). Online music communities: Theory, research, and practice. In B.-L. Bartleet & L. Higgins (Eds.), *The Oxford handbook of community music.* New York: Oxford University Press.

Chapter 3
Inclusive and Empathetic Perspectives

The healthy community is one that leaves the [. . .] integrity of each individual intact. The only thing we have to bring to community is ourselves [. . .] It is ultimately the best gift we can give others.

Parker J. Palmer[1]

This chapter is about creating space for others. With the recognition that within the dominant sector of society lies power and privilege, community music builds on the premise that all are welcome and that those with influence must exert intentional energy to provide access to any and all who wish to be in the community. In western cultures, research affirms that 'membership in the white middle-class group affords individuals within this group certain privileges in society', while those outside of this group experience challenges (Dei et al., 2000). This situation exists because society is influenced by the norms established by the dominant group (Gay, 2004).

Participatory Music as 'Open-Door' Policy

Widely cited in community music circles is the notion that the act of making music in the company of others is an 'act of hospitality, a welcome [. . .] to those who want to participate in active music doing [. . .] a gesture toward an open-door policy, a greeting to strangers, extended in advance and without full knowledge of its consequences' (Higgins, 2012, p. 142). Not all music experiences are hospitable, and no doubt the reader has had personal encounters, or at least knows of such where fear, judgement and possibly even trauma prevailed. Systems of music education that privilege goals of musical perfection and competition have resulted in a myriad of performance anxiety symptoms and even a waning passion for music in those who once claimed a strong appetite for music study and growth. Whether striving for technical and stylistic perfection, or as simple as the adage 'no pain, no gain', we are witnesses to what some have called abuse in the music studio and ensemble setting. Juanita Epp and Alisa Watkinson (1997) suggest that any practices and procedures that adversely impact individuals by burdening them psychologically, mentally, culturally, spiritually, economically or physically are considered to be abusive. Influenced by sociologist Pierre Bourdieu, they go so far as to call it systemic violence. It includes practices and procedures that prevent participants from fully experiencing learning and growth, thus harming them.

Especially in North America, community music is most evident through volunteer ensembles comprised of amateur musicians who seek to enhance their personal and social lives through membership in a choir, band or other group. For many ensemble directors, there is pressure and expectancy for performances of a high standard, to be competitive and even to compete in local and national festivals. However, a community music perspective would include other priorities, such as asking if the musicians are enjoying themselves, do they find the music uplifting, is the audience engaged and finding the music beneficial? The social, inclusive and musical aspects are of equal importance. In contrast with traditional performance conventions, the ranking of talent and competition often results in depriving students more than serving them.

Process and Musical Potential

Lee Bartel and Linda Cameron (2004) have pointed out applications to music in the contexts of social norms and expectations in academic and conservatoire systems. Identifying three types of problems – music-related dilemmas, musical expressivity-technical proficiency and student (participant)-related dilemmas – they note that many decisions made in the assumed interest of musical growth are not actually student- or participant-based. The primary focus on the second area, musical expressivity-technical proficiency, results in mistakes becoming glaringly obvious. Mistakes must be corrected at all costs in order for performances to be deemed acceptable. Artistic excellence is associated with technical perfection and to achieve this end, the personhood of the musician may be compromised or even sacrificed. The mistake is, of course, in the emergence of the binary of process versus product. These need not be mutually exclusive. Community music values process, but insists on the rigor of developing musical potential to the fullest. The question must be applied to all instructional and leadership processes; do the ends justify the means?

How to manage and direct criticism in the interest of advancing musicianship becomes an instructional choice on behalf of the facilitator. If the criticism targets the inability of the participant to meet the expectation, whether due to lack of talent, stubbornness, lack of effort or focus, etc., then the person's character is likely to be impugned. This is misdirected criticism, often stemming from the psychological state of the facilitator as much as from the proficiency or lack thereof of the music participant. This is seen frequently as a perpetuation of the teaching style that the facilitator experienced from influential mentors and instructors in their own musical growth journey. We find ourselves teaching the way we were taught, continuing in a cycle of learning that is difficult to break. However, positive feedback can serve to motivate and inspire and may help to achieve the desired outcome. Self-confidence and a deeper level of engagement can be the result of positive and complimentary commentary on areas such as effort, expression, energy and so on. Such helpful feedback builds a spirit of empathy and self-worth in both individuals and the collective (Bartel, 2004).

Phil Mullen
Community Music Engagement with Children and Young People in Challenging Circumstances

Phil Mullen is a widely respected community music facilitator with an international presence. He has engaged in a diverse range of projects and events, leading thousands of participants into creative and inspiring music making. Music Inclusion is an example of a nationally funded programme that Phil served as an evaluator. Its aim was to ensure that children and young people in challenging circumstances are able to access music-making opportunities. Including both non-formal education through inclusive music-making activities, and formal education through music services provision, this programme addresses youth who find themselves in what Phil defines as one or more of the following situations:

1. Children, because of where they live, find themselves in an economically deprived situation, or are in rural isolation;
2. Children with disabilities, impairments and/or cognitive differences. Examples: visually impaired, deaf, those with autism;

3. Children who are challenged in life at the moment of engagement: those who do not live with their parents, children who are bullied or are bullies, those suffering bereavement or have been hospitalised;
4. Children and young people with challenging behaviour.

Phil, working in mainstream educational settings (mainly schools), deals with children ages 12 and under who do not have access to youth clubs or do not have the usual opportunities for social occasions. Schools are where they are found, especially in an era of declining funding for community children's programming. Phil works on the 3:30 theory; based on classes of 30 students, most often 3 will have difficulty in engaging, which may be for a variety of reasons. Phil works with these. In highly deprived wards (based on the social deprivation index that takes into account education, economics, standard of living, etc.), there is an increasingly growing population of vulnerable children and youth.

In practice, Phil asks, 'with these particular students, what is it we need to do?' He does not espouse that community music is one set practice or ideology. As differences emerge with children in challenging circumstances, practice must move beyond the generic theories and into contextualised applications.

For children finding themselves in economically deprived or rural isolation situations, it is all about trying to connect them with opportunities. Sometimes it means travel, although much can be achieved using online resources. Phil sets out to work with the student's potential; what they can achieve, who they are, where they are going, all in the interest of aiming higher in life.

For those with impairments or cognitive differences, he finds and addresses the barriers that impede them from making music. Assistive music technology, especially the use of digital tablets such as the iPad, is increasingly finding its way into use. How can the curriculum be adapted, the music made meaningful, and what kind of instruments are available or can be devised to make the music accessible?

Those who are vulnerable due to current circumstances demand a wide range of leadership approaches. Phil uses an emotionally intelligent approach, recognizing that their feelings in large part are affecting their lives.[2] Youth who are abused or part of gang culture have experienced deep levels of emotional trauma. When music opportunities are oriented towards the emotional-feeling needs of the student, it has the capacity to open up pathways for the release of those feelings and create opportunities for reflective thinking.

Phil notes, and studies support this, that children with challenging behaviour have poorer academic and life outcomes (Deane, Holford, & Mullen, 2015; Harrison & Mullen, 2013). Their life arc is worse than the others. It is essential to recognise the complexity of their situation. In accepting what the child is bringing, accepting the child but not necessarily the behaviour, a space is created for safe, creative expression. The facilitator must be very aware of levels of energy and anxiety, and respond accordingly.

Specific skills sets embrace the reflexivity of leadership in these settings. The 'lesson plan attitude' does not work in this field. This does not mean that one is sloppy or unprepared. Skeletal planning that includes how to set up the environment, a sequence of strategies to be used and other general outlines of the plan are important. But rather than a fixed idea of all of the steps, the facilitator seeks to build on personal values and from those values and beliefs derive what they are hoping to accomplish. It is to be open . . . open to what the student brings, and open to the process and outcomes. The final product is not necessarily in mind until it reveals itself in due time.

Phil also believes in structured reflection. He feels we have the language of contemplative practice, but the practice is still slowly emerging. The field of community music has some way to go to offer professionals opportunities for structured reflection that align with their own skill sets and ways of working. An important leadership skill is being able to guide participants in a type of dynamic reciprocity – reading and responding in ways that helps move towards musical outcomes, personal outcomes and social goals. Personal musicianship is developed, concepts of self and well-being are supported, and group cohesion and the ability of the individual to find their way into a group are all intertwined.

An example of Phil's facilitation strategies with elementary-age children includes an opening session where ground rules are established. What are the expectations of our class community? Members of the group will say how they want to be treated so a really good group can be built. The authoritarian leader role is gone. Behaviour management is now on the students' terms and the demonstration of this group spirit is manifest in how the students act out their own established protocols.

Next, once the ground rules are clear, a song is made of these rules. The students write the lyrics and Phil helps set the chord progressions and they have a go at the first line. The students speak or rap the lyrics, or even begin to sing it. The contour of melody emerges and they all can work on shaping it more definitively together. This now becomes the opening song for every session. It is their 'first song' and it reminds them of their own created terms of conduct.

Phil uses a variety of repertorial material that gets them feeling secure. Template songs with simple parts, or with openings where they can invent parts, lead them into more complex processes. It all depends on what is going to work in that specific situation.

Phil reminds us that we are to be free as a music educator and musician, and the central point is to be responsive to the reading of the group. It is about context and being in-the-moment with that group.

Extended strategies include taking some inventory of what the group wants to do. Do you want to sing? Write something? Percussion? Technology? Play instruments? Some groups can make these choices. Phil does not approach this as a fixed planning strategy but rather, he may sometimes make decisions and be a directive leader on one occasion and then return to the same group on another occasion, and circumstances may be right to open up the student leadership a bit more. In dealing with children with challenging behaviour, it is very important to get the 'read' of the group right in terms of sharing ownership. Too much control on Phil's part may be disempowering whereas too little may open the door for a negative form of chaos. The work is totally context-dependent and is continually changing.

In other contexts, Phil may use warm-ups or initial activities that provide a strand that moves into a completed composition. Or, he might devise and introduce a framework for improvisation so that the beginnings of a composition can evolve. For example, one might begin with a little exercise and evolving from that another decision is made. Then we ask, what do we need to do to this piece so that we would be happy performing it, and as the various musical challenges are addressed, the piece takes shape and form. Over time, something quite wonderful emerges.

As Phil works with emerging community music facilitators, he stresses creative group work, extended periods where the group does this together. They reflect on their learnings from those extended situations. Reflective questions probe for responses, such as what did the music develop? What creative decisions were made? How did you feel? How was the group cohesion? What worked? Didn't work?

Phil underscores that developing these skills requires time. Shadowing the experienced facilitator in a mentoring environment provides support as the emerging leader takes more risks and employs more creative practice. He recommends that setting up a project while there is still support as a student is an excellent experience. And, remember, mistakes are learning moments, and need not be crises!

In conclusion, Phil believes that as community music continues to develop globally, and continues to serve in activist settings, such as working with children and youth in challenging circumstances, the practice will broaden and many will get good fairly quickly at running a group that feels good about itself. It will continue to distinguish itself from formal education. Phil believes that within his own work, community music must stay focused on personal transformation. He does not necessarily feel the whole field must follow this as there are different understandings of the term community music with different emphases in careers. However, the area of personal development and indeed transformation has been vital for community music practice and those with that interest can follow it to a deeper level. In situations where social factors work against them, and societal stereotypes become negative baggage that they carry, he believes 100 percent that community music programmes are a prime site for transformation.

Phil's experience tells him that transformative work with individuals in challenging circumstances may not be successful in short sessions. It may require years of sustained support and practice. If we are to be serious about change and society enhancement through community music, then long-term planning and funding is the only way to achieve the real potential.

Community music in practice, then, seeks in a spirit of empathy and inclusivity to consider music making for the benefit of others, to play, sing, compose and improvise with other humans in mind as recipients or co-musickers (Carpenter, 2015). Using a range of instructional and leadership strategies as outlined in Chapter 4, community music facilitators seek to balance their experience with the skills and abilities of the individuals they are working with. The challenge of the task is to place the act of musicking over a value solely based on the final outcome. Goals include providing space for musicians to achieve their potential rather than aim for perfection, for them to engage fully as participants, and to bountifully partake in the musical, social and cultural journey on route to whatever destination awaits.

Culturally Responsive Workshop Characteristics

Circumstances and realities do impose conditions on the empathetic context described above. With an approach of respect and an understanding of the diversity of abilities and needs of others, community musicians recognise necessary boundaries and engage in the construction of norms to create safe places and open spaces for all who come. Empathetic stances in community building do not infer that there are no expectations or a lack of protocol in the processes. Those who enter under the premise and invitation of hospitality must themselves embody those characteristics of respect, sensitivity and generosity. A helpful perspective is found in educational pedagogy that we will call *culturally responsive leadership*.

Culture goes much deeper than typical understandings of ethnicity, race and/or faith. It encompasses broad notions of similarity and difference and it is reflected in our participants' multiple social identities and their ways of knowing and of being in the world. Our participants must see themselves reflected in the experiences that community music provides. Facilitators must know and build on prior knowledge, interests, strengths and learning styles. Differentiated instructional strategies provide a wide range of methods and opportunities for participants to demonstrate . . . to make evident their musical growth as well as their personal challenges with music.

Let us consider the following questions:

- What does a workshop or instructional space look like, sound like and feel like when we encourage reflection, honour the community and support authentic collaboration among facilitators and participants?
- What does a workshop or instructional space look like, sound like and feel like when it is inclusive and when instruction is responsive to the full range of participant diversity?
- How do we work with the greater communities to develop an authentic appreciation for the importance of being culturally aware and responsive?
- What is the impact on our music participants when we do not acknowledge the complexity of culture and difference?
- How can we lessen dominant perspectives in our practice so that contributions from different backgrounds can be better understood and integrated into musical practices?

The following are some inquiry questions for culturally responsive facilitators:

- What questions might we reflect upon to examine our own biases towards diversity and cultural responsiveness?
- How might we integrate specific life experiences of our participants into daily instruction and learning processes?

Those engaged in this work of responsive leadership are committed to the collective, not merely individual empowerment, such that the impact of this approach is directed towards making change for all members of society (Ladson-Billings, 2011). As facilitators in community music, we must be prepared to include everyone while also being committed to the individual; the journey towards equity and inclusivity seeks to empower each member in the community environment. This approach affirms the personal cultural capital that each participant brings to our midst.

Donald Devito
Engaging with an Adaptive Curriculum for Diverse Learning Contexts

Donald DeVito is a Music teacher at the Sidney Lanier Centre, Gainesville, Florida.[3] The Centre is a state school for children with severe disabilities, and is accessible for students between the ages of 4 and 22. The participants in Don's music activities all have a variety of disabilities including autism, Prader Willi and Down syndrome, Schizophrenia, severe intellectual and physical impairments. There are also students who are in need of behaviour-related support systems, primarily juvenile justice prevention. Don is the first certified music teacher the school has attracted in its 40-year history. He states that his reasoning for maintaining his position as a music teacher at the school, rather than pursuing a university lecturer position for instance, is a result of the enjoyment he consistently gains working within the environment and alongside his students. Although the Sidney Lanier Centre is essentially a state school, Don is able to lead sessions as a community music facilitator rather than a music teacher. From this vantage point, he is able to observe each student's needs and if necessary can adjust sessions in response. He doesn't force anything upon the students, and if something isn't working as well as it should be, he won't give up; he will adapt this until he feels progress is being made.

The second context of Don's work takes place through the development of a music and special education programme at the Notre Maison Orphanage in Port au Prince, Haiti.[4] He links both locations, in the United States and in Haiti, through personal visits and telecommunications. Technology has also enabled Don to employ the skills of international music educators who are interested in developing adaptive curriculum and there are regular sessions that bring guest musicians into the classrooms via programmes such as Skype. As a result of these collaborations, he is able to educate his students on a variety of different cultures and cultural musics. One particular community music project, with which Don and his students engaged, was called DIScoveringABILITIES and was performed in the Carnegie Hall, New York. This was a large-scale collaboration between students from New York and New Jersey and musicians from African, Irish and Brazilian backgrounds.

Don sets out to engage his students in musical activities that will provide some life skill foundations. He encourages his students to engage with people in a range of different settings, from taking them to the grocery store, to inclusion activities with other school students younger than themselves, and also getting them to take part in competitions not necessarily open for involvement for children with disabilities. As the schools he works in are self-contained settings, these type of activities encourage his students to engage with people they wouldn't usually engage with. As a result of this, the students gain confidence that they can apply to other aspects in their lives. In addition to this, Don also gives his students leadership opportunities. He teaches codes and rhythm signals for blind, hearing-impaired and intellectually disabled students and encourages them to learn to adapt and take up leadership positions to give them an enhanced sense of musical engagement.

When asked what the essential personal qualities in enabling effective music making with this type of client group are, Don replies, patience and a confidence in the pedagogical approach. He qualifies this by adding:

> It takes a great deal of time and patience when teaching 160 students with every disorder, mental health and need for behavioral support that you can imagine. Keeping in mind the Sidney Lanier setting is designed as a school with the same benchmarks and standards of an academic music education organisation found in a US public school.

Don is always mindful with regard to the importance of 'accommodation for all learners', and he believes that the facilitation and communicative aspects of group activities brought through the approaches associated with community music have been critical to the successes of his programme. At the heart of Don's pedagogical approach is flexibility. Reliving participants' anxiety by enabling choice is vital. For example, the group deciding on the first activity:

> I have found that students with significant anxiety that can lead to behavioral outbursts appreciate being able to have a say in the first activity of the class. This way they know exactly what is going to be asked of them when they enter the room and everything tends to go smoothly from that point. Even five minutes of a preferred activity to start can create a consistently open and accommodating environment.

Understanding music theory has also been of great benefit to Don and he sees this as a vital skill in what he does. In some situations, he takes their stories or poems, often written around the challenging situations or experiences they have faced, and generates melodies that fit the words to create songs that the participants feel they own.

Don's advice to musicians wishing to work in this area is to always 'have a game plan for what you envision with your group but be prepared to change on a moment's notice. Allow the participants to determine the path that the activity takes.' He outlines a situation that highlights some of these points:

> When I learned that I would have 7 new classes of students from kindergarten through age 22 with behavioral and mental health needs, I had a preliminary activity planned using the materials and instruments I had in my classroom. By the end of the first week, through listening and communicating with the students on what we did and what their interests were I altered the course of the term.

In this example, Don organised different approaches for each class that included working together with rock instruments employing garage band strategies similar to those discussed by Lucy Green (2008). Another example involves students with significant behavioural needs that were not being met by other education establishments in the district. Don facilitated an inclusive community choir teaching portions of a song in their separate classes, then bringing them together for a performance:

> I taught Down on the Corner by Creedance Clearwater Revival on voice and percussion to a high school class of students with disabilities (the north section of the school) and taught the guitar rift to a class of students with behavioral needs (the south section of the school). They were brought together to form a combined ensemble.

These strategies have had the effect of diminishing the fear of failure and increasing the acceptance of others.

When working within these contexts, Don states that facilitation, observation and age-appropriate material are three key facets of the work. Collaborative partnerships are also very important and he advises community musicians working in these contexts to think outside of their immediate locality for potential creative partners as he feels international collaborations have largely benefited his work. An illustration of this is the work with Arthur Gill, a music educator working with children with disabilities in Pakistan. Connecting through a UK funding agency Gill was able to raise £20,000 to enhance his knowledge, which enabled him to engage over 500 children in his country. Additionally, Don was able to visit the University of London to attain training in new approaches in categorizing behavioural interaction for children with disabilities. Both he and Arthur were able to apply the latest approaches in special education straight into their classrooms.

As illustrated by both Don and Phil, one of the challenges in creating an empathetic space for musicking is to find ways to recognise and hear each other's voices. An example of the inclusive honouring of voice is those working in critical race theory issues who embrace and engage in narrative practice (Delgado & Stefancic, 2012). Storytelling is a very important, rich and creative way to provide information and meaning about the experiences of participants from diverse backgrounds.

Community music's equivalent to storytelling is constructed and re-constructed sound, both made individually and with others. Safe spaces are created through the intervention of the facilitator. Musical pathways are developed as participants become more aware of themselves and those in community with them. When this practice enables one to hear with the whole being (and often we hear in ways that we are not verbally possible to express), it might be considered an empathetic practice, an act of hospitality. It is in the invitation to hear in nuanced ways that opens up the potential opportunities of feeling the 'otherness' with authentic and grounded perspectives. Empathetic practice is key to the building of communities, and developing the capacity to show empathy towards the challenges that are being faced daily by those around us enables us to value the realities, the good and the bad.

Inclusive Action in Participatory Music, Personal and Social Well-Being

Community music facilitators are musicians who nurture the identities of participants through inclusive active participation in music. These musicians frequently inhabit those pockets of society where populations are marginalised or disadvantaged. The foundational premise in community music is that the personal and social well-being of those in the group is as important or more important that the mastery of musical skills and polished performances (Veblen et al., 2013). People who find themselves in disadvantaged situations, including migrant populations, at-risk youth, the elderly, incarcerated, those with post-traumatic stress conditions and those suffering from a variety of abusive experiences or from physical or mental challenges, may all find a place of acceptance and worth through music intervention and participation.

Among the many examples around the world of populations that are disadvantaged and neglected are the Native Peoples of Canada. In 2015, the Truth and Reconciliation Commission Report[5] submitted 94 *Calls to Action* in response to the years of hearing testimonies of witnesses to the atrocities committed by dominant settler culture programmes. A drumming circle made up of women and youth were called upon to provide traditional First Nations song and dance for events and ceremonies at the time of the release of this report. This case study explores the work of the Good Hearted Women Singers and their leader, Kelly Laurila.

Kelly Laurila
Keeper Of Song, *Mino Ode Kwewak N'Gamowak* (Good Hearted Women Singers)

Twenty years ago, Kelly attended a Pow Wow at Six Nations, Ontario, and at the beginning of the event was first confronted with the Big Drum. She was literally overcome with emotion and could not stop crying. She wondered why it was so powerful. She consulted an elder who responded, 'your heart remembers when your mind does not'. This began a journey of retracing her own heritage and roots, and finding the Anishinabe people, connecting to her own heartbeat and to the heartbeat of the land. This journey has been challenging, profound and deeply rewarding and, at the time of writing, Kelly is well into her PhD programme in social work, and the leader, or 'Songkeeper' of *Mino Ode Kwewak N'Gamowak*, the Good Hearted Women Singers. As facilitator of this drum circle, it is she who holds the memories and teachings of songs and passes them on exactly as she has been taught. In each song, the roots are acknowledged – who taught it, where it came from and what is the purpose of the song. There are specific songs for specific occasions and

Figure 3.1 *Mino Ode Kwewak N'Gamowak*

in some contexts where there are those who do not know the teachings, certain songs cannot be sung, for as Kelly explains, 'we would be hurting those who do know'.

The context of the drum circle is a community within a community – in this case, an urban Indigenous drum circle within the city, a community of women and youth coming together for collective singing, healing and being with one another. There is something about identity and culture that we spend our lives seeking, and the drum circle helps to give confidence to *just be* within the traditions of the First Peoples. Healing comes from the drumming and singing, from being together in community, and from honouring the protocols of the teachings and traditions.

Kelly was part of the group that in 2003 was formed by a community elder and local Métis[6] musician to provide a place where Indigenous women and youth could learn the teachings and traditions of their ancestry. Membership in the group was diverse at that time, and is even more so today. Some came, knowing their Aboriginal roots, their First Nation, and could clearly identify with that ancestry. Some from settler ancestry have joined, only to learn later that they came from First Nations ancestry. Often, parents who lived in the dominant settler culture would not acknowledge their Aboriginal ancestry and the descendants did not learn of their own heritage. Being a 'native Indian' was considered shameful and not to share publically if avoidable. Kelly was aware that she was a *Sáami*, an Indigenous nation from northern Scandinavia (Finland), but she was raised as a Canadian girl with an Irish background. She carries with her the tensions of identifying as both Indigenous and settler.

Some members of the group who are settlers came seeking spiritual connections to the drum, knowing the injustices of the past and in search of some resolution in their own lives. The diversity of the members of *Mino Ode Kwewak N'Gamowak* is an important and welcomed aspect of the group, creating a rich texture of personal stories of lives of challenge, abuse and often trauma. Kelly is learning these stories of how healing relationships are created through drumming and singing as part of her doctoral research.

Kelly has been gifted with many traditional teachings. She has learned from her elders that one should never be identified through negativity. An essential quality of leadership within a community drum circle is knowing when to respond to something and when to let it be. She practices the strategy of emphasizing the positive in order to erase the negative. Her authority is derived in that she was gifted the leadership from the founding elder. Kelly would not feel enabled to facilitate the group without this gifted authority. She continues to meet with the elder and it is at these meetings where she can express her own doubts about her heritage and deal with the meaning of the music and the role of the song in this ongoing journey.

Whatever is done within the circle, it must contribute to the building of good relations. The context must be kept in perspective with words always said in a positive way where the musical instruction, pronunciation, drumming pulse and the overall spirit of the music are all emphasised in the affirmative. There is also an awareness of the presence of ancestors in this experience, a presence that guides the teachings and instruction as songs are learned, drummed and danced, and ultimately handed down to others.

A typical meeting of the *Mino Ode Kwewak N'Gamowak* might include the following components. Ritual is very important for the cultural acknowledgement it brings, but also for the safety and comfort with doing this every week, providing the knowledge that the members will know what to expect.

Smudging

The event begins with a cleansing in the smoke of burning sage and participants invite the smoke into their presence to prepare themselves spiritually, emotionally, mentally and physically in order to be ready to be in circle with themselves individually and with others.

Pray

All join hands in the circle, extending our left hand up to the person on our left and right hand down to the person on the right. In this way, each is receiving the prayers with our left hand and giving with our right hand. Nobody is left out of the prayers in the circle. We give thanks for all we have, water, land and all that is within creation. We ask for prayers for those who are struggling and for community at large. There is a saying called 'all our relations'. We say this at the end of each drum circle. It reminds us that we are all connected to all beings in our world. We cannot exist without the help of all our relations.

Sing

A welcome song is always sung, including a welcome for everyone including the ancestors from the spirit world.

Seven Grandfathers

Seven candles are lit, representing the seven grandfathers of love, honesty, respect, humility, courage, truth and wisdom. In this ritual, women and/or youth may share their story of any of those grandfathers, making it very conscious that they are not just singing but are building relationships. How they walk their lives in a good way will impact others.

Songsharing

When singing, all of the prayers and teachings are remembered. At this stage members are invited to share. If a member is coping with bereavement or trauma, illness, family or child issues, a healing song (e.g. Bear Song) is sung. Collectively, the circle gathers around that particular woman and with song comes healing. When the drums resonate with the body, the body is changed and as the person senses a spirit of healing, the whole group also experiences the healing. There is always a place for singing special songs for individuals who are having challenging or celebratory events in their lives.

Each person is invited to bring a song. The women talk about their song before they share it, and then all are welcome to join her in the song. But, through song we have each other to carry the song through. Each person will take a turn to lead a song and then we all sing together. We learn the songs as we go. It is okay if mistakes are made, because we will learn as we go to correct them. Each person talks about the song before they share. Each person brings their own nation's song (e.g. Haida Gwaii, MiqMaw, Cree, Anishinabe, Haudenosaunee, Cherokee) and others have offered songs. Kelly invites them to go around the circle until each member has had a chance to lead a song (like passing the feather). If a song is new and someone does not know it, it can be led again. The learning is by oral practice and memory. The practice to 'trust that you will get the song' and that trust is both in process and in the teachings. Not all have learned that teaching of look, listen, listen again with patience. There is much to be learned also in noting what they are not saying.

When songs have been shared, the drumming and the dancing within the circle comes to its conclusion with a travelling song. This closing song regretfully bids farewell to the ancestors, the drum beat slows, and the rehearsal comes to a close.

Kelly remarks that while this should have been so obvious, it is within the hearing of the stories of the women that the circle is what is so important. The circle addresses the emotional, spiritual, physical, mental and relational healing each week. Her research reveals that the circle represents knowing, being, seeing and doing, the circle of life. Sometimes the group withdraws from the busy pace of public performing just to be in the circle together, to stop and remember their roots and to have sacred time. In these times set aside for themselves, they are reminded that the urban setting is a struggling terrain with tensions arising within the public-private and urban Indigenous influences pulling on them.

The group is inclusive and sensitive to each member's particular values. In particular, gender concepts are honoured and welcomed. Sensitivities around identity, clothing and openness to all people are practiced. There are those who can be called to lead within the circle and learn the teachings. Kelly is particularly encouraging of the youth to take on more responsibilities. New songs are introduced and many decisions are made collectively. At times, issues need to be addressed and direct, honest, open but always kind discussions take place to resolve matters and move forward.

Those who experience the Good Hearted Women Singers in an event may not know which one is Kelly. There is no identification or exceptional public role that would point her out to those who do not know her. The circle is completely inclusive with shared leadership and a generous spirit of contribution from each of the members. The intentional interdependent nature of the group is key to its power and effectiveness. It is a model for leadership that is nurturing, respectful and fully hospitable.

This description is found on the group's website:

> Our drum group reflects a sweetgrass teaching. One blade of sweetgrass by itself is not very strong. It can break easily. When several blades of sweetgrass are braided together, the sweetgrass is strong and cannot easily be broken. The singing and drumming helps us to find the strength to keep going. A woman may feel reluctant and not have the confidence to lead a song, but she gives it a try because she knows that the others

Figure 3.2 Good Hearted Women Singers Benefit Concert

will be there to pick up the song if she falters. That song will be carried on, just as we all must carry on with our lives, no matter what. Just as the braided sweetgrass is strong, our 'knowing' that we have the strength and support of one another helps us to carry on.[7]

As community music practice embraces the engagement of the disadvantaged, community musicians seek to meet the challenges of diversity, inclusivity and equity in the provision of opportunities for creating, improvising, performing alone and in groups, exploring the music of others, and sharing the deepest of human expression. As boundary walkers, community musicians must be secure in their own identity and personhood: grounded, centred and able to navigate a wide range of challenges. A balanced, healthy approach to one's quest for a fully active life is one that considers work, creativity and caring as mutually complimentary dimensions of engagement. Work is often driven by external forces, by necessity or demand. Creativity is driven by inner motivation, imagination and vision. Caring is borne out of compassion for others, an act of nurturing, which in turn makes us aware of others in community. Work, creativity and caring can become empathetic acts as we live out our lives within the perspective of inclusivity and hospitality.

At the edges of society, music brings its sounds and silence . . . bursts of sonic energy and seemingly empty spaces where modes shift and excitement builds or tension is released. On the margins and along the boundaries, the community musician walks among the voices that are often silenced by systems of oppression, systems that are faced on a daily basis. Walking the boundaries is potentially disruptive and challenges the familiar practices. The uncertainty and ambiguity found in the margins, however, open up limitless possibilities. This disruptive energy potentially becomes a central force in maintaining life and vigour, in shaping and reshaping practice and in developing community and relationships. Not without its challenges, working from perspectives of inclusivity, empathy and hospitality provokes and disturbs the static state of traditional music education and in so doing resists a fixed state of conditions and constancy. It is within that context that the act of making music together is an act of hospitality.

Questions and Topics for Discussion

1   Discuss the concept of inclusive, hospitable music making. How does it look, sound and feel in the various settings you as a reader experience?

2   It is noted that often music-making decisions are not made with the participant in mind. Provide some examples of how musical problems are approached in your settings and how musical growth can be achieved that is participant based.

3   Discuss these questions presented earlier in this chapter: (a) What does a workshop or instructional space look like, sound like and feel like when we encourage reflection, honour the community and support authentic collaboration among facilitators and participants? And (b) What does a workshop or instructional space look like, sound like and feel like when it is inclusive and when instruction is responsive to the full range of participant diversity?

4   Having read the three approaches to facilitating musical practices in diverse and vulnerable communities, consider this question, presented earlier in the chapter: How can we lessen dominant perspectives in our practice so that contributions from different backgrounds can be better understood and integrated into musical practices?

Notes

1   Palmer (1990).
2   Goleman (1995).
3   http://lanier.sbac.edu
4   www.raysoh.org/projects/notre-maison-orphanage/
5   www.trc.ca/websites/trcinstitution/File/2015/Honouring_the_Truth_Reconciling_for_the_Future_July_23_2015.pdf
6   In Canada, the Métis are Aboriginal people, descendants of First Nations and European ancestry, primarily from the Algonquian and French.
7   http://minoodekwewak.wix.com/goodheartedwomen

References

Bartel, L., & Cameron, L. (2004). From dilemmas to experience: Shaping the conditions of learning. In L. Bartel (Ed.), *Questioning the music education paradigm. Volume II of the series 'Research to practice: A biennial series.'* Toronto: Canadian Music Educators Association.

Carpenter, S. (2015). A philosophical and practical approach to an inclusive community chorus. *International Journal of Community Music, 8*(2), 197–210.

Deane, K., Holford, A., & Mullen, P. (2015). *The power of equality 2: Final evaluation of youth music's musical inclusion programme 2012–2015*. Retrieved from http://network.youthmusic.org.uk/learning/research/power-equality-2-final-evaluation-youth-musics-musical-inclusion-programme-2012–20

Dei, G. J. S., James, I. M., Karumanchery, L. L., James-Wilson, S., & Zine, J. (2000). *Removing the margins: The challenges and possibilities of inclusive schooling*. Toronto: Canadian Scholar's Press.

Delgado, R., & Stefancic, J. (2012). *Critical race theory: An introduction* (2nd ed.). New York: NYU Press.

Epp, J. R., & Watkinson, A. M. (Eds.). (1997). *Systemic violence in education: Promise broken*. New York: State University of New York Press.

Gay, G. (2004). Beyond Brown: Promoting equality through multicultural education. *Journal of Curriculum and Supervision, 19*(3), 193–216.

Goleman, D. (1995). *Emotional intelligence: Why it can matter more than I.Q.* New York: Bantam Books.

Green, L. (2008). *Music, informal learning and the school: A new classroom pedagogy*. Aldershot: Ashgate.

Harrison, C., & Mullen, P. (Eds.). (2013). *Reaching out: Music education with hard to reach children and young people*. London: Music Mark.

Higgins, L. (2012). *Community music: In theory and in practice*. New York: Oxford University Press.

Ladson-Billings, G. (2011). Asking the right questions: A research agenda for studying diversity in teacher education. In A. Ball & C. Tyson (Eds.), *Diversity in teacher education* (pp. 383–396). Lanham, MD: Rowman and Littlefield.

Palmer, P. J. (1990). *The active life, a spirituality of work, creativity, and caring*. San Francisco, CA: Jossey-Bass.

Veblen, K., Messenger, S. J., Silverman, M., & Elliott, D. J. (Eds.). (2013). *Community music today*. Lanham, MD: Rowman and Littlefield.

Chapter 4
Strategic Leadership and Facilitation

One of the marvelous things about community is that it enables us to welcome and help people in a way we couldn't as individuals. When we pool our strength and share the work and responsibility, we can welcome many people...

Jean Vanier[1]

Facilitation, Definitions and Applications

The community musicians featured throughout this book illustrate the diversity of the practice. Underlining all the work, however, are sets of key skills that can be clearly identified. Under the umbrella term 'facilitation', deriving from the French *faciliter* (to render easy) and the Latin *facilis* (easy), community musicians have been concerned with encouraging open musical dialogue among different individuals with differing perspectives. A concise description of a community music facilitator might be: a self-reflective musician who has a variety of human, processual, technical skills and knowledge, together with a variety of experiences to assist groups of people to journey together to reach their musical goals.[2] From the perspective of those featured in this book, facilitation can be understood as a process that enables music participants to harness the flow of their creative energy in order to develop and grow through pathways specific to them as individuals and the groups through which they are involved. In this context, facilitation does not mean that the music leader surrenders their leadership responsibility, merely that the control is relinquished. For example, the facilitator will constantly call upon their ability to 'read' the responses of individuals and the group as a whole, constantly monitoring the nuances of interactions. The facilitator will need to be articulate, skilled in providing clear instruction and information to whatever extent the group requires it. The musician may at times need to challenge and provoke, and alternately reassure and encourage, responding to their knowledge of each individual.

Rebecca Gross
Finding Voice in the Choir

Rebecca Gross is a community musician who facilitates groups, workshops, choirs and projects for people of all ages in and around the North East of England. She became interested in music at a very young age; however, it wasn't until later on in life that she decided to focus on working with people to create and perform music. Her parents never thought that music could be a career and initially wanted Rebecca to be a medical doctor as she was gifted in the sciences. Resisting her parents did cause difficulties but eventually Rebecca undertook a music degree, followed by a Masters of Arts, and then a Master of Education. It was, however, when Rebecca took part in a community music project that she realised this was the type of music making she was most interested in. She recalls:

> I participated in a community music project which had a profound impact on me. I thought 'Woah' I want to do what he does because what he has done has touched my heart and I am a different person and can be more of myself because of the facilitation. I got way more involved than I thought I was going to and I came out of it a transformed person. And so because it happened to me, that's what I'm looking for, for other people.

For Rebecca, the essence of being a community musician is the ability to adapt to an ever-changing environment. 'You need to be able to relate to the people in your group', she says; 'you need to understand their needs and feel committed to the fact that every single participant is a stakeholder in the process'. Rebecca works with a variety of age groups, from toddlers to elderly people. She finds that the main skill a community musician needs is adaptability. She believes that one's core skills should remain the same; however, the ability to adapt allows the facilitator to relate to people in each group they work with. In addition to this, she also believes that inclusivity is another important feature of being a community musician. She feels that every single person has the right to access sessions, on their own terms and at their own pace.

The choir is a setting in which Rebecca does a considerable amount of work. As a facilitator, she believes in equality. For example, she feels that everybody who participates should have equal access to any material, such as sheet music or lyrics. Furthermore, she prepares herself to ensure she knows every note of every song in order to be able to correct something if it goes wrong. In addition to this, she feels that individuals are better when they sing together. One example of this is her work with Whitby Community Choir. This particular choir, with the guidance of Rebecca, organised an annual street choir festival. As a result of projects such as this, the choir feels like a community organisation helping to make a change in their area; however it is the singing that makes it special and encourages members to stay. Rebecca explains that there is an amazing supportive culture within the group and she asked, 'Would this be the same if it was a different kind of social group? Is it the singing that makes it special?'

> Overwhelmingly, it was the singing. It was the fact that it was *a cappella*, and they felt exposed and they needed to step up and be heard because if they weren't singing nobody would hear anything. I have seen those moments where lives are changed. For instance, one lady came and joined the choir and then she said 'I love this so much that I want to do it every night'. So she set up her own little choir and got new people who were in her circle of friends to join it and then she said 'oh this is really hard I didn't know how hard it would be, I'm going to bring them all back to choir'. So it was just, it has a life of its own and it is because we sing.

It is clear that Rebecca cares very deeply for those that decide to work with her and this comes across through the ways she approaches her work. She is not a 'glory seeker' and she strongly believes that one quality that allows her to connect with her participants is that she considers that the most important voice in any session is that of the participants, not her own. This shows the mutual respect that Rebecca upholds throughout all sessions she facilitates. She does not set herself up as being remote from anyone, she partakes in each session with the participants, both physically and emotionally. Rebecca's work appears to be selfless as she facilitates sessions to benefit the participants, not herself:

> The most important voice in the room is their voice, not mine. My job is to find out what they need, find out what they think they need and find out what I think they need. And rather than compromise between the two, try and do it all. Try to listen for that unspoken dialogue that's going on. Listen to when people stop and say 'I need to tell you this thing about me'. Not dismissing it as unimportant, really taking it on. Because

sometimes people have these real open hearted moments when they're sharing something they might not have shared to anybody else. And in that moment you're privileged to be the person who they're talking to. So you've got to respect and value that privilege.

In addition to long-term work such as music tots and community choirs, Rebecca also partakes in short-term projects. One recent project that she facilitated, in 2014, was called 'Wish You Were Here', as part of the Yorkshire Festival celebrations for the Grand Depart. Rebecca gained funding through North Yorkshire Music Action Zone (NYMAZ)[3] and, with inspiration from Cecil Sharp, the English folk song collector, created the project that encouraged young people to work with community music groups to compose songs about the places they lived in. She administered two of the eight groups and observed the other six. This was an interesting experience as she found a broad contrast in facilitation strategies throughout the other groups. Reflecting on one of her groups, she notes,

> They [the participants] wrote this amazing song about Botton and about how it is to live in this lonely place. And I thought it was a really good song. I only had to trim it down, I kind of did that producer thing where I was like 'right, okay, no that's way too long'.

It seemed clear to Rebecca that some of songs emulating from other groups had more character and influence from the facilitator and consequently lacked input from the community participants. This demonstrates the fine lines facilitators walk when working creatively with groups – providing a working space that enables individual input and ownership rather than a vehicle for the group leader's work.

As Rebecca is primarily a freelance community musician, although she is affiliated to various organizations, she feels that this can sometimes lead to feeling isolated. She is on the board of 'Sound Sense', the UK's national community music members association,[4] and therefore has the advantage of being able to meet other practitioners and discuss their practice. Furthermore, she identifies other practitioners with whom she has either a similar approach, or has similar work:

> We'll have a meeting and then we'll say 'right, this is our CPD [Continuing Professional Development]. We're going to meet, we're going to talk about our practice, we're going to explore difficulties and problems that we're having, look for new ideas' and those meetings, those moments are really really really valuable. And can provide those moments of insight.

This is beneficial to her, as a facilitator, as she is able to discuss her practice, explore problems and look for new ideas with other community musicians, rather than alone. This is why Continuing Professional Development (CPD) is an important aspect of Rebecca's life:

> I think that, as a freelancer, it's your responsibility to take control of your CPD, and I think that anybody who is a freelance community musician that isn't engaging in CPD in an active way really should be asking themselves why they're not.

One way of doing this is getting involved with other community music projects and Rebecca uses this technique to shadow other workers, watch performances and reflect on what she thought the strengths and weaknesses are: 'There's no better way to improve your practice than to steal somebody else's best bits. It's a proven fact!'

Rebecca believes that anyone wanting to become a community musician should do so because they have a heart for wanting to share music and use it to make a change in peoples' lives.

> I feel sometimes people decide to pursue a path into community music because what they really want to be is an orchestral musician or a classical singer, but there isn't any work so this will do. In my experience these are the people that find the work the least fulfilling.

Rebecca is emphatic in saying that community music work demands an expertise and commitment – it's not just something you can do effectively if you are filling in time waiting for something else. From a facilitator's point of view, she believes that to work within the field you should be prepared for it to change your life, as you will not be emotionally immune to the process people who you're working with are going through.

Facilitation, Essential Qualities

Within the act of facilitating, there may certainly be a starting point, but the rest of the process need not be as certain. This is supported by our case studies that seem to challenge any sense of a predicable ending to group creative music making. Facilitators therefore, offer routes towards suggested destinations and are ready to assist if the group journey becomes lost or confused, but they are always open to the possibility of the unexpected that comes from individuals in their interactivity with the group (Higgins & Campbell, 2010). They also need to be organised and plan their approach well, aware of imposed time frames and restraints and the intended musical goals that must fit within these. Aims and objectives may be set but an insistence on particular musical outcomes and procedures to get there are not held onto at all costs. This is not an easy task because within any group there are a multitude of fine lines between leading and controlling.

Facilitators need to be creative, able to improvise and think 'on their feet', and ensure variety and appropriate pacing so that the group is carried along by their own momentum, energy and sense of flow. Most critically, if each of these skills is understood as a kind of 'tool', it is not the range of tools available but the facilitators' choice of the most appropriate tools for the task at hand that most distinguishes their work (Howell, Higgins, & Bartleet, 2016). As previously argued, facilitation 'is an art', whether or not it takes place in an arts-based context (Higgins & Campbell, 2010, p. 9). The personal attributes of the music facilitator also play an important role. Effective leadership benefits from a certain amount of charisma and likeability, the ability to remain positive and calm in less predictable environments and a willingness to be open to one's own learning taking place alongside that of the participants. Underpinning this range of skills and attributes is an understanding of musical excellence that is defined both through the quality of musical outcomes and the quality of the social bonds that are created through the process (Turino, 2008). In other words, facilitators understand that the personal and social growth of participants is as important as their musical growth.

Chris Bartram

Selecting the Right Tools from a Broad Toolkit of Skills and Activities

Chris Bartram is an experienced freelance community musician, music educator and trainer. He has worked with many of the UK's leading regional and national arts organizations, including Opera North,[5] Manchester Camerata,[6] The National Centre for Early Music,[7] Sing Up,[8] Jessie's Fund[9] and Accessible Arts and Media.[10] He has worked extensively with people with learning and communication disabilities, including projects with young people with Autism and Asperger's Syndrome. When interviewed, Chris says that he has always worked in a wide variety of contexts and environments as a freelance community musician, and has always tended to think of himself somewhat as a generalist, a 'jack of all trades'. This has meant that Chris's skill set is such that he can be effective in many different and demanding contexts, pulling upon a broad 'toolkit' of skills and activities in order to respond to situations as they arise. Because of his good working knowledge of a wide range of musical styles, genres, forms and structures, Chris is both flexible and adaptable. He is able to play guitar and piano as supporting instruments and also possesses some basic knowledge of technology, including sound systems, and various music technology software, for example, Pro-tools and Audacity. He also stresses that through his working life there has always been a demand for knowledge of other art forms because the community music work he has been involved with often takes place across artistic fields. These types of skills, coupled with an ability to 'read' a room quickly, to understand where the participants are at, and be able to move in and between different environments and activities, have meant a steady stream of employment. Chris also puts this down to the ability to listen carefully and to explain concepts simply and straightforwardly to people who may not be trained in music.

When thinking about his own career and reflecting on the types of personal qualities that have been important, Chris lists the following as consistent and essential: a belief that all humans are inherently creative and inherently musical; a genuine sense of fun, engagement and enthusiasm – but also being able to be 'real' and honest with people; flexibility, adaptability; compassion, empathy; discipline, and a sense of professionalism; personal integrity; endurance and resilience, that is, being able to hang in there when the going gets tough, when things are not 'going well'. With this much experience, Chris can offer some keen insights into the mechanics of community music work. He notes that one facilitation strategy he is using increasingly across all the sites he works in is a willingness to do less and to just wait. An example of this is described in the work with Jessie's Fund where he creates plenty of silence and space, noting that 'this has paid off many times, leading to "breakthrough" moments for individuals'. This strategy of being in the moment has also been part of the creation of a recorded soundscape he has completed with mental health service users. During this project, the group decided the content and structure and Chris was there to 'offer' musical knowledge and support. Both he and his collaborator explained to the group their proposed working methods before the project started and then set up open-ended discussion sessions, thus enabling the group to talk freely. Chris felt that this process led to a reduced sense of expert control and placed the responsibility of the work with the participants and as such increased the sense of ownership for the group.

One of Chris's projects has been leading a choir, open to people who use mental health services. Communitas,[11] as they are known, is connected to a university and provides opportunities for young community musicians to learn their craft. Chris talks through how he engages the aspiring music facilitators using three stages of development: (1) Start by getting the students to develop their own warm-ups, so that they get a sense of standing in front of a large group. Give some broad feedback, stressing the positive things that they are doing. (2) When they are more confident, ask them to teach a round as the follow-up to the warm-up. Talk in detail with them about key aspects of call and response teaching, such as using hand gestures, listening to the choir when they sing phrases back, offering minimal instructions and working with the sound being made. (3) Get the students to teach a song. The students should choose the song themselves, so they have ownership and a sense of responsibility.

Chris's other work includes mentoring staff who support some of his music participants. More often than not, they have no music training. Staff are, Chris notes, understandably nervous and unsure. In this context, he aims to work initially with simple activities that do not necessarily need any specific musical knowledge, starting by modelling the activity, then working together until they can run the activity themselves. This whole process is always supported by regular discussion, which is typically organised in blocks: 15 minutes of planning; 30 minutes music making; 15-minute reflection and planning for the next session. As a community music educator, Chris offers the following tips for those wishing to work in this arena:

- To get as much practical experience as possible in as many different environments as possible, supporting other community musicians, talking with staff who work with the various client groups, etc.;
- To embrace as many forms of music as possible (styles, genres, forms and structures, and so on);
- To build up the broadest 'toolkit' of ideas and activities on which to draw as needed;
- To develop some knowledge of other art forms that can interact with music;
- To have at least one supporting instrument (e.g. piano, guitar);
- To assume that the participants will be willing to take part and throw themselves into the activities.

Rebecca and Chris demonstrate a range of facilitation approaches, although some very clear common qualities emerge. It is noted that in both case studies, the leader must at various times be adaptable and flexible, creative, nimble thinkers, open to possibilities, organised, discerning of their participant group, and able to walk the fine line between leading and controlling. Chris notes that selecting the right tools for the task is just as important as having a wide range of facilitation and musical skills. There is another quality that community music facilitators must exhibit and that is passion.

Passion and Building Trusting Relationships (Nikki-Kate Heyes)

Nikki-Kate Heyes (full case study featured in Chapter 8) believes that being passionate is an essential personal quality needed to enable effective music making with a client group. She believes that making music and enabling people to make music is a very personal activity and therefore providing inspiration can be very difficult unless the facilitator is driven by passion with 'head, heart and hands'. Through reflective questioning, she discovers the reasons why people become participants in music activities and, thus, she observes how music is an important means to understand their own identity. In addition to passion, Nikki-Kate uses empathy, ensuring a connectivity with participants, a positive 'anything is possible' approach, imagination and creativity all supported by resourcefulness and resilience.

As a facilitator, Nikki-Kate does not feel she has formal formulaic strategies. Every situation is different and it is important that she reflects in order to better understand how a process, event or piece of work has developed. Patterns of work have emerged throughout her 25 years of experience and these patterns may form a facilitation strategy that she relies on in her practice. She insists that this strategy includes a confidence that takes people on an imaginative journey of musical risks and challenges.

For Nikki-Kate, success is evident when the group takes ownership and begins to provide their own commentary on the project. True success is when the facilitator can be an audience member and celebrate the end result of the participating team. Her mantra 'never repeat the same workshop twice' is a great challenge not to revert to 'old faithful' ideas and to ensure that one keeps the work fresh and full of vitality. And most importantly, she reminds us to continuously listen to the group, tune into their energy and build trusting relationships.

As a practice, community music has always been concerned with relationships both in terms of the individual, the group and the wider connections among those with whom they are surrounded. This is why an analogy of the parent-child is a useful mirror of the facilitator-group relationship because we have all somehow been involved in this reciprocal event. This can be expressed in the following way.

A young child needs clear instruction and boundaries to feel safe and secure. This is the premise for the young child to begin to grow and develop. As the young child grows, the parent needs to step back a little, letting go a touch more as the years go by. The child must face some milestones alone, yet looks towards the security of the caring parent who is ready, waiting and expecting to offer comfort, support, guidance and perhaps redirection. As the child moves into adolescence, the parent needs to release the reigns further, allowing the young adult to overcome challenges, encounter new discoveries and develop their self-assurance. With the aim of enabling the development of autonomy, the diligent parent will carefully consider when to sensitively step in with offers of support, guidance, advice or comfort.

We may have experienced a parenting style that was intrusive and gave us little freedom to discover ourselves. Alternatively, we may have experienced a childhood where the adults in our lives adapted their parenting style to suit our changing needs. It is this latter ideal that seems to express the fundamentals of the group-facilitator relationship. Within this bond is the ability to sense what is needed and to be able to offer an accurate response in an ever-changing environment and a multitude of situations. Most of us will have experienced a range of different styles of guidance and support throughout our lifetime, and in recalling some of the feelings and messages we received from different approaches, we have a useful tool for developing ourselves as skilled facilitators of the musical event (Higgins & Campbell, 2010).

Dana Monteiro
Building Community through Samba Culture in an Urban High School

Dana Monteiro is a high school teacher at the Frederick Douglass Academy (FDA) in Harlem, New York City. This is a school where over 200 students play samba every week on instruments imported from Brazil. Students learn traditional Rio-style samba with singing entirely in Portuguese. FDA is an urban school and can be a challenging environment for teaching. Classes are overcrowded, the building is too small, discipline is an issue, students cut classes frequently and are constantly moved, making classes mixed in terms of education experience. All of these issues, Dana explains, makes planning difficult and are barriers to the formation of a successful music programme. Despite all these 'barriers', Dana has built an extraordinary music programme, engaging the entire school in active musical doing. It all started when in 2002, prior to the Brazilian music programme, music classes at the FDA were not popular. The band programme had been in steady decline and in order to re-establish it the school administration hired trumpeter Dana Monteiro as its new

Figure 4.1 Dana Monteiro and Samba School

music educator. After trying for four years to revitalise the band programme Dana felt that he had made little progress, numbers were still low, the young people did not seem interested, there were significant decreases in class sizes and a there was a growing transient student population. While on vacation in Brazil, Monteiro met some Pagode musicians who encouraged him to visit a local escolar de samba. It was at this event that Monteiro witnessed young people engaged in non-formal musical experiences and thought that this approach to making music might resonate with his students back in Harlem (Higgins, 2016).

Multicultural Curriculum and New Kinds of Educational Settings

Dana attributes some of this success to 'not being a perfectionist' – always needing to keep classes moving along and interesting. He notes that 'if I were to stop everything to make each rhythm perfect before teaching new material, I would lose the interest of my population, who are young and more interested in what's happening in the present moment'. Because the young people are susceptible to outbreaks of disruptive behaviour, Dana places 'energy' as an important attribute in his work and admits he is often exhausted after work: 'My job is quite physical. With my client group, I must demonstrate the willingness to exert energy to inspire them to match my energy. It allows me to will them to play correctly and to learn.' In efforts to inspire the student population to try new things, Dana has explored other percussion traditions himself and brought these back to his school. For example, they have introduced Uruguayan Candombe and Cuban percussion into their programme. As he states,

> With both, I am a novice, but I have found that I can learn together with my students just as effectively as I can teach them from the position of expert. When the students are your equals, everyone can be equally satisfied and encouraged by success.

This way 'teacher' and students are always on a musical journey together. Dana believes that musicianship is vital. A trumpet player before becoming a percussionist, Dana's musical knowledge enabled him to respond to the environment he was working in. Clear communication and ability for clarity of explanation have been critical for the programme's growth. He recounts:

> I think I am able to divide complex skills into manageable parts. I believe I am able to think from the perspective of the novice, because not too long ago I was in their shoes. I knew nothing about samba when I started teaching it.

His work as a band conductor has also set him in good stead providing skills in keeping track of rhythmic complexity and an ability to sort out musical problems whilst keeping the ensemble moving along.

Co-dependent learning is an important aspect of Dana's work, particularly peer-to-peer learning. In other words, he is not responsible for all of the teaching; the students take responsibility and understand the importance of learning from each other. Music notation is never used but rather listening, copying and modelling become the primary ways the students learn. Dana proudly admits that many of his players are now better models than he! In some instances, his role has become to conduct the actions of the class as a whole while the intense deep learning takes place between student to student. In this way Dana always champions student leadership: 'We always appoint two students to be directors. They are given responsibilities such as conducting, instrument maintenance, logistics and have a voice in the selection of repertoire and events that we decide to play at.' These actions have empowered the student body to such an extent that when Dana can't attend an event they are playing at, the students go on their own as they are perfectly capable of organizing themselves independently.

Figure 4.2 Samba School

Dana's work is interesting from a community music perspective because it offers some interesting crossover between community music and an aspect of music education sometimes referred to as cultural diversity in music education (Campbell et al., 2005; Kors & Schippers, 2003). According to Huib Schippers (2003), the term *cultural diversity* is understood as a dynamic concept, a neutral indication for the presence of more than one culture in any given situation. The term is being used here to refer to (1) content – that is, music from various cultural backgrounds, and (2) people, especially a mix of ethnicities. Cultural diversity, then, references different approaches to music making or systems of musical transmission and learning. As an orientation within the broader area of music education, cultural diversity emerges through the growth and developments of multicultural education (Banks, 1996; Gibson, 1976; Grant, 1977; Sleeter, 2005). Multicultural education arose from the diverse courses, programmes and practices that educational institutions devised to respond to the demands, needs and aspirations of the various pressure groups, such as the women's rights movement, those advocating equality for the disabled, senior citizens and the LGBT communities. Grounded in a vision of equality, multicultural education served as a mobilizing site to support and advocate social justice and democracy. During the 1980s, however, complacency and backlash began to replace a general sense of optimism. It was argued that the *multicultural curriculum* was insufficient on its own to redress disadvantage among pupils from minority backgrounds (Nieto, 2010). Programmes that supported the values and practices of *cultural pluralism* (a term used when smaller groups within a larger society maintain their unique cultural identities) were added to the mix, but had little impact on the continuing transmission of the dominant culture within schooling. Valuing democracy with diversity in ethnicity, language, lifestyle and tradition, cultural pluralism rejects the notion of the cultural 'melting pot' that characterises the multicultural condition (Duarte & Smith, 2000). The increased attention towards the idea of cultural pluralism, ignited by both ethnic and women studies, for example, broadened the conceptual field through interdisciplinary debates that resisted assimilation because it emphasises cultural sameness rather than cultural diversity.[12] The demand for structural changes within institutions created pressure that eventually led to the creation of new kinds of educational settings for learning about a range of musical cultures (Drummond, 2005; Volk, 1998). Institutions such as the Conservatory of Amsterdam,[13] Copenhagen Rhythmic Music Academy,[14] Malmö Music Academy (Sweden),[15] Queensland Conservatorium (Australia),[16] Irish Academy of World Music and Dance,[17] SOAS[18] and the World Music and Dance Center, Rotterdam[19] serve to illustrate this.

Doug Friesen
Creative Processes with Listening as an Empathetic Act

Doug Friesen facilitates workshops for students, educators, musicians and those in interdisciplinary arts in Canada, Central and South America. As a student of Canadian composer R. Murray Schafer,[20] he has adapted and extended Schafer's creative work that is grounded in intense, intentional listening, listening to the world, each other and creatively interacting with both through documenting, reflecting, improvising and composing.

In order to be effective, Doug approaches participants as a learning member of a larger community. As much as is possible, time is taken to build trust and co-create goals for work. The hope is to welcome the vulnerability of all involved in order to enable individual and group change to occur – an openness to not knowing, to creative listening and interaction being a self-cultivating 'end'.

After intentional listening, Doug strives to make music as soon as possible, choosing games or exercises that practice and explore social interaction. He says, 'There is nothing stopping us, no matter who the participants, to create an environment of music making within 5 minutes.' Drawing upon the work of Schafer, John Stevens,[21] Pauline Oliveros[22] and others, Doug builds self-awareness, reflection and critiquing right from the start. 'What did this feel like?' 'What did you like about this?' 'Was the learning difficult?' are the types of probes he uses to elicit thoughtful responses and conversations.

An example of a facilitation strategy involves asking participants to breathe, relax and recall an early sound memory, perhaps the earliest they can remember. Standing in a close circle, imitate these sounds as closely as possible, trying to make a sound when no one else is, perhaps after some space. Then when an ending presents itself, ask participants to think of a more musical way to make this sound, perhaps shaping it by changing volume, pitch, speed, duration or intensity – again trying to make the sounds when no one else is, maybe imitating or reacting to other sounds and waiting for an ending to present itself. In some groups, such as his recent work in Brazil, this could go on for many minutes as people are listening, reacting to, shaping the sounds and adding movement, then, as if by accident, as a group, slowly or quickly ending together.

Other times, he has led silent sound-walks for focused group listening. He recalls a recent walk through Mexico City evolving into a composition that started with listening (a huge construction site seemed to pause suddenly as the group walked past), shifted to interaction (imitation and dissonance) and ended with a group coyote call.

Figure 4.3 Doug Friesen Workshop

Doug suggests that this work is not non-traditional. It can remind us of how music might have begun, discovering breath and sound. Leadership in these workshops is creating a space to meet each other halfway to create and shift. What participants already know and have experienced is not only important, but also essential. Doug illustrates in his work that a variety of approaches in building on the prior knowledge and experience already present in the room can be successful.

This all comes from a place of humility. Doug says that listening is an empathetic act . . . listening keeps us in tune with our surroundings. He still gets nervous when working with a room full of strangers, but he honours the process of taking time to listen and let things happen in each unique setting.[23]

Chiefly concerned with how to get people involved in active music making, community musicians place an emphasis on inclusivity and thus work towards this ideal by having strategies of effective group work embedded within their approaches to pedagogy. In simple terms, how one speaks to people, how one greets them, how one responds to their questions and idiosyncrasies are all vital ingredients in participatory music encounters. Just like the parent-child relationship cited above, during these processes it would be expected that the group looks towards their facilitator for reassurance, clarity, direction, encouragement, guidance or shaping. In these instances, community musicians seek to find a comfortable balance between being prepared and able to lead, and being prepared and able to hold back. This balance provides pathways for the group to discover their own journey of musical intervention. Facilitators are therefore never static in one approach or another, but rather move in and out of roles as the group dictates.

Indicators of Success (Gillian Howell)

In Chapter 2, Gillian Howell described her work with refugees and asylum seekers in Australia. Here, she talks about her workshop strategies and how she goes about organizing the content: 'My workshops usually run for 90 minutes in the English Language Schools and across a pre-determined stretch of time, for example, 90 minutes per week for ten weeks.' The class is fairly long for the types of people she is working with, but this duration enables her to include a variety of activities within the weekly workshops, for example: A range of songs, playing of instruments, playful warm-up tasks and games that develop focus, spontaneity and rhythm and creative development, are the essential components of each session. Gillian is always mindful of how much new material she can introduce to students in any given workshop. She feels that it is important for the students to experience at least some material that is familiar, so that they can enjoy feeling confident and secure. This often includes repeating the same sequence of warm-up games and tasks for four consecutive weeks. Similarly, once a new song has been taught, Gillian and the participants will sing it together for the next four to five sessions at least. The number of weeks of necessary repetition are not set in stone as things like this are decided according to how the group is responding on a given day. Familiar material can settle and calm a group; however, sometimes, too much familiar material can provoke impatience or less engagement.

The creative development work is focused around producing new music and takes place in small increments evolving over a number of weeks. Throughout the 10-week period, Gillian and the participants develop new musical material for the group composition projects. Although this is the focus, Gillian's process includes brainstorming, discussions and visual arts in order to build specific vocabulary and phrases that can be used in song lyrics. Early on in a 10-week project, the group will move fairly quickly from one activity to the next, giving the students opportunities to play a variety of instruments, skill-based games, share different musical knowledge and ideas from their countries of origin, and start to reveal their different strengths and preferences. As the project progresses, the group will spend greater chunks of time on their original musical content, which leads to the final couple of sessions where the majority of time is spent rehearsing, refining the transitions between sections, familiarizing and memorizing in preparation for a performance to other classes and parents at the end of term. At the end of the project, children usually have two opportunities to perform their original compositions, both during a school assembly and at an end-of-term concert presentation. However, given the transitional population of the school, music created in one term cannot usually be performed in a subsequent term if the students have left the school to move on to a mainstream setting.

In determining whether or not the project has been a success, Gillian states:

> I have never been required to assess the 'success' of the projects by the schools, or by the arts organisation or funders that placed me there, although I have been asked to evaluate the different outcomes that I've observed over the course of the project. There haven't been any 'unsuccessful' projects, because the very fact that they happen at all is seen as a positive and desirable thing.

Nevertheless, there are a number of things that Gillian looks for while the project is in process and when the project has concluded. These are her ways of understanding the project's impact on the students and a mechanism for critiquing her own work. In no particular order, they include:

Happiness: Are the students smiling? Laughing? Are they relaxed with each other and with the teachers? Do they move with enthusiasm into the room? Towards instruments? Towards me? Towards each other?

Engagement: Are we creating material that seems relevant to the students and their experiences? Are people joining in, and in what different ways are they participating? Are they volunteering ideas and information? Are they physically as well as mentally engaged in the activities?

Social relationships: Are they getting to develop and strengthen social bonds with each other through the music activities? Is everyone in the group included, and are any exclusions being addressed through the music activities? How have their interactions with teachers and other adults changed in the music project? Can we see evidence of these social developments being transferred to their participation in other classes or in the playground as well?

Confidence and esteem: Are the students building confidence and acquiring new skills? Are they demonstrating, showing or helping others how to do things? Are they happy to perform? Do they feel good presenting their work to others? Are they proud and able to identify the work as their own, as well as a collective achievement?

Learning: What are the ways that students are demonstrating what they have learned? What new things can they do? To what extent have they taken on roles such as leaders or demonstrators or helpers? Have they developed new technical skills on the different instruments being introduced? Are they motivated by their progress and the idea of mastery?

Musical: Has the group created music that they are all finding interesting, engaging and effective? Is it catchy, so that students and staff leave the music workshops humming or singing, or with an appealing 'ear worm'? Does the music reflect a diversity of student input, and musical contributions? Does Gillian feel musically satisfied by what the group has made; does it satisfy her own aesthetic sensibilities?

Gillian makes an interesting point here and admits that appealing to her own aesthetic sensibilities may not necessarily be the point as she is not the focus of the workshops; 'yet I feel that if I am not excited by the project and the material, then it has missed its mark slightly. I want to love it too, and I trust my own reactions to the music that evolves as markers of a successful project'.

At different times, donors and host organizations have asked Gillian to complete evaluation forms. Recognizing that these are important from a funding perspective, she admits frustration at times because the questions can miss the mark for understanding the project holistically and notes that the 'success' of a project will always be greater than the sum of its parts. It is therefore important to contextualise the project in order to embed each child's experience within the project as a whole.

Did we make music together? Did we grow and change and learn through the process? Was it a positive and affirming experience for everyone? Did they appear to feel confident and proud of their work by the end of the project? I want to be able to answer 'Yes' to each of these questions in order to feel a project has achieved what it could, and been fit for purpose.

When asked about advice for those wishing to work in community music contexts, Gillian suggests that one should always look towards the participants for musical input. She makes the point that many people have skills and talents that they have never been asked to share before. In her context of working with music in English Language Schools, it may have been one of the first places where they shine and can take on leadership roles, particularly for those with severely disrupted prior schooling. Engaging in community music activity can be a positive experience, helping learners build resilience and maintain a sense of confidence in their capacity to be successful. Music lessons can play a critical role in building the foundations for their future learner identities.

Conclusion

Facilitation necessitates trust in the ability of others to process the musicking materials and ideas that are suggested or gently shaped, as well as to submit to the inventiveness of others, no matter how difficult this may be. As our case studies illustrate, trust is learned through listening to participants and enabling them to work together. By establishing a secure but flexible framework from the outset, it is possible to give over the control to the group and to trust in the direction it takes. In giving up control, the possibilities emerge for musical outcomes that are unpredictable and only evident in their unfolding. Music becomes an invention personal to the participants, owned by the participants, and meaningful to the participants, with the potential to generate an experience that can shape, create and mould identity. In short, music-making experiences such as those expressed by our featured musicians can be uncompromising, personal and 'alive' – a process that evokes a telling of 'their' story over ours. The self-worth that comes to individuals within a facilitated group from being 'allowed' to invent is powerfully affirming. Participation in shared learning has then the potential to work towards emancipation and empowerment; open-ended community music making places ownership of the resultant musical outcomes in the hands of participants, at the same time as encouraging their continued musical growth. These ethical commitments imply a hospitable welcome that is central to the music workshop experience, an idea inherent within much of the work being discussed.

Questions and Topics for Discussion

1. How does the term 'facilitate' define as different from traditional music leadership terms such as conductor, director or even teacher? How can the more traditional roles be more facilitative?

2. Based on the studies in this chapter, what emerged for you as the key or essential skills of community music facilitation?

3. Educational practices today are frequently based on a set of curriculum outcomes and administrators often require a pre-formed lesson plan that is faithfully followed. In what ways does community music depart from this process? How are community music practices similar to traditional classroom instruction? Explore these processes.

4. How is creativity an essential quality in community music practice? Provide some examples of creative music leadership where the facilitator moved from the prepared plan in order to meet the challenges of the moment. Expand the discussion to how this process might be applied to more formal instructional settings.

5. The ability to break complex skills into manageable parts is cited in this chapter. Start with what you might consider to be a complex skill and describe the various components. How might you break it into smaller parts and then build it into a practice?

6. With the cooperation of others, plan and deliver a music workshop where you draw upon both preparation and reflexive decision-making. Invite your participants to comment on what worked best in your workshop and what could be strengthened.

Notes

1 From *Community and growth* (Original Title: *La Communauté: Lieu de Pardon et de la Fête*). See Vanier (1989).
2 Adapted from Hogan (2002, p. 57).
3 NYMAZ is a youth music development charity, which champions the transformative potential of music for children and young people. We know that music has the power to change lives – it can raise aspirations, enable personal and social development, and enhance career prospects. See www.nymaz.org.uk/
4 www.soundsense.org/metadot/index.pl
5 www.operanorth.co.uk/
6 www.manchestercamerata.co.uk/
7 www.ncem.co.uk/
8 www.singup.org/
9 www.jessiesfund.org.uk/
10 www.aamedia.org.uk/
11 www.yorksj.ac.uk/converge/converge/archive/communitas-choir.aspx
12 The idea of cultural pluralism in America has its roots in the transcendentalist movement and was developed by pragmatist philosophers such as William James and John Dewey, and later thinkers such as Horace Kallen and Randolph Bourne. One of the most famous articulations of cultural pluralistic ideas can be found in Bourne's essay, 'Trans-National America' (Bourne, 1996).
13 See www.ahk.nl/en/conservatorium/study-programmes/bachelor/music-in-education/
14 See www.rmc.dk/en/programmes_of_study/
15 See www.mhm.lu.se/
16 See www.griffith.edu.au/music/queensland-conservatorium
17 www.irishworldacademy.ie/
18 www.soas.ac.uk/music/
19 See www.wmdc.nl/en.html
20 For example, *The rhinoceros in the classroom* and *A sound education* (Schafer, 1975, 1992).
21 See *Search and reflect* (Stevens, 2007).
22 See *Deep listening* (Oliveros, 2005)
23 For more information see: www.creativemusiced.wordpress.com; www.patria.org/arcana; www.paulineoliveros.us

References

Banks, J. A. (1996). *Multicultural education, transformative knowledge, and action: Historical and contemporary perspectives*. New York: Teachers College Press.

Bourne, R. S. (1996). Trans-National America. In W. Sollors (Ed.), *Theories of ethnicity: A classical reader* (pp. 93–108). Washington Square, New York: New York University Press.

Campbell, P. S., Drummond, J., Dunbar-Hall, P., Howard, K., Schippers, H., & Wiggins, T. (Eds.). (2005). *Cultural diversity in music education: Directions and challenges for the 21st century*. Brisbane: Australian Academic Press.

Drummond, J. (2005). Cultural diversity in music education: Why bother? In P. S. Campbell, J. Drummond, P. Dunbar-Hall, K. Howard, H. Schippers, & T. Wiggins (Eds.), *Cultural diversity in music education: Directions and challenges for the 21st century* (pp. 1–11). Brisbane: Australian Academic Press.

Duarte, E. M., & Smith, S. (Eds.). (2000). *Foundational perspectives in multicultural education*. New York: Longman.

Gibson, M. A. (1976). Approaches to multicultural education in the United States: Some concepts and assumptions. *Anthropology & Education Quarterly, 7*(4), 7–18.

Grant, C. A. (1977). *Multicultural education: Commitments, issues, and applications*. Washington, DC: Association for Supervision and Curriculum Development.

Higgins, L. (2016). My voice is important too: Non-formal music experiences and young people. In G. McPherson (Ed.), *The child as musician* (2nd ed., pp. 594–605). New York: Oxford University Press.

Higgins, L., & Campbell, P. S. (2010). *Free to be musical: Group improvisation in music*. Lanham, MD: Rowman & Littlefield.

Hogan, C. (2002). *Understanding facilitation: Theory and principles*. London: Kogan Page.

Howell, G., Higgins, L., & Bartleet, B.-L. (2016). Community music practice: Intervention through facilitation. In R. Mantie & G. D. Smith (Eds.), *The Oxford handbook of music and leisure*. New York: Oxford University Press.

Kors, N., & Schippers, H. (2003). *Sound links: From policy to practice – cultural diversity in ten easy steps*. Rotterdam: Academy of Music and Dance.

Nieto, S. (2010). Multicultural education in the United States: Historical realities, ongoing challenges, and transformative possibilities. In J. A. Banks (Ed.), *The Routledge international companion to multicultural education* (pp. 79–95). New York: Routledge.

Oliveros, P. (2005). *Deep listening: A composer's sound practice*. Lincoln, NE: iUniverse.

Schafer, M. R. (1975). *The rhinoceros in the classroom*. Canada, CA: Universal Edition Ltd.

Schafer, M. R. (1992). *A sound education*. Ontario: Arcana Editions.

Schippers, H. (2003). *SoundLinks*. Retrieved from http://www.cdime-network.com/sl/0303201641360211

Sleeter, C. E. (2005). *Un-standardizing curriculum: Multicultural teaching in the standards-based classroom*. New York: Teacher College Press.

Stevens, J. (2007). *Search and reflect* (2nd ed.). London: Rockschool.

Turino, T. (2008). *Music as social life: The politics of participation.* Chicago, IL: University of Chicago Press.

Vanier, J. (1989). *Community and growth.* London: Darton, Longman and Todd.

Volk, T. M. (1998). *Music, education, and multiculturalism: Foundations and principles.* New York: Oxford University Press.

Chapter 5
Mindfulness, Activism and Justice

Justice is the prophetic invitation to do what needs to be done to enable the poor, the disadvantaged and the neglected, to participate in the resources and wealth of the community. Injustice is the outcome of having skewed neighbourly processes so that some are put at an unbearable disadvantage.

Walter Brueggeman[1]

Music's Role in Enacting Justice

A prevailing historical perspective in mainstream music education has been that the work of music is essentially in the aesthetic realm and is not necessarily connected to political issues, public policy or social concerns (Dalhaus, 1989; Hamilton, 2007; Scruton, 1999). Popular advocacy movements supported by scholarly research have touted by-products of music study such as discipline, academic achievement and self-identity building as justification for including music in the school curriculum (Babo, 2001; Chan, Ho, & Cheung, 1998; Danaher, 2013; Haanstra, 2000; North, Hargreaves, & O'Neill, 2000). Beyond the institutional study of music, modern history shows that music has been central to most activist movements (Danaher, 2013), and the songwriters and composers continue to remind us that music inspires, educates and can even seek to enact justice and play a role in reaching those in need of hope. Music has been used by justice causes as a way to engage and maintain participation from a broad base of the population.[2]

Attempts to tightly define community meet resistance. However, it is generally agreed that a community is made up of people who share a common vision, perspective or some other aspect of human life. Diversity within a community can create incompatibility amongst its members, and as political scientist Mark Mattern points out, for a diverse population to effectively act on its purpose, there is 'this need for collective political action' (1998, p. 11). Community music practice was borne out such an action, borne out of a need to service a neglected sector in society and activism has been at its very core from the start (Higgins, 2012).

In *Rhythm and Resistance*, Ray Pratt (1990) observes, 'No music alone can organise one's ability to invest effectively in the world, [but] one can note powerful contributions of music to temporary emotional states' (p. 39), and it is during these windows of heightened social awareness that music coalesces people into action. Perhaps it is music's ability to reach the whole person, emotions, body and mind that brings within a shared community that sense of social well-being that enables music to play a role in movements of peace, conflict resolution and social justice (Miller, 2000). Music may serve as inspiration for people to examine aspects of social justice such as 'accepting others, challenging discrimination, examining privilege, and rejecting violence' (Levy & Byrd, 2011, p. 64). Music can also inspire people to take action around societal problems such as 'poverty, racism, abuse, and addictions and such global issues as hunger, disease, and war' (White & McCormack, 2006, p. 122).

A profound example of an occasion where music provided a means to galvanise the expression of a nation is found in the response of the Norwegian people to Anders Behring Breivik's mass murder of 69 children on Utoya Island, 8 citizens and the wounding of hundreds more in Oslo's public buildings in 2011. His extremist views on immigration, Muslim immigration in particular, drove him to commit this unthinkable crime. They gathered by the tens of thousands, aiming to face down terror with the power of music. Inspired by a Facebook-organised protest, Norwegians flocked to public squares across the country, ignored the drenching rain and lifted their voices in song. Some said that they hoped Breivik might even hear their voices as they fought back with a weapon of their own. Their weapon: a children's tune that he claims has been used to brainwash the country's youth into supporting immigration. Pete Seeger's *Children of the Rainbow* was sung defiantly in Norwegian and again in English.

> A sky full of stars, blue sea as far as you can see
> An earth where flowers grow, can you wish for more?
> Together shall we live, every sister, brother,
> Young children of the rainbow, a fertile land.[3]

It is amazing that such a simple, pretty little song could represent the anger and grief of a nation, while simultaneously giving voice to their deep expression of justice. In the communal singing of a simple children's song, the nation's commitment to each other was reaffirmed in the face of efforts to divide them and distance them from their core values.

There are other examples of where song has accelerated justice causes into a resolution, most often a peaceful one. One thinks of the stories from a World War One battlefield where, on Christmas Eve, allied troops heard the German soldiers singing *Stille Nacht, Heilige Nacht,* resulting in a brief truce where gifts were exchanged, football games broke out and the effect on the men was such that they were removed from the front lines. Through the power of music, these warriors were contaminated by peaceful feelings to the extent that they were unfit to continue in the role of front-line soldiers (Smithrim & Upitis, 2003).

The Singing Revolution is a story of awe-inspiring magnitude that illustrates a situation where community song changed the course of modern history. The Revolution started in the summer of 1987 when mass protests by the Estonian people began against Russian occupation of their country. In the June evenings of that year, over 10,000 people a night packed the Tallinn Song Festival Grounds, where they sang patriotic and national songs – songs forbidden by the Soviet regime. In September of 1988, 300,000 Estonians gathered to continue their protest and to hear Trivimi Velliste make the first public demand for independence. The years from 1987 to 1991 were filled with numerous such public demonstrations, as well as a great deal of political manoeuvrings, the sum of which is known as the Singing Revolution. On 20th August 1991, Estonian politicians declared the nation's independence even as Soviet tanks were rolling through the countryside to quell the movement (Thomson, 1992).

These are powerful examples of music's ability to create community for the purpose of mobilizing change. Singing, that uniquely human practice that uses an instrument given to all of us at birth, can enact justice, calm anger, bridge mighty chasms between opposing forces, and most important of all, heal our spirits.

Sing Fires of Justice
Festival of Song and Word

Sing Fires of Justice started as a choral workshop for community and church choral directors. While the need for enhancing choral singing in the community was primary, the organizing committee sought a deeper purpose that would help the participants and members of the audience to focus on some area of social or cultural concern. Having recently celebrated the 10th anniversary of the Sing Fires of Justice Festival of Song and Word, the event is now a pillar in the community for music and justice. Scholars meet to discuss peace and conflict, justice and activism. The community context now involves an interdisciplinary team (Community Music, Seminary, Religion and Culture) and a multi-faith steering committee (Muslim, First Nations, Christian, Jewish, Buddhist, Secular Spiritual) who provide leadership in creating a community music event that focuses on such justice concerns as poverty and homelessness, education, eco-justice, peace and conflict, and the missing and stolen Indigenous women.

The event has taken on several forms, including a two-day academic symposium asking the question 'What now?' after reflecting on 10 years of activity, a choral workshop and rehearsal (singers made of up community, faith-based and university members). The culminating event is a public service concert, where various faith traditions offer musical welcomes, choirs provide anthems and improvised musical responses, and a keynote speaker provides context and challenge for all gathered.

There is a team of scholars, community activists and musicians who meet semi-regularly throughout the year to plan. Each person on the team brings

Figure 5.1 Sing Fires of Justice

a unique strength, whether it be musical leadership, cultural scholarship, activist perspectives and faith-based practice.

Once the general planning has been completed, the specific skill sets required are:

- Musical facilitation with musicians who bring a range of abilities and cultural practices. Besides choral rehearsing, group improvisation creates possibilities for cross-genre performances, and opens windows for a variety of possibilities;
- Wider understanding of practice with diverse populations who have a single mind towards peace and justice activism;
- Inclusion of audience in singing and response to spoken word is facilitated through carefully constructed programming and the creating of an atmosphere of community where taking risks is safe and encouraged;
- Network building in order to widen the boundaries of who participates and what is accomplished.

The following are taken into consideration in terms of facilitation:

- The key is planning and strategically mobilizing the plan;
- Each facilitator has a role that includes, beside the music facilitation, marketing, recruiting, budget, library, hospitality (nourishment and fellowship times) and designing the programme itself;
- Reflexive practice and flexible goals enable the facilitators to respond in the moment in order to provide rich and meaningful experiences for the volunteer musicians.

Many participate in Sing Fires of Justice to enhance their personal musicianship. They are able to achieve musical goals in this context that are not possible on their own or in their smaller local settings. Student singers are given leadership roles as they appear, and aspiring community music and music education majors participate with their own future projects in mind.

Here are important tips that we have discovered:

- Trust your team partners in the planning process;
- Widen the boundaries of participation . . . open the door wide;
- Be prepared. Do not waste the time of others with uncertainty or miscues on the part of the leadership;
- Respect those who bring aspects of culture or faith that are unfamiliar to you;
- Undertake careful evaluation of the event in order to inform future planning.

Research with the participants indicates that in most there is a value base that responds to the goals of addressing the fault lines of modern society, the deep and perplexing problems that marginalise, judge and prejudice the majority against various minority sectors (Willingham & Ludolph, 2013). Sing Fires seeks to transform societal norms that include:

- The significance we ascribe to instrumental reasoning, which can calculate the costs, but not the value, of everything;
- Our reliance on the economy as the most important measure of meaning;
- The diminished sense of community in a world dominated by individualism and fear of 'the other';
- Our neglect, even at times disdain, for the intangible, the difficult-to-measure – intrinsic values, human feeling, inventiveness and imagination, the life of the spirit.

Grounded in socio-political activism, community music embraces a 'dimension that includes symbolic values, inter-institutional relations, conflict, and negotiation' (Kleber, Lichtensztajn, & Gluschankof, 2013). The typical practice of the conservatoire model is to create technically sound and expressive performers and ensemble leaders who efficiently polish their charges into a mistake-free group of musicians for public presentation. However, the act of 'musicking' (Small, 1998) embraces the entire context of the composer, performer, listener and all of the attendant players that make music participation possible. This also includes a commitment to social justice awareness – a knowledge that our ecological and societal responsibilities are not disparate components from our artistic endeavours.

Creative Tensions Between Activism and Contemplation

In addressing social and cultural concerns, an activist musician might be considered a fully alive and functioning musical contributor to society. To be fully alive is part of the activist life. To be aware of the responsibilities of good citizenship, to influence decision-makers for morally good causes, to open up one's music making to a wider social network are indications of a vibrant and animated spirit. We live in a culture that privileges action. In earlier societies, contemplation was valued more highly than action (Arendt, 1998). In order to meet material needs, people needed to be active. The reader might recall that Plato's model person was the philosopher king who led a society whose primary responsibility was to be thoughtful and reflective. This shifted with the rise of science, the Industrial Revolution and the emerging consumerist society that found value primarily in the accumulation of goods. Thus, the need to be active and less contemplative became prevalent.

There is a yin-yang aspect to activism – a tug-of-war that pulls and tempers the frenzy of activity with the escapism of contemplation and mindfulness. To be an activist, one must also be contemplative and reflective. When the creative tension between activism and contemplation is abandoned, both ends of the rope fly apart into madness (Palmer, 1990). Several community music programmes include mindfulness as an important personal practice in developing a sensitivity to the inner realm that guides and informs action (Miller, 2000). For example, at Wilfrid Laurier University in Waterloo, Canada, community music graduate students are required to engage in a daily contemplative practice and to journal their responses. The student chooses a practice that works for them, and there is 10-minute table sharing that opens each class. Students are able to voice their experiences in the safety of a collaborative small group, usually three, and in so doing expand their own sense of mindful contemplation.

True activism also includes caring, drawing upon the empathetic energy as more fully described in Chapter 3. Compassion for others can take on individual and personal forms, but also is demonstrated through movements for political and economic justice – justice that speaks on behalf of others whose oppression diminishes us all (Palmer, 1990).

Debbie Lou Ludolph
and a Community Choir, Inshallah

After a study trip to Palestine-Israel and sharing in some of the Palestinian songs used in community and in worship, Debbie Lou Ludolph responded to the request, 'Go home and sing our songs as a way to tell our story!' The choir Inshallah was formed, and approximately 20 people from the Waterloo Region community, Ontario, came together to sing songs of faith from around the world. It was open, with a simple agenda to nurture a connectedness to all of humanity through song and to sing against the ideologies and ethnocentrism that suggests otherwise. There was a solid sense of purpose within the group – that of enacting justice through song as an expression of faith and solidarity.

Since 2007, Inshallah has swelled to over 125 in number and continues to welcome people of all ages, abilities and cultural-religious backgrounds.

Figure 5.2 Debbie Lou Ludolph and Inshallah

In 2009, The Kanata Centre for Worship and Global Song, located within the Waterloo Lutheran Seminary, Wilfrid Laurier University, was established out of the work of Inshallah, offering a space where justice could be understood through dialogue, research, worship and music.

Debbie Lou sees her role primarily to create an open and hospitable space for safe participation in music making. 'Hospitality is non-negotiable,' states Debbie Lou, 'and we keep learning what that means!' Where those with previous choral experience may expect the traditional musical hierarchy, here it is firmly established that there is shared leadership. Members of the choir are invited to offer leadership in language coaching, musical styles and performance practices. Together with her team of volunteer facilitators and students, she has created a culture that offers a variety of ways into the music. There is space for degrees of participation. For the trained musicians, there must be opportunities for reading music and personal musical growth. The non-readers find success in rote singing and learning in the aural tradition. This balance is tricky and Debbie Lou focuses on the goal of participation rather than perfection.

Authentic presence is a key aspect of Debbie Lou's leadership. 'I have to be centered and prepared and know why I am doing what I am doing, and then I can see and hear what emerges and engage in play.' She also points out that part of her self-work is continuing to learn about 'otherness'. As other groups partner with Inshallah, she intentionally works 'on her own stuff' around embracing that which is not familiar in her own experiences.

Rehearsals are 90 minutes where there is freedom to play. She comes with a plan, overall goals and at the same time is spontaneous and creates playful exercises in the moment, which unlock the singers physically, musically and spiritually, so that they are able to engage fully with the music and the experience. Setting the frame for the rehearsal with simple paperless songs that reference the connectedness to God, each other and all of creation creates an environment where the rest of the repertoire is set in that vision. Teaching about the context of a given song allows the singer to deepen engagement and critically reflect on its meaning for activism. What does it mean to sing another culture's song in our culture? What is our government or faith community doing to create peace and healing in that situation? Singers are frequently invited to share with a neighbour (the singer next to them) what the material means to them in this context.

As a facilitator in a community music setting, Debbie Lou brings her own formal musicianship and theological training as foundation, but finds herself working in the boundaries of genres and practices that she personally is not highly skilled in. The choir and community guests with different cultural/faith experience help in deepening the understanding. Within the mix of what happens at rehearsal is vocal technique, but it might be 10 minutes of paperless music and vocal exercises to free body and voice and the choir members likely would not call it vocal technique. Inshallah singers have responded that working hard at the edge of their musical ability can be challenging but rewarding, and when something is mastered there is great satisfaction in returning to it over and over. In addition to the musical growth, a study (Ludolph 2009) suggested that Inshallah singers had grown in their understanding of common humanity and difference, of song's contribution to deepening prayer and expressing joy, and had been moved towards activism and personal growth.

A credit course, Inshallah is now offered for students in any of the university degree programmes. It is important for the students to understand that this is not 'fun in the sun in Mexico', but that the reason for doing the global song has people behind it. The intent of the course is to understand the larger purpose of singing the global song in a western culture, and the perspective that experience brings in providing space for positive activism and in seeking justice. The choir responds beautifully to peer leadership. They all want to be part of the learning and growing. 'I do not own the space,' says Debbie Lou. 'This cuts through the cultural understanding of what a conductor and choir is. Here it is shared leadership.'

Debbie Lou offers several tips for those engaging in this type of work:

1. Know your community and have the support of others who share your dream.
2. Don't be afraid of mistakes and risks.
3. Use musical language that is accessible to the singers.
4. Contextualise your mission: who is the 'other' for your community? How can we create a space to sing with those who are outside the dominant culture? For example, faith wise, Inshallah is situated within the Lutheran Christian tradition . . . how do we sing with Buddhists, Muslims, First Nations people, dance with Wickans?
5. Be ready for resistance . . . music purists, theological conservatives . . . LEARN TO MANAGE TENSION! (Tension is not always a bad thing.)
6. Be open to surprises – see them as opportunities . . . Listen intently.
7. Find a partner or community to reflect with.

Action as Risk-taking: Social and Cultural Capital Building

Educator and activist Parker Palmer (2007) describes one aspect of the nature of action as that of risk-taking. Perhaps the greatest risk is that of self-revelation – revelatory of our own faults, failures and shortcomings. Acknowledging that activism and contemplation are potentially risky activities opens up the pathways of deeper understanding and personal growth as contemplative activists. Activism hinges on at least two possible approaches, the instrumentalist activist and the expressive activist. The instrumentalist activist engages in a means to a predetermined end, governed by the logic of success and failure – a process that values success over learning or relationships. Most would consider that among the most successful of all modern activities, science is one that does predicate its value on success and failure *per se*, since for the pure scientist, failed experiments provide stepping stones towards finding the truth in subsequent studies.

Alternately, the expressive activist engages in the expression of a conviction or value, a goal that lies within the personal with intrinsic rather than extrinsic attributes. How does one engage the authentic self in incorporating those values that enable the process to value means over end? How might outcomes of the expressive activist be more in line with a larger sustaining truth or ideas that challenge and transform? Community music seeks to align itself with important causes of humankind, to enact justice, to enhance lives and to engage in community building in what might be described as social innovation and cultural capital. 'When an act is true to one's nature it is more likely to have outcomes that are true to the field of action' (Palmer, 1990, p. 24). The message: Be true to yourself and act accordingly.

Benefits of Civic Engagement

Civic engagement is a positive form of active participation in a social context. Studies show that civically engaged citizens experience many benefits; they are healthier, happier and even live longer (Pancer, 2015). Engaged young people benefit as well, with healthy relationships and less resulting mental and physical health issues. Community music, like other civic and community activities, is designed with a purpose in mind, bringing diverse individuals together to create something more than they are able to achieve on their own. Community music and other arts groups enhance the life of the community on many levels, including the individual's sense of purpose and worth. Sociologists Piliavin and Siegl (2007) refer to this sense of purpose as 'mattering', claiming that by engaging and participating in such groups the participants exhibited healthier lives, both physically and psychologically.

Role of Larger Collective in Self-Identity

Lee Willingham (2001) notes, 'There is an "alchemy" that happens when a balance is present between one's own individual reasons for belonging to the group, and the true sense of the community expectations, both musical, and social' (p. 90). Community engagement, while dependent upon an individual act of participation, connects the musician to something larger, fulfilling that need to belong to something greater than one's self. Belonging to the larger collective is part of defining self, an aspect of how we self-perceive, a way of telling ourselves 'that is who I am' (Spangler, 1996, p. 1). The importance of one's sense of self or self-identity is symbiotic with the community identity and serves as the starting point to action. The beliefs and values of individuals are both shaped by and act in shaping those social values that give a community its *raison d'etre* and are key in engaging the processing of serving justice in the interest of enhancing the lives of those in the collective. In order to fully and deeply engage in systemic change, one must answer the question 'Who am I?' both in the individual sense, and as a person in community.

Mary Cohen is a social capital builder through a prison choir, where the identity and personhood of the singer are honoured as an individual of worth, regardless of whether they are incarcerated or outsiders.

Mary Cohen
Oakdale Prison Choir

Mary first contemplated the idea of choral music for incarcerated people when in 2002 she attended an East Hill Singers Prison Choir concert in an area church and was inspired by the idea. While completing her PhD, she served as a Special Projects Coordinator for Arts in Prison, Inc., where she supported arts instructors to lead programmes at the Lansing Correctional Facility, which strengthened her resolve to continue with these activities. Upon relocation to Iowa for her position at the University of Iowa, she initiated a prison choir through a series of collaborative connections. Goals included a positive experience for a sector with few artistic expressive outlets, and in parallel, to explore community-engaged scholarship through such partnerships. To help her prepare for the challenge, Mary researched and wrote a number of papers and book chapters on prison choirs in other places that put her in a good place to initiate the Oakdale project.

At the outset, Mary learned that a key component is building mutual respect – respect among singers, warden and prison staff. More than 20 outside volunteers learned guidelines for participating in the choir, and with the image of a village in mind, in partnership they committed to a long-term plan. She

Figure 5.3 Mary Cohen, Oakdale Prison Choir

cites the communication of a clear purpose as essential to moving the process forward. The purpose must meet the needs of the men in the prison along with the women and men from outside who come together to sing as well as the needs of the group as a whole. These are addressed through a set of prepared guidelines that include such aspects as selecting appropriate language (avoid outside references such as going shopping, etc.) and structuring the interactions so that people can make positive connections (reflective writing, musical biography, etc.).

She also has clear strategies about the rehearsal seating so that choir members can interact with one another. Within each rehearsal, the members sit in mixed formation, move to their vocal sections, sometimes move back to mixed or semi-mixed formation and then conclude in a standing circle. As seating changes are made, the members are encouraged to say 'hi' to each other and exchange greetings. Rituals are important, and Mary also values changing the activities for variety. At the end of each practice and concert, the choir sings 'May you walk in beauty'. 'Hi fives' of support are exchanged, building on feeding and growing the dynamics of hope. The guiding framework for Mary's dissertation and the development of the theory of interactional choral singing pedagogy was Christopher Small's concept of musicking. This principle embraces the social element as a very important component of music making – on the same level as musical elements. The participants exemplify this premise in their engagement with each other on a variety of social levels.

One of the goals of the Oakdale Prison Choir is to build social cohesion. This depends upon direct connection and collaboration among the participants. Musical leadership skills emphasise vowel and pitch matching, clear consonants and strong attention to text. Mary's role is varied: conductor mostly, sometimes at the piano, sometimes sharing the leadership with singers. For the May 2016 concerts, members created arrangements for their chosen song.

New songs are introduced by rote, by listening to a recording, by reading the lyrics expressively and by reading traditional notation. The group uses solfege in warm-ups and applies solfege to learning melodic phrases of new songs. They are invited to express what they think the lyrics are saying to them. With a number of original songs performed each season, as the group learns to perform these songs, the choir creates slight revisions of the songs.

Mary mentors others who are starting prison choirs. She insists they carefully consider the purpose for starting a programme. She encourages them to explore the concepts of restorative and transformative justice. They become aware of the 'us-them' binary that leads into stereotypes and myths about incarcerated people. The overarching theme is to find new ways of building community in the context of singing – a singing community of care.

Mary concludes by encouraging those engaged in prison choirs to follow the guidelines, protocols and requirements of prison administration. This is a long-term investment. It is the establishing of a village, not a summer camp (Cleveland, 2000). Make as many connections as possible. Keep lines of communications open. Try to understand what the participants are about and what is going well for them. What new ideas might they have for growth and new directions? Always consider what the greatest good for the group and for society is. Be willing to make changes and adapt to allow the programme to develop for the greatest good![4]

Activism demands change. Social innovation is an act of change-making that might be described as ideas (products, services and models) that 'simultaneously meet social needs and create new social relationships or collaborations' (Grisolia & Ferragina, 2015). Those who want to change the world come in many shapes and sizes. We often think of social innovation as resulting in changes that transform our culture or our economy writ large. It may be so. Alternately, social innovation can profoundly enhance communities with gentle nudges and still small voices. Community music, when practiced by fully alive participants, is by its very nature a social innovation and cultural capital-building enterprise.

Merely enabling activism through music does not ensure that desired results are produced. Social and political contexts may limit outcomes. We keep in mind that 'the value of music as an *alternative* communicative forum' (Mattern, 1998, p. 144), existing alongside a myriad of social justice practices, continues to flourish and influence justice concerns as it is embodied by participants who share that community common vision, those values and perspectives.

Questions and Topics for Discussion

1 Discuss the role of song/music in protest movements. How does it work? What aspects of community-engaged musicking are able to advance sociocultural causes?

2 Sing Fires of Justice is a community music event that raises awareness of a social cause. Discuss the role of music in this context. Think of your own setting where you might introduce music to bring community together to enact justice. How might that look? What are the challenges or obstacles?

3   Discuss these examples of societal norms as outlined in the chapter:

   - The significance we ascribe to instrumental reasoning, which can calculate the costs, but not the value, of everything;
   - Our reliance on the economy as the most important measure of meaning;
   - The diminished sense of community in a world dominated by individualism and fear of 'the other';
   - Our neglect, even at times disdain, for the intangible, the difficult-to-measure – intrinsic values, human feeling, inventiveness and imagination, the life of the spirit.

4   In what ways can community music practice provide a balance to what might be described as a consumerist, individualised society?

5   What is the individual's role in a collective setting? How does one maintain and develop self-identity as part of the collective?

Notes

1   Brueggemann (2001).
2   www.wired.com/2011/12/occupy-wall-street-music/. See also Norton (2011).
3   www.independent.co.uk/news/world/europe/thousands-defy-anders-breivik-with-childrens-song-in-norway-7681732.html
4   See also Cleveland (2000).

References

Arendt, H. (1998). *The human condition* (2nd ed.). Chicago, IL: University of Chicago Press.

Babo, G. D. (2001). *The impact of a formal public school instrumental music instruction programme on an eight grade middle school student's reading and mathematics achievement.* (PhD)., Seton Hall University, NJ (Dissertation Abstracts International, 62 (04), 1277A).

Brueggemann, W. (2001). *The prophetic imagination* (2nd ed.). Minneapolis, MN: Augsburg Fortress.

Chan, A. S., Ho, Y. C., & Cheung, M. C. (1998). Music training improves verbal memory. *Nature*, 396, 128–29.

Cleveland, W. (2000). *Art in other places: Artists at work in America's community and social institutions.* Amherst: Extension Service Press.

Dalhaus, C. (1989). *The idea of absolute music.* Chicago, IL: University of Chicago Press.

Danaher, W. F. (2013). How I've understood music's role in activism. *Mobilizing Ideas.* Retrieved from https://mobilizingideas.wordpress.com/

Grisolia, F., & Ferragina, E. (2015). Social innovation on the rise: Yet another buzzword in a time of austerity1? *Salute e Società, 1,* 169–79.

Haanstra, F. (2000). Dutch studies of the effects of arts education programmes on school success. *Studies in Art Education, 42*(1), 20–35.

Hamilton, A. (2007). *Aesthetics and music.* New York: Bloomsbury Publishing.

Higgins, L. (2012). *Community music: In theory and in practice.* New York: Oxford University Press.

Kleber, M., Lichtensztajn, D., & Gluschankof, C. (2013). Diverse communities, inclusive practices. In K. Veblen, S. J. Messenger, M. Silverman, & D. J. Elliott (Eds.), *Community music today* (pp. 231–45). Lanham, MD: Rowman and Littlefield.

Levy, D. L., & Byrd, D. C. (2011). Why can't we be friends? Using music to teach social justice. *Journal of the Scholarship of Teaching and Learning, 11,* 64–75.

Ludolph, D. (2009). *Global song in a Canadian church context.* (Unpublished master's thesis). Waterloo Lutheran Seminary, Waterloo, ON.

Mattern, M. (1998). *Acting in concert; Music, community, and political action.* New Jersey, NJ: Rutgers University Press.

Miller, J. P. (2000). *Education and the soul.* Albany, NY: SUNY Press.

North, A. C., Hargreaves, D. J., & O'Neill, S. A. (2000). The importance of music to adolescents. *British Journal of Educational Psychology, 70*(2), 255–72.

Norton, Q. (2011). Beyond blowin' in the wind: The music of occupy wall street. *Security.*

Palmer, P. J. (1990). *The active life, a spirituality of work, creativity, and caring.* San Francisco, CA: Jossey-Bass.

Palmer, P. J. (2007). *The courage to teach.* San Francisco, CA: John Wiley and Sons.

Pancer, S. M. (2015). *The psychology of citizenship and civic engagement.* New York: Oxford University Press.

Piliavin, J. A., & Siegl, E. (2007). Health benefits of volunteering in the Wisconsin longitudinal study. *Journal of Health and Social Behavior, 48*(4), 450–64.

Pratt, R. (1990). *Rhythm and resistance: Explorations in the political uses of popular music.* New York: Praeger.

Scruton, R. (1999). *The aesthetics of music.* New York: Oxford University Press.

Small, C. (1998). *Musicking: The meanings of performing and listening.* Hanover: University Press.

Smithrim, K., & Upitis, R. (2003). Contaminated by peaceful feelings, the power of music. *Canadian Music Educator, 44*(3), 15–17.

Spangler, D. (1996). *The call.* New York: Riverhead Books.

Thomson, C. (1992). *The singing revolution: A political journey through the baltic states.* London: Joseph.

White, C., & McCormack, S. (2006). The message in the music: Popular culture and teaching in social studies. *Social Studies, 97*, 122–27.

Willingham, L. (2001). *A community of voices a qualitative study of the effects of being a member of the Bell'Arte Singers.* Toronto: National Library of Canada.

Willingham, L., & Ludolph, D. L. (2013). *Sing Fires of Justice: Exploring the impact of a community-based music and social justice tradition.* Paper presented at the Festival 500: The Power of Song, Memorial University, St John's, NL, Memorial University, St John's, NL.

Chapter 6
Wholeness and Well-Being

I think music in itself is healing. It's an explosive expression of humanity. It's something we are all touched by. No matter what culture we're from everyone loves music.

Billy Joel[1]

Participatory Music Making as 'Spaces' Promoting Health

The purpose of this chapter is to consider questions surrounding issues of community music practice, health and the wellness of being. As previously discussed, music is inherently a social act, a space where people come together and negotiate journeys through sound. Community musicians' emphasis on participation, people and places puts an onus on engaging with others, and interactions of this nature can, by default, generate excellent spaces through which health and well-being can be promoted. Participatory music making has, then, presented a multitude of opportunities to explore the entire range of health-related issues; isolation and loneliness (Clift et al., 2008; Cook, 1986); communication (Aldridge, 1991; Neugebauer & Aldridge, 1998; Miell, Macdonald, & Hargreaves, 2005); disabilities (Ockelford et al., 2005); cognitive among older people (Coffman, 2002; Davidson & Faulkner, 2010; Hays & Minichiello, 2005); rehabilitation (Batt-Rawden, 2006); alleviating depression (Guetin et al., 2009; Siedliecki & Good, 2006); pain relief (Brown, Chen, & Dworkin, 1989); psychological measures of quality of life (Lu, Lu, & Liao, 2008); anxiety (Bulfone et al., 2009); emotional well-being (Juslin & Sloboda, 2001); and also the effects of community psychology (MacDonald, Kreutz, & Mitchell, 2012).

Multi-Dimensions of Well-Being

Although not without its critiques, health is described by the World Health Organisation (WHO) as a 'state of complete physical, mental, and social well-being, and not merely the absence of disease or infirmity'.[2] This presents a definition of health that embraces the multi-dimensions of well-being, which can be described in turn as an active process of becoming aware of, and making choices towards, a healthy and fulfilling life.[3] To a large extent, wellness comes about through self-reflexivity, a conscious, self-directed and evolving process of achieving full potential that involves a multidimensional and dynamic approach to lifestyle. Notions of health and well-being that are intrinsically linked with music have become an important contemporary theme in arts research, sparking a host of activity that includes organised groups such as: The Arts and Health Australia,[4] The Global Alliance for Arts and Health,[5] Sidney De Haan Research Centre for Arts and Health,[6] Centre for Arts and Humanities in Health and Medicine[7] and The International Union on Health Promotion and Education.[8] This has also spawned focused publications such as *The Arts and Health: An International Journal for Research, Policy and Practice*[9] and *The Journal of Applied Arts and Health*.[10]

In trying to elaborate reasons why music can be directly associated with health benefits, Raymond MacDonald et al. (2012) distil the following possibilities as to why music produces beneficial health effects. Music, they say, is ubiquitous, emotional, engaging, distracting, physical, ambiguous, social, communicative and affecting both behaviour and identity. Unravelling these ideas, they suggest that the impact of music on our health is far greater than the many anecdotal stories we can all tell. Community singing has been a research domain that appears particularly to have been impactful and is illuminated well by Stephen Cliff (2012; Lee, Stewart, & Cliff, 2017) through his work at the Sidney De Haan Centre.[11] This work is underscored by an initiative, led by Live Music Now but involving organizations from the care sector and the arts sector, to have a choir in every care home in the UK.[12] One reason for this growth has been the advances in research strategy and method, for example, approaches that are neurological, philosophical, pain management interventions, epidemiological and sociological as well as attempts to engage quantitative designs that mobilise concepts such as empowerment and social inclusion (Daykin, 2012).

Nick Rowe
Converge

Converge is a partnership between York St John University and Tees, Esk and Wear Valleys National Health Service Trust in the UK. The project delivers educational opportunities, support and guidance to people who use mental health services in that region of the UK. This remarkable project is driven by two imperatives: the need for recovery-orientated, non-stigmatizing educational opportunities for people who are experiencing mental health problems; and to provide opportunities for university students to learn through working alongside people who use mental health services. Accordingly, the aims of the project are: (1) to offer high-quality educational opportunities to people who use mental health services in the York area; (2) to challenge the dynamics of social exclusion that makes it difficult for people who use mental health services to access good quality educational and employment opportunities and (3) to provide an opportunity for university students to work alongside people who use mental health services, enhancing their employability and 'real-world' experience. What distinguishes Converge from other projects is that it offers a model of collaboration between a university and a mental health service provider seeking to make a real difference in the lives of users of mental health services, full-time students and the university community. Through the project each can learn from, and alongside, the other because it matches the 'core business' of its key providers: The university educates its students, the health service has a valuable provision for its clients and full-time students complete their modules.

Converge contributes significantly to mental health provision through opening the university and its resources to mental health service users and providing educational opportunities that promote hope and aspiration for the future whilst challenging the corrosive effects of the mental illness identity. Offering courses in sports and exercise, theatre, dance, fine art, creative writing, psychology, life coaching, public speaking, facilitation, business start-up and music, Converge has approximately 22 courses with over 150 participants. The courses in music are particularly oriented around composition and songwriting and a weekly choir called Communitas. University staff and students are involved in the delivery of the courses; currently, four people with lived experience of mental ill health are paid tutors on Converge courses and nine Converge students are part of university undergraduate or postgraduate programmes. As well as their programmes for learning, Converge also offers a Discovery Hub, which provides a signposting service for people who use mental health services. This feeds into an information service surrounding the current learning opportunities in the community helping to support individuals currently registered with the

Figure 6.1 Communitas Choir

Community Mental Health Teams and Assertive Outreach Team to connect to community learning opportunities and bridge the gap between secondary care services to mainstream community resources.[13]

Nick Rowe is the director of this project and has a background in psychiatric nursing and drama therapy. When asked what he believes to be the essential personal qualities in enabling effective art-making with his client group, he reflects back to his time as a drama therapy facilitator and describes three key attributes: (1) a capacity to listen, (2) being attuned to the pace of others, and (3) the ability to be as flexible as possible, always able to adapt to changing circumstances. Nick underlines how essential an experience and deep knowledge of the art form itself is, describing that personal experience and reflection on how the art form has been helpful in one's life are paramount.

Social inclusion is at the heart of what Converge sets out to do. Social isolation is one of the most intractable problems for people who have experienced mental illness. Converge students consistently tell Nick that engaging in the project promotes a sense of belonging and increased social integration. As Nick recalls, one Converge student recently said:

> Converge has been the best thing to support me, it has helped me to stay out of hospital by providing engaging activities which engage me as a whole person. It also gives me a community to be part of.

Wholeness and Well-Being **111**

Converge offers valuable opportunities to university students. In the academic year 2014–15, 93 students were involved in Converge either helping to deliver courses or by supporting participants. This is experience that enables students to develop an understanding of mental health that not only enhances their employability on graduation but also enables them to develop arts-leadership skills.[14]

Community Music and Therapy (Community Music Therapy)

A historic review of music in society reveals that it has always been linked with curative, therapeutic and other medical values (MacDonald et al., 2012; McClellan, 2000). The field with the longest history of explicit connection to music relating to health and well-being is music therapy. With a history dating from around the early twentieth century (Bunt & Hoskyns, 2002), music therapy has had an emphasis on the therapeutic relationship between the client and the therapist. Through various interventions, the therapist uses music as the primary means of establishing and maintaining a positive benefit for the client (Trondalen & Bonde, 2012) and requires the authorised professional competency of a trained music therapist (Bruscia, 1998). Keen not to claim territorial ground and to ensure an interdisciplinary discourse, Brynjulf Stige (2012) defines music therapy as the study and learning of relationships between music and health. In this formulation, he acknowledges that there are a number of fields that have a stake in this endeavour and community music is certainly one of these areas of practice having particular synergy with community music therapy (CoMT).

As a result of exploring different and alternative approaches to music therapy, CoMT is not restricted to working with clients in hospitals or other health settings (Stige & Aarø, 2012). As an evolving practice within music therapy, CoMT is a way of doing and thinking about music therapy in which the larger cultural, institutional and social context is taken into consideration (Ruud, 2004). As a collaborative and proactive approach to health, development and social change, CoMT involves an awareness of the broader systems that music therapists work within and is characterised by collaborative and context-sensitive music making, focused on giving 'voice' to the relatively disadvantaged. By questioning what Gary Ansdell (2014) describes as the 'consensus model',[15] this approach marks a shift from the traditional medical model that has a focus towards finding a cure and the reduction of symptoms. CoMT as a practice embraces ideas firmly linked to empowerment, prevention and health promotion. These approaches are resonant with a broader move towards more participatory models of healthcare provision.[16] From the perspective of those working this way, recipients of care do not have things done on them but become full partners in the process (Tsiris, 2014). This provides the contextual backdrop against which a number of music therapists are now working – domains that may be described as previously occupied by community musicians (Wood & Ansdell, 2017). One might say that music therapists are expanding their practices to becomes more politically and socio-culturally sensitive whilst community musicians are more consciously working alongside participants towards health-related outcomes. Some of these gestures have been termed as health musicking, which is described as a concept initially developed as a way of rethinking music therapy theories (Stige, 2002). As an idea, health musicking can be used to describe how musical encounters can offer certain health effects created through participant involvement in a given situation (Stige, 2012) and are excellently exampled in the book *Musical life stories: Narratives on health musicking* (Bonde et al., 2013). Projects of this nature have their purpose in the promotion of health in the widest possible sense rather than in the healing and treatment of people.

Phoene Cave
Freedom through Singing and Holistic Practices

'No one has died from singing!'

Phoene Cave is a vocal coach, community music choir leader, trainer and music therapist. She brings these elements together in a wide range of projects with a current focus on music in health, which seeks to engage participants holistically through an emphasis on creativity, empathy and humour. Phoene explains that, in 2008, she answered an advertisement for a singing teacher to work with patients with chronic lung disease at the Royal Brompton Hospital in London. Funded charitably and managed by Royal Brompton and Harefield Arts, the Singing for Breathing project was inspired by Bronchial Boogie, an Oldham project using brass instrumental teaching to improve respiratory health and raise self-esteem in asthmatic children.[17] Phoene felt her music therapy training, along with her knowledge of vocal anatomy as a vocal coach and physiology as a shiatsu practitioner, gave her the skills required.

Phoene describes the wards with frail people in nightwear, many linked to oxygen cylinders to assist their breathing.

Figure 6.2 Phoene Cave

> One woman said to me incredulously, 'I can't even speak, let alone sing.' She did sing, though, and told me how much better she felt afterwards. It took her back in body, mind and heart, to a time when she danced and felt alive. Music has the power to do that.

Phoene says that singing together on the wards gave patients an opportunity to connect in song with each other, as well as different members of staff. This provided a sense of communion and connection on the wards.

> We would sing as the cannula went into the back of the hand. We would sing as bloods were taken. Nurses, porters, physiotherapists would join in a chorus as they were passing through, and consultants would smile. The patients would dance in nightgowns around portable intravenous drips, hoping the wires would not get tangled! Many times, the singing could heal the strain of visiting sick relatives in hospital, in a way words never could. An aunt seeing her niece sing for the first time in years wept with joy; a brother pulled out his mobile phone and found the words to a song so he could join his wheezing sister, as he watched the breath soften and the colour lift in her cheeks with every verse.[18]

For the purpose of sustainability and good practice, Phoene has been funded by the British Lung Foundation to train 30 Singing for Lung Health practitioners to set up other groups in hospitals and the community across the UK.[19] Each trainee attends a practical weekend course and leaves with information on how to set up groups and with tailored handouts highlighting content and delivery methodology. They can they choose to receive two hours of Skype mentoring with Phoene and access a Facebook page for peer mentoring.

It is interesting when Phoene considers the essential personal qualities in enabling effective music making with this client group. She points towards her difficulty in finding effective group leaders, suggesting that some of the population of musicians may find challenges around empathy and responsiveness, if their training has focused on performance and technical excellence. Conversely, she points towards those musicians who are well-versed in facilitation techniques but are very limited in terms of vocal anatomy and physiology. In short, essential qualities are described as 'patience, patience, patience' and 'empathy, empathy, empathy' aided by confidence and a passion and knowledge for what you are doing. Confidence comes from these qualities but Phoene takes time to explain that the work can be effectively delivered by both extroverts and introverts. 'As long as you know absolutely what you are doing and why you are doing it and always be prepared to use reflective practice.'

For the work Phoene does with the British Lung Foundation, a detailed knowledge of the human vocal and respiratory mechanism is vital both in healthy individuals and those compromised by a chronic lung disease. This knowledge, coupled with a strong sense of personal kinaesthetic awareness and proprioception, enables the would-be facilitator to engage with participants holistically, drawing out music making that is intrinsically connected to the body. She suggests that if you don't have physical awareness and understanding of what is happening with your own breath and voice mechanism, you are less likely to be able to observe what is happening with your participants. Although music leaders cannot change the pathology of what goes on inside a lung, they can certainly help people understand how they may be restricting their own breath use. A broad repertoire of material and a feel for structured and measured pace is vital – as is an ability to craft a session but also the sense to know when you need to throw it all out of the window and be receptive to what is going on inside of the room. For those who want to work in this field, Phoene says:

> I want physically aware practitioners to move with the ebb and flow, but not so loosely that there is no sense of structure, pace, boundaries, start, middle and end, as that is equally unhelpful. Know when to loosen the reins and when to pull it back. What to pull it back into and knowing why you have made that decision.

In determining whether or not her work is 'successful', Phoene has developed a six-point criteria.

The fundamentals of Singing for Breathing are to:

1. assist participants to develop awareness of their postural and breathing patterns;
2. change old habits through learning new exercises;
3. return to a more natural breath pattern and reduce 'top up' breaths (with the focus on primary not secondary muscles);
4. extending out breaths through sung phrases and developing muscle memory through repetition;
5. exploring a vocal production that is supported by the whole body;
6. building breath stamina, and having fun.

Each of these statements outline what Phoene would hope the participants are able to do after a period of time. Conscious that they are physical rather than musical, Phoene has been challenged by some who ask whether she is running a physiotherapy group or a choir. She says:

> Both. It is providing music for health as well as well-being. When participants are singing they are not overly conscious about their breath use, as one singer told me, 'Oh my god that was amazing I just sang for 16 beats in one breath without stopping and I didn't even notice because I was so caught up in the song I wasn't thinking about my breathing.'

Appropriate evaluation continues to be vital, not only to capture efficacy but also to capture funding – this means mixed methods of both regular NHS questionnaires as well as capturing quotes and stories. The anecdotal feedback continues to be overwhelmingly positive and includes statements such as:

> 'I can walk further before becoming breathless'

> 'It has taught me to extend my outbreath and to avoid using inhalers. I am better able to cope when I get out of breath on stairs or slopes'

> 'I can now walk up a hill and not get too breathless and daily feel an improvement. The singing also makes me feel better in myself'

> 'My breath control, stamina, motivation and outlook on life have all improved . . . made me more confident about taking a chance . . . and to sing out'

'My whole body feels so much different from tension to relaxation. Something medical intervention won't achieve!'

Amongst the stories people tell, the respiratory medical experts continue to research the best methods to capture the evidence base required for the Clinical Commissioning Group or public health funding.

The British Lung Foundation training is also being evaluated to ensure not only that trainees are getting the information they need, but to define what constitutes a Singing for Lung Health group, as opposed to a more generic singing for well-being group. Phoene applauds the power of group singing, but questions when community musicians work without the side-point criteria and the group turn up for a sing-song and don't focus on repertoire with appropriate phrase lengths to target breath support management. It is great that they are enjoying the music making activity but if the focus is meant to be targeting lung capacity it would be difficult to say in truth that the sessions were successful. It all depends on the objectives.

Phoene offers some targeted advice for a sustainable career as a community musician suggesting that neither a course nor observation is enough but rather in combination alongside some systematic mentoring. Pointing towards continual professional development, she makes a strong case in advocating that community musicians should regularly invest in their training, and finds it disconcerting when practitioners do not plan for this or are not willing to upgrade their current skill sets and knowledge.[20] In a final reflection, Phoene says:

> Looking back retrospectively I have ended up at this extraordinary place through pure chance – I'm a qualified Shiatsu practitioner who found body work through singing and teaching singing and realizing that people might not sing very well if their bodies were messed up. I have practiced yoga and danced on and off for over 25 years which adds to the mix. Think broad and think about how you can invest in yourself as a musician – jam, play and learn to breath.

For both community music and CoMT, Christopher Small's (1998) notion of musicking is of particular significance providing the practices with a conceptual fulcrum through which to discuss music as a performance activity. With this idea guiding some of the thinking, CoMT provides challenges for major reassessment of performance's place within music therapy. As Gary Ansdell suggests, CoMT is developing 'a more nuanced understanding of the affordances and varying suitability of the private and public aspects of musicking within broadly-defined therapeutic contexts' (Stige et al., 2010, p. 186). This is illustrated through examples that include: how neurological impairment can bring about disconnection in body function, self-image, relationships and social structures; how being active in music can provide pathways from therapy to community; creating environments where songwriting can be used to explore the difficulties of losing a spouse; and how leading a choir can help patients share something positive with others (Ansdell, 2014).

Addressing Mental Health through Musicking (Way Ahead, Simon Procter)

Simon Procter's work at Way Ahead presents a good illustration of CoMT. Located in London, in an environment that has high levels of unemployment, crime and incidences of mental illness, Way Ahead is a non-medical community resource centre for people with experience of mental health problems. Not part of any statutory services, it is funded by a yearly grant from the local health authority, social services and an assortment of charities. A management committee, which includes service users and local people, runs the centre, endeavouring to create an environment in which members can value their individuality and their culture through a sense of community. The centre is designed to help people experience their capacity for well-being, rather than focus on their medical illness. In an effort to alleviate isolation, there are no doctors, nurses or patients – just members. There are no experts – just workers. There are no case history files and no classification of members on the basis of diagnosis (Higgins, 2012). Members are welcomed to the centre based on who they are rather than a personification of a history or diagnosis. Way Ahead is, as Procter (2004, p. 224) describes, 'a haven from psychiatric orthodoxy'. Extending Small's notion of musicking, this work engages with each member in such a way to draw him or her into 'co-musicking', with all the interpersonal and creative demands that this presents. Through co-musicking, Procter seeks to create a shared musical history that is not documented for others to pick over, but experienced by each musician in their own unique way. Without interventions, Procter believes that he could not offer his co-musickers significant opportunities for empowerment and enablement.

With the frames of CoMT, health musicking and well-being in mind, Carol Beynon, Kathy McNaughton and Betsy Little have their focus on practitioners who are always mindful of issues relating to wholeness and being.

The People We Are
The Intergenerational Choir

> Music is a part of being human . . . To those lost in dementia, music can have a power to restore them to themselves and to others, at least for a while.
>
> Oliver Sacks[21]

Every Thursday afternoon, two dozen teenagers get off the bus, ready for something that no one wants to miss – Intergenerational Choir rehearsal, a community/school-based project created by the Alzheimer's Society of London and Middlesex (ASLM) in Canada. The ASLM turned to Medway High School to find strong young singers, and to the Sisters of St Joseph, just down the road, to create a choir that could socialise and rehearse in their wonderful home. Five sectors of the community comprise this choir: persons with dementia (PwD) who are members of the ASLM, their caregivers, high school student singers, their music teacher and several Sisters of St Joseph. This initiative was inspired by a volunteer with the ASLM – a retired teacher who believed in the benefits of music and intergenerational learning. She had read about the possible therapeutic benefits of singing for persons with dementia.

Carol Beynon brings a research perspective on intergenerational singing to this project, which, in this setting, is defined specifically to bring two generations

Figure 6.3 Intergenerational Choir

together in a mutually beneficial learning situation. The programme is designed to benefit older singers and, equally so, the teenagers. Kathy McNaughton, a high school music educator, provides the practitioner's view. Both are experienced choral leaders and music educators, and their work was also motivated by the early onset diagnosis of Alzheimer's disease of a beloved colleague, a choral educator and highly respected community musician. He and his caregiver wife were invited to join the choir, and to participate in singing and co-conducting the intergenerational choir. As the disease progressed quickly, his musical mind remained lucid, so even in later stages he was able to masterfully conduct the choir in repertoire that had been familiar to him.

This is not a residential programme in a long-term care facility (although people in LTCs are invited to attend if they can); rather, it is a community-based programme that requires transportation for both people diagnosed with Alzheimer's and for the students from the high school to the chapel at the Sister's home. Thus, one of the original purposes of establishing the Intergenerational Choir was to provide a weekly two-hour respite for caregivers who are generally responsible for round-the-clock care for their loved ones. Some caregivers do take advantage of the time to run errands, but many stay to experience the renewed sense of self in their loved one, which occurs in the intergenerational choral environment. Many caregivers have joined the choir as they feel uplifted as well by the singing. Kathy notes that 'as they see a change in their loved ones' attitude and behavior, they want to be part of the process. How could they not be involved with such a positive experience?'

The choir provides a positive bond for adolescent youth and older singers to build connections. While some of the older participants were fine singers who come to refresh their former musical abilities, others have no singing experience and come for the camaraderie, the enjoyment of singing in a group and the outing. The students provide both a social and musical bridge to connect to the older singers, to make new friends, to learn about lives lived and to share experiences.

Established routines are important. As the students get off the bus and enter the Sisters of St Joseph's spacious and welcoming foyer, they meet their older friends and move into the chapel intermingled with each other. This 'meet and greet' moment is one of great expectation and joy on the part of all involved. Reuniting with singing partners each week is a key part of the ritual. Once they are seated and greeted, Kathy welcomes them and makes a few comments. (Incidentally, Kathy tries to speak to each singer and get the latest news from them before rehearsal begins.) Successes are recognised, both those of the seniors, but also the accomplishments of the students. Notice is also given when the news is sad or of a loss within the group.

Once the opening has played out, they sing a familiar song, something known to them or music that has recently been worked on. At the time of writing, they have been opening with 'Oh, What a Beautiful Morning' from Oklahoma. New material and the familiar are interchanged throughout the rehearsal so that there is a focus on new learning and remembering. The Intergenerational Choir performs in concerts and has sung at conferences as well; having a public event on the calendar provides a goal to strive for. Knowing that they have work to do is a huge motivation for full investment in the music learning process. They may start out with unison singing, but eventually part singing is introduced and more complex multi-part arrangements are frequently performed. Students help the older singers when needed, and while the various stages of the progressive disease are evident, the inclusive spirit and culture of the group creates a space for all to contribute, regardless of their musical or intellectual abilities.

Each rehearsal concludes with the Irish Blessing, and as they sing 'May the road rise up to meet you', the anticipation of next week's rehearsal is often accompanied with the question 'Are they coming back?' It is noted that for some later stage patients, one of the few things they can recall in their weekly schedule is Thursday's 3 pm choir rehearsal. Some have been known to ask their caregivers each day, 'Is it Thursday at 3 o'clock?' The routine ends each week with a social time with refreshments that lasts about a half-hour. The cookies and drinks cannot be missed as it is a special time for the generations to chat and laugh together.

The routine of greeting, sharing, singing together and socializing results in a multidimensional experience of socio-relational development, robust physical and mental activity of singing/learning and the aesthetic-cognitive processes of combining text and music for all participants in a mutually beneficial manner.

Both Carol and Kathy agree that a strong working knowledge of how to sing well and how to work with diverse individuals is an essential quality for the choral director of this programme. Musical styles, the ability to adapt the voice to a range of reportorial demands and having a sense of realistic musical expectations are key ingredients. Kathy balances the diversity of the singers' needs and preferences from those who want a full choral experience with polished, performable pieces with those who want a sing-song hour. Presenting a positive attitude, being open, friendly and affirming that the person really matters, providing lots of communication and sharing warmth through relationships are leadership necessities. Newer members need lots of encouragement, but so do the teenagers, many of whom are experiencing such a situation for the first time in their lives. For all participants, making mistakes is a concern, saying the wrong thing, getting the words wrong is embarrassing and the usual preconceived fears of not being good enough are all addressed and dealt with in a positive, non-judgemental way. The sense that they are accomplishing something important and significant is key. Singing on Thursday afternoons is not just another event on the weekly schedule; it is a time where profound personal and community experience is shared and important achievements are recognised and celebrated.

Choosing the music to be sung is one of Kathy's challenges. Persons with Alzheimer's disease or other dementias range in age and some are in their fifties. The 'songbook' of WWII or the traditionally used Christian hymns that are often used with seniors are not what many of the participants know or relate to. The music of the 1960s, 70s and 80s are the songs they connect with, and finding or creating arrangements of popular music in that era is important. Sometimes a group of singers will express its dislike for a certain piece of music in the repertoire. Kathy must weigh these opinions against the wishes of the whole group, and decide whether to drop the piece, or persevere. (Unlike a school setting, where the teacher typically selects the repertoire, this choir – including older and younger singers – feels it has ownership to shape those decisions.) The high school students know current choral repertoire and when appropriate, a newer contemporary selection is introduced.

Kathy applies her music education experiences to this choir: listening for things that need improvement, deciding what to address and what to let be, knowing what concepts to try, and reading the mood of the singers. Moods, of course, can change quickly, and being able to respond instantly is critical. Humour and friendly banter are healthy components of this environment. Sometimes the singers just sit and laugh. Watching to see where to lighten the mood is important, more so than getting the music perfect. Carol adds that an excellent teacher can make it work because music educators are accustomed to working with diverse, heterogeneous groups and become adept at adapting instructional strategies to a variety of learning contexts. Teachers have the advantage of possessing a variety of pedagogical tools for dealing with various situations and are able to translate their knowledge into useful strategies in this environment.

This choir is now overflowing with members and is at full capacity. Plans are under consideration to create another intergenerational choir in another area of the city with another school and members of the growing set of singers with dementia along with caregivers. Issues such as accessibility (e.g. curbs, steps, bumps that impede the use of walkers), expenses, transportation for both students and older singers, changes in location and leadership and so forth are a reality, all of which require a significant investment of resources by the ASLM. Currently the programme is funded through generous donations and foundation grants.

In thinking about what is necessary to create and maintain such programmes, Carol raises the issue of where accessible seniors' centres are located. For example, in Ontario, when new schools are built, they must accommodate a day-care centre and this access to early childhood education for collaborative learning is useful in many ways. Her view is that retirement residences, seniors' centres and long-term care facilities should be built near schools so that intergenerational or multigenerational interaction is easily accessible and supported. No one in current society has ever been around just their own peer groups throughout their lives; they have always lived in multigenerational settings. She advocates for co-care facilities that combine day-cares, schools and seniors. Music in such a setting is natural in relationship building, enhancing community culture and providing profoundly important experiences for all.

Participants have claimed that they feel like new people by the end of the rehearsal. The agitation that is a real aspect of those living with dementia is, in many cases, replaced with calmness, less anxiety, aggression and better sleep after rehearsal, lasting anywhere from 4 to 24 hours. The participants want to come back and are usually delighted to enter the setting once again. There is, however, a sense of both joy and loss as they leave for another week. For a brief two hours during the Intergenerational Choir rehearsal and social time, the persons with dementia and their caregivers leave behind the challenges and struggles of their lives and become active learners themselves as well as friends and mentors to their younger partners; the high school students find themselves as learners and trusted singing partners to their older friends; and, the Sisters of St Joseph are integral as singers and hosts as they play an important role in strengthening and developing new, reciprocal relationships with students and the community.[22]

Conclusion

Issues pertaining to the health and well-being of human populations appear to be significant agenda items of many governments today. As an international phenomenon, health inequalities are connected to social inequalities relating to social status both in life expectancy and quality (Department of Health, 2010) and as a consequence directly relates to our well-being. The challenges are of course far-reaching and extremely complex; however, it does seem that music can play a role in directly impacting our health and thus improving our well-being. This matters because it adds to our life expectancy, improves recovery from illness and is associated with positive health behaviours throughout the lifespan (Department of Health, 2014). This is also important because it has implications for treatment decisions and cost – in other words, increased funding for health-related arts projects can, ultimately, reduce the healthcare cost burden. In short it might make economic sense to fund community music or CoMT projects if research can adequately support its positive and lasting impact to matters relating to health and well-being.

The three case studies throughout this chapter illustrate different approaches to working within this area. First, Converge highlighted the importance and effectiveness of institutional collaboration by creating a partnership between a health trust and a university. By creating a mutually benefitting relationship, both parties enrich their experiences and increase the chances of providing both effective support in the now, and well-informed practitioners for the future. Second, the work of Phoene Cave offers insight to the possibilities of an interdisciplinary community musicians, one whose skill base intersects between community music and music therapy. This type of activity is reflected in the scholarship of CoMT where notions of how a music therapist engages with people are challenged. Finally, the Intergenerational Choir deepens our insight into the impact that singing together can have and demonstrates the extent and capacity musicking has in creating reciprocal, healthy relationships.

Those we interviewed all flagged up how vital patience and empathy are to this work. This, laced with being attuned to the group and an ability to be flexible in circumstances that constantly shift, resonates with community music work more generally. Working with music in health settings can clearly be rewarding for both the musician and the participants, and it would appear that anyone wishing to enter the field should be mindful of the benefits their work has on the health and well-being of their participants, but also acknowledging the wider benefits to the locality and its population.

Questions and Topics for Discussion

1 What are some ways that music produces beneficial health outcomes? Discuss these in terms of your own experiences and observations.

2 Mental health is the subject of considerable attention. Explore resources that address music and mental health and consider such practices as are outlined in this chapter as examples of music participation enhancing the lives of those living with mental illnesses.

3 What is music therapy? How is it used in clinical settings? Explore community music therapy as the 'consensus model' and its value. How can community music therapy address those who are in disadvantaged settings?

4   Discuss Christopher Small's idea of 'musicking' in the context of health and well-being, and then explore 'co-musicking' as defined by Procter in this chapter.

5   How might an intergenerational setting for community music be advantageous to the health of all ages represented?

Notes

1   Billy Joel: The Rolling Stone Interview, 6 November 1986.
2   http://pnwf.org/html/h.HTM#health www.who.int/en/
3   www.nationalwellness.org/?page=AboutWellness
4   www.artsandhealth.org/
5   www1074.ssldomain.com/thesah/template/index.cfm
6   www.canterbury.ac.uk/health-and-wellbeing/sidney-de-haan-research-centre/sidney-de-haan-research-centre.aspx
7   www.dur.ac.uk/cmh/cahhm2/
8   www.iuhpe.org/index.php/en/
9   www.tandfonline.com/toc/rahe20/current
10 www.intellectbooks.co.uk/journals/view-Journal,id=169/
11 www.canterbury.ac.uk/health-and-wellbeing/sidney-de-haan-research-centre/research-projects/home.aspx
12 www.livemusicnow.org.uk/lmn_news/item/68951/date/2015-04-24/title/a_choir_in_every_care_home
13 www.higheryork.org/discoveryhub
14 For further information see Rowe (2015).
15 The consensus model is a 'thinking tool' to help an understanding of how music therapy has, over the last two decades, gradually drawn towards a consensus in the practice and within the theoretical models used to legitimates such practice.
16 https://en.wikipedia.org/wiki/Participatory_medicine; http://participatorymedicine.org/
17 See Andrew (2008) and www.theguardian.com/society/2007/sep/05/guardiansocietysupplement.health1
18 See Andrew (2008) and www.theguardian.com/society/2007/sep/05/guardiansocietysupplement.health1
19 www.blf.org.uk/
20 Pheone mentioned some of the following as good examples of training within the area of music and health in the UK. Opus (www.opusmusic.org), Wishing well. (http://wishingwellmusic.org.uk/) and Kutulia Music (http://www.kutuliamusic.org).
21 Sacks (2008, p. 385).

22 www.alzheimerlondon.ca/; www.youtube.com/watch?v=L5o3Nh6ydbo; CBC Radio Documentary: The Person I've Become – an Alisa Siegel Documentary (available online at CBC Radio Podcasts, *The Sunday Edition*, aired 17 April 2016)

References

Aldridge, D. (1991). Physiological change, communication, and the playing of improvised music: Some proposals for research. *The Arts in Psychotherapy*, *18*, 59–64.

Andrew, W. (2008). Bronchial boogie. *The Journal of the Royal Society for the Promotion of Health*, *128*(6), 287–88.

Ansdell, G. (2014). Revisiting 'Community music therapy and the winds of change' (2002): An original article and a retrospective evaluation. *International Journal of Community Music*, *7*(1), 11–45.

Batt-Rawden, K. (2006). Music: a strategy to promote health in rehabilitation? An evaluation of participation in a 'music and health promotion project. *International Journal of Rehabilitation Research*, *29*, 171–73.

Bonde, L. O., Ruud, E., Skanland, M. S., & Trondalen, G. (Eds.). (2013). *Musical life stories: Narratives on health musicking*. Oslo: NMH-pubikasjoner.

Brown, C. J., Chen, A. C. N., & Dworkin, S. F. (1989). Music in the control of human pain. *Music Therapy*, *8*, 47–60.

Bruscia, K. (1998). *Defining music therapy* (2nd ed.). Gilsum: Barcelona Publishers.

Bulfone, T., Quattrin, R., Zanotti, R., Regattin, L., & Brusaferro, S. (2009). Effectiveness of music therapy for anxiety reduction in women with breast cancer in chemotherapy treatment. *Holistic Nursing Practice*, *2*(4), 238–42.

Bunt, L., & Hoskyns, S. (Eds.). (2002). *The handbook of music therapy*. Hove, East Sussex: Brunner-Routledge.

Cliff, S. (2012). Singing, wellbeing, and health. In R. MacDonald, G. Kreutz, & L. Mitchell (Eds.), *Music, health, and wellbeing* (pp. 113–24). New York: Oxford University Press.

Clift, S., Hancox, G., Morrison, I., Hess, B., Stewart, D., & Kreutz, G. (2008). *Choral singing, wellbeing and health: Findings from a cross-national survey*. Retrieved from Canterbury.

Coffman, D. (2002). Music and quality of life in older adults. *Psychomusicology – a Journal of Research in Music Cognition*, *18*, 76–88.

Cook, J. (1986). Music as an intervention in the oncology setting. *Cancer Nursing*, *9*(1), 1–45.

Davidson, J. W., & Faulkner, R. F. (2010). Metting in music: the role of singing to harmonise carer and cared for. *Arts in Health*, *2*(2), 164–70.

Daykin, N. (2012). Developing social models for research and practice in music, art, and health: A case study of research in a mental health setting. In

R. MacDonald, G. Kreutz, & L. Mitchell (Eds.), *Music, health, and wellbeing* (pp. 65–75). New York: Oxford University Press.

Department of Health (2010). *Our Health and Wellbeing Today*. Retrieved from London:

Department of Health (2014). *Wellbeing: Why it matters to health policy*. Retrieved from London.

Guetin, S., Sousa, B., G, V., Picot, M.-C., & Herisson, C. (2009). The effects of music therapy on mood and anxiety-depression: An observational study in institutionalised patients with traumatic brain injury. *Annals of Physical and Rhabilitation Medicine, 52*(1), 30–40.

Hays, T., & Minichiello, V. (2005). The meaning of music in the lives of older people: a qualitative study. *Psychology of Music, 34*(4), 437–51.

Higgins, L. (2012). *Community music: In theory and in practice*. New York: Oxford University Press.

Juslin, P. N., & Sloboda, J. A. (Eds.). (2001). *Music and emotion: Theory and research*. New York: Oxford University Press.

Lee, P., Stewart, D., & Cliff, S. (2017). Does group singing affect quality of life? Evidence from Australian choirs. In B.-L. Bartleet & L. Higgins (Eds.), *The Oxford handbook of community music*. New York: Oxford University Press.

Lu, X., Lu, Y., & Liao, X. (2008). Study on influence of music therapy on quality of life of cancer patients. *Chinese Nursing Research, 22*(1B), 106–08.

MacDonald, R., Kreutz, G., & Mitchell, L. (Eds.). (2012). *Music, health, and wellbeing*. New York: Oxford University Press.

McClellan, R. (2000). *The healing forces of music: History, theory, and practice*. Lincoln: iUniverse.

Miell, D., Macdonald, R., & Hargreaves, David J. (Eds.). (2005). *Musicical communication*. Oxford: Oxford University Press.

Neugebauer, L., & Aldridge, D. (1998). Communication, heart rate and the musical dialogue. *British Journal of Music Therapy, 12*(2), 46–53.

Ockelford, A., Welch, G., Zimmermann, S., & Himonides, E. (2005). Sounds of intent: Mapping, assessing and promoting the musical development of children with profound and multiple learning difficulties. *International Congress Series, 1282*, 898–902.

Procter, S. (2004). Playing politics: Community music therapy and the therapeutic redistribution of musical captial for mental health. In M. Pavlicevic & G. Ansdell (Eds.), *Community music therapy* (pp. 214–30). London: Jessica Kingsley Publishers.

Rowe, N. (2015). Creating a healing campus: A partnership between a university and a provider of mental health services. In B. Cozza & P. Blessinger (Eds.), *University partnerships for community and school system development: Innovations in higher education teaching and learning* (Vol. 5, pp. 119–34). Bingley, UK: Emerald Group Publishing Ltd.

Ruud, E. (2004). Reclaiming Music. In M. Pavlicevic & G. Ansdell (Eds.), *Community Music Therapy* (pp. 11-14). London: Jessica Kingsley Publishers.

Sacks, O. (2008). *Musicophilia: Tales of music and the brain*. New York: Vintage Books.

Siedliecki, S., & Good, M. (2006). The effect of music on power, pain, depression and disability. *Journal of Advanced Nursing, 54*(5), 553–62.

Small, C. (1998). *Musicking: The meanings of performance and listening*. London: Wesleyan University Press.

Stige, B. (2002). *Culture-centered music therapy*. Gilsum, NH: Barcelona Publishers.

Stige, B. (2012). Health musicking: A perspective on music and health as action and performance. In R. MacDonald, G. Kreutz, & L. Mitchell (Eds.), *Music, health, and wellbeing* (pp. 183–95). New York: Oxford University Press.

Stige, B., & Aarø, L. E. (2012). *Invitation to community music therapy*. London: Routledge.

Stige, B., Ansdell, G., Elefant, C., & Pavlicevic, M. (2010). *Where Music Helps: Community Music Therapy in Action and Reflection*. Farnham: Ashgate.

Trondalen, G., & Bonde, L. O. (2012). Music therapy: Models and interventions. In R. MacDonald, G. Kreutz, & L. Mitchell (Eds.), *Music, health, and wellbeing* (pp. 40–62). New York: Oxford University Press.

Tsiris, G. (2014). Community music therapy: Controversies, synergies and ways forward. *International Journal of Community Music, 7*(1), 3–9.

Wood, S., & Ansdell, G. (2017). Community music and music therapy: Jointly and severally. In B.-L. Bartleet & L. Higgins (Eds.), *The Oxford handbook of community music*. New York: Oxford University Press.

Chapter 7
Culture of Inquiry

. . . for those of us who understand life, figures are a matter of indifference.[1]

(The Little Prince)

Research informs us that the arts are a means of knowing and learning; that they contribute to a culture of permanence; and that they are a means of connecting humans to the world beyond.[2]

Role of Research in Emerging Field of Community Music

As a scholarly enterprise, community music is garnering the interest of an increasing amount of people who seek to explore the field's theory and practice from a researcher's perspective. This chapter does not provide detailed methodologies on how to conduct research (a number of resources are listed in the bibliography), but rather, it explores and describes a range of project ideas that guide the direction of the field of community music. Research in this field may take a rather macro focus with topics such as the effect of music in a social context, or the impact of a project on a school district. Other research interests include more micro action-research probes, such as the effectiveness of a certain facilitation strategy, or the success of various approaches to specific participant segments. In order for this trajectory to continue to develop and grow, a culture of inquiry needs to be encouraged and maintained. New publications are in process at the time of writing, including authored and edited books. *The International Journal of Community Music* has compiled a robust collection of peer-reviewed articles capturing a diverse range of interests and investigations where community music has place alongside and within inter-related disciplines.[3]

From our experience, it would seem that reflective practice, in the way philosopher Donald Schön (1991) might describe it, is embedded in the thinking-in-action processes of community musicians. Our case studies support this and underline a commitment to do the very best work within the contexts they find themselves. Although it appears from our research that an ongoing process of reflection is what community musicians just do, we wonder if this can be described as a culture of inquiry. Most practitioners do appear to reflect deeply about the projects they are running, asking questions about the process, the participations, the relationships within the group and the music being created. These types of procedural questions point towards the care many community musicians have for those they make music with and reflect both dedication and a belief in the power of music.

Examples of Graduate Research Projects

As a practice that has grown into a field, higher education courses straddling both undergraduate and graduate studies have contributed to the relatively new phenomenon of community musicians generating and executing research projects. The existence of community music graduate programmes has proffered interesting new perspectives in terms of research projects and methods. For example, Masters students at Wilfrid Laurier University in Waterloo, Ontario, Canada, have embarked on studies that, among others, explore the impact of music in medical settings, with newly settled immigrants, business, in faith-based communities, schools and the private studio. Examples of these are briefly referenced.[4]

A study, using qualitative ethnographic methods, invited veterans from recent conflicts to share their stories with secondary school students who were writing songs about the effects of post-traumatic experiences. Through a singing-songwriting-themed process, the voices of teenagers amplified the expressions of the veterans through newly created songs, presented in schoolwide assemblies. The researcher explored the impact on student engagement, musicianship and perspectives on war, justice and levels of civic engagement. The students took musical risks and these were noted in focus interviews and personal statements as having profound, lasting impacts on both the veterans and the young singer-songwriters.

A study was carried out on the effects of gender on the lives of teenage guitar players. The purpose was to understand how teenagers view gender in relation to music in their personal lives and in the media. Using nonprobability purposive sampling, students were interviewed, responses analysed and results showed heightened awareness in sexist lyrics, gender roles in media, use of various instruments by gender and the sense of popular music as a marketable commodity geared towards various demographics.

The collaborative experience between symphonic string players and indie rock bands was explored using workshops and creative presentations, culminating in a public event where classical symphonic themes were reimagined with rock instruments embedded with string players, and flipped with string players creating music with the rock bands. This genre mashup has legs! These musicians are currently collaborating on a recording project and have planned to continue their musical relationships.

An oncology department in a large regional hospital agreed to have ukulele instructional sessions as part of the programming for patients undergoing chemotherapy. For 6 weeks, a facilitator led a number of participants into the world of playing the ukulele, and the researcher did pre-post interviews. The results were overwhelmingly positive, and the motivation for continuing to learn the instrument has continued with several of the original participants. The personal narratives from the participants bore out the belief that music making has healing capacities, in body, mind and spirit.

One graduate, working in a faith-based music community, discerned that the key principles that inform the practice of community music are the same as those that sit as central to the ethics of many faith traditions. The studies conducted led to transformational changes in worship through the facilitation of creative and innovative musical participation from the congregations. The benefits of the study were shown to include an increase in the level of confidence of leadership and congregation, an increased sense of empathy among the participants and a renewed focus on inclusivity and participation. The process of exploring strategies and approaches for change resulted in an enhanced faith community music experience and an encouragement for the possibilities of gifts-centred music making within the context of corporate worship.

Dave Camlin
Informed Practice at the Sage Gateshead

As the growing interest in community music continues to emerge through courses and programmes in higher education, it is important to explore some aspects of practice that are continuously informed and improved through practical research. Dave Camlin, as Head of Higher Education at the Sage Gateshead in the North East of England, is a songwriter, composer, teacher and researcher. He has had an influential role in the development and running of the community music undergraduate programme and, through his research, he pushes us into philosophical discussions around what it means to be musical. Through his work, he opens spaces to consider dialogical ways to interact with people while challenging us to consider how we understand the strategies and practices around person-centred musical learning (Camlin, 2015). Like many community musicians, the context of Dave's work has changed as his musical career has progressed. At the start of his career, he was a singer-songwriter regularly gigging with a band. This meant that his practice as a community musician took on a focus of songwriting – an extension of his professional self. This also included working with ensembles and music production, often with young people in non-formal music-making contexts. As his own music career evolved to include an increased amount of singing and music teaching, his community music practice shifted accordingly. For example, he currently runs two community choirs in the 'Natural Voice'[5] tradition in west Cumbria and Gateshead as well as leading a programme of undergraduate music training at Sage Gateshead, a course of study that Dave hopes will prepare students for a sustainable career in participatory music making.

When asked about the essential personal qualities in enabling effective music making, Dave lists six key ideas. First, he cites empathy as the ability to apply a 'theory of mind' to put yourself in someone else's shoes and understand

Figure 7.1 Dave Camlin, Human Music Project, Sage Gateshead

their motivations, challenges and ambitions. Musicality follows because community musicians need to be confident at applying their musicianship in different contexts in order to effectively lead people on their personal musical journeys. Third, community musicians must be willing to take risks and be openly vulnerable in terms of their own authority, always challenging their power. There must be a genuine interest in dialogue and conversation, a strong sense of humour and finally knowing 'why' one is engaging in any particular activity as well as knowing 'how'.

Whilst reflecting on his own practice as a facilitator, Dave points us towards one of his articles where he states, 'Success is like quality, it's contingent on the situation' (Camlin, 2015). This is important because it reminds us that although the etymology of facilitation literally means 'to make easier', what makes something easy is different for different people. Dave examples this with the following story:

> When I first teach something to one of my choirs, we learn as much of the material aurally first, so that the notation-phobic members don't get anxious, but doing this can make the notation-dependent members anxious, so it's always a balance. I have to 'read' the room very closely for signs of anxiety (the signs of which can often be very subtle things, and out of people's conscious awareness like a slightly furrowed brow or a tapping foot) and adjust accordingly. If the 'dominant response' is an aural one, then people are 'making' music rather than 'reading' it when it comes to performance. I also make sure there are MP3 recordings available of whole songs and individual parts, as they help reinforce accurate aural learning during personal practice.

Putting this into practice, the 'biggest buzz' for Dave is when the group he is working with relaxes and simply enjoys being 'in' the music. This is connected to a belief that having fun in a social context is a critical aspect of music making:

> feeling part of something bigger, and really 'connecting' with the other people you're 'musicking' with. In rehearsals that means there's always a big emphasis on 'feeling' the music in your body, and developing a collective sense of 'entrainment' to reinforce the interpersonal connections that music brings.[6]

Getting the participants to use their bodies is an important aspect of Dave's style and he encourages the choir to move around the room during rehearsal, singing, dancing and 'playing' together. From Dave's perspective, this helps the group cohere and be more confident with each other by lessening individual self-consciousness. In performance, this translates into something joyful and celebratory, which can be both compelling and uplifting. This can have the effect of encouraging audience participation both in terms of the event itself and for future involvement.

Turning towards the undergraduates students he works with, Dave says he recognises the importance of dialogue – a central part of his conceptual work. He recalls that by the time a new cohort of students starts a degree, 'a lot of them are already fantastic technical musicians'. Where he thinks his skills are useful is in helping them to realise that they have the resource within themselves for self-development. As an example, Dave points to how this approach worked with a student with a number of physical disabilities. In this instance, the person had to learn that their way of making music – while not conventional – was still valid. This helped Dave to understand the power of the community music facilitation as much as it helped those he works with to develop their own pedagogical approach:

> I think this kind of dialogue, where I'm learning as much as the student, is very empowering for all concerned. I'm very heavily influenced by the philosophy of Critical Pedagogy, and believe that music is a vital part of our 'ontological and historical vocation to be more fully human'.[7] So at the back of my mind when working with students, I'm always thinking about how their musical development might contribute to their actualization as human beings, and how it will also help them to be better teachers. I find that helps enormously to be more objective about music teaching-learning situations, and to locate this kind of learning dialogue inside longer-term learning goals.

In discussions about developing leadership, Dave points to a number of initiatives such as the dialogic peer mentoring work of Reflect Lab, Music Lab, and ArtWorks' Peer Artist Learning project.[8] Dave sees leadership as a mindset and a way of being in the world, rather than any predetermined or prescribed set of skills, stating that 'I think of it as "agency" as much as I think of it as "leadership" – developing agency means also knowing when to be a good follower as well as how and when to step into the leadership role.' Again, Dave believes that reflective dialogue is at the heart of developing leadership and agency. You make sense of your practice by talking about it and getting other people's perspectives on it – challenging your assumptions when necessary in order to develop. In this way, reflective dialogue helps the facilitator to develop insights into their practice that is not always easy when you work in isolation. We can, as Dave suggests, get caught up in our own habitual ways of thinking and doing: 'we need to have our preconceptions disrupted if we're going to bring about shifts in our professional (or personal) identity'. Liking it to filling a vacuum, leadership means taking responsibility rather than waiting for someone else to give it to you. As Dave notes:

> Some of my most formative experiences of developing my own agency as a 'leader' have come about when I've been willing to put myself into a vacant space, and take responsibility, so I try to facilitate situations for other people where they have to do the same. The impetus for agency comes from asking yourself the question that the Russian poet Irina Ratushinskaya asked herself in prison, 'If not I, then who?' and I think the other question that goes along with that is, 'if not now, then when?'[9]

From Dave's account, a leader is the person who does something rather than waiting or hoping for someone else to do it on their behalf, suggesting that 'we make the road by walking' (Horton & Freire, 1990). This is an invitation to 'get involved' and learn how to do the work by being part of it. Make your work about you, your passions and the people you work with. 'If you don't feel confident about yourself and your current skills, borrow someone else's confidence in you! Who thinks you can do this? Why trust your own self-doubt

Figure 7.2 Dave Camlin, Sing 4 Water Project

over their confidence, especially if they have more experience than you?' In his typically encouraging way Dave advocates that,

> If someone asks you to be involved in something, no matter how unconfident you feel about it, say 'yes'. They think you can do it, so maybe they're seeing something you can't yet. As songwriter Rikki Lee-Jones says 'the world you make inside your head is the one you see around you', so imagine a world that has you following your heart and your musical passion, and draws people into it, inspiring everyone who's involved. What does it look like? What kind of things are you doing? Who else is there? What are they doing?

Science-Art Dualisms (Elliott Eisner)

Dave Camlin's study illustrates the ongoing questioning and active researching that guides and informs decisions. His work is orientated around an open attitude of curiosity and inquiry. Probing questions such as 'how did this work?' and 'what could be improved?' seem to be everyday practice. With intentionality and basic record keeping, these questions and subsequent actions form the basis of a culture of inquiry. There is also place for formal research, but it need not necessarily be daunting in proportion or massive in scope. Practitioners who are active, reflexive, in-the-moment musicians may mistakenly resist the notion of research in practice. In the current academic culture, scientific methods are considered to be fail-proof and reliable. We who live, work and think within artistic contexts must consider a wide range of means of knowing and doing, remaining open to a variety of methods and approaches.

Since the turn of the twentieth century, the arts have declined in social practice and importance, as industry, commerce, consumerism and technology have driven human and cultural development. Science was considered dependable; the artistic process was not. Science was cognitive; the arts were emotional. Science was teachable; the arts required talent. Science was testable; the arts were matters of preference. Science was useful; the arts were ornamental. Art was a fall-back position.[10] The dualism of science-art is, in fact, a fairly modern condition and it is essential for musicians and music facilitators to embrace the scholarship that the arts embody. Qualitative methods such as ethnography, narrative inquiry, observation and grounded theory honour the nuanced and expressive qualities that emerge when humans and music intersect.

Examples of Research Processes in Doctoral Programmes

We have already pointed towards other fields of music scholarship that have resonance with community music: scholars from music education (Allsupp, 2016; Elliott & Silverman, 2015; Jorgensen, 2003; Woodford, 2005), music therapy (Ansdell, 2014; Stige et al., 2010) and applied ethnomusicology (Barz & Cohen, 2011; Pettan & Titon, 2015) – all argue for a broader and inclusive music making. This has given community music scholarship greater visibility and consequently brought some experienced practitioners into the folds of doctoral study. For example, Ruth Currie and Joanne Gibson, both PhD candidates from the UK but also experienced practitioners, were asked to discuss what impact the doctorial process was having on their professional practice. Ruth suggests that the process is affording her the opportunity to explore theoretical perspectives on music making, facilitation and relationships within her reflective practice. She continues:

> As a workshop leader, I have identified how research in the field of community music can support my facilitation in traditionally music education-based settings, and I am experiencing the benefit of considering these two research fields in partnership. Engaging with community music from a research perspective has created opportunities for me to work with, and learn from, a rich variety of people whom I may have never encountered. It is the inquiry evolving from the field's wide-ranging experiences and approaches that is deepening my questioning. This is not only in the questioning of my own practice, but my questioning of the role and responsibility of the field of community music and how this can be supported, through evidence, shared learning, and exploration throughout the international community.
>
> As a researcher, having the experience of my practice as a workshop leader and school teacher provides me, as I'm sure it does all facilitators, with a wealth of questions and aspirations for our work in this field. Being able to explore some of these questions is not only exciting, but I feel intrinsically at the core of my music-making philosophy; to support not only my own practice, but the practice and development of the wider community of music-makers and facilitators through linking and experiencing theory and practice.

Joanne Gibson frames the context she previously worked in by saying:

> Throughout my practice as a community musician (and before I even realised that my practice was community music) I have been concerned

with '[. . .] doing things right as well as doing the right things' (Arévalo, Ljung, & Sriskandarajah, 2010, p. 39). By this I do not mean 'right' in the sense of perfection, but in the sense of meaning and purpose. Guided by my understanding of music-making with people as a continuous journey of learning, exploration and discovery, I have shaped my practice through questioning and an ongoing process of reflection, reflection-in-action and reflection-on-action.

Reflective practice, with a focus of both 'on' and 'in' is critical to the ongoing professional work of the community musician. For Joanne, the process of self-reflecting questions arises before, during and after the projects she is involved in. She is therefore continually reflecting on how to work with and for the participants underpinning this process with questions surrounding the music-making context, process and product, the role of the community music facilitator, project sustainability, project purpose and meaning and whether '[she is] doing the "right" thing'. Since beginning her PhD research journey, Joanne has been able to develop these skills in new ways and although early into the process has been able to identify the potential for the profession. She remarks:

> Although I have always been aware that I reflect (indeed self-reflection was repeatedly encouraged on my Masters programme) and that I ask a lot of questions, adapt my methods and explore new ideas, I never assimilated this to research through practice. It is only recently that I have begun to associate my practice with research, or rather praxis, through embarking upon PhD study with the International Centre for Community Music, York St John University. Locating my reflective practice within a critical framework has developed my thinking and understanding as 'Spontaneous concepts, in working their way "upward" toward greater abstractness, clear a path for scientific concepts in their "downward" development towards greater concreteness' (Nelson, 2013 p. 63). Growth in community music research, alongside recognition given to the culture of inquiry that community musicians work within, has exciting potential to support the field through new insights and understanding.

There is then clear evidence to suggest that community musicians are working together in order to generate a sustainable environment of self-reflexivity, research and scholarship. For some there has become a merge of the *community musician-self* and the *scholar-self* blurring the distinction between traditionally understood 'professional' and 'academic' practices.

Research strategies including narrative inquiry (M. S. Barrett & Stauffer, 2009), autoethnography, (Brochner & Ellis, 2016; Chang, 2008; Davis & Ellis, 2008, Ellis & Bochner, 1996), community-based research (Boyd, 2014) practice as research (E. Barrett, 2010; Biggs & Karlsson, 2011; Nelson, 2013; Smith & Dean, 2009), and arts-based research (Finley, 2008; Leavy, 2015; McNiff, 2008) have opened up the possibilities for ways to 'answer' questions through strategies and methods that resonate with the practice itself.

Four Hypothetical Research Vignettes

Building upon the examples above, we provide four hypothetical research vignettes. Each illustration begins with a question pertinent to community music and is then followed by a short descriptive passage that serves to outline a possible research scenario.

1. What are the motivations for adults to join a community music project?

    Due to the success of last year's community music event, a retelling of local folk tales and stories, a notice in the cities performing arts newspaper advertised this season's project.

    > Your local art museum and gallery has just reopened after an extensive refurbishment. We are offering the garden space as a site for a visual art and music installation. We would like you and your groups to explore the theme of personal identity.

    Over a period of 3 months, those that signed up for the project made a three-dimensional visual representation of themselves using found materials. These ideas acted as stimulus for music improvisation and composition. During the art-making process, the community musician/researcher had time to bond with participants, building mutual respect, trust and friendship. This enabled in-depth questioning relating to the central question as regards the motivations for adults to join a community music project. Conscious of the researcher's motives, the participants felt close to the project and this began to influence the process and the artefacts that were being produced. The final display and performance presented an extraordinarily rich complement to the academic paper.

2. How effective are the music-making strategies of community music facilitators within a school environment?

As part of a general music curriculum, students work collaboratively in small groups to write and arrange their own songs. Non-formal music-making strategies are employed, as these are deemed a key feature in community music. Throughout the 12-week project, the teacher/researcher and the students examined the experiences using interviews, journals and video diaries; each group decided that they would like to present their songs through a public sharing. The performance is framed by the teacher/researcher as a research project and consists of the music plus interjections of the video diaries and interviews.

3. What role can music play in the development of community within an area designated as showing significant signs of social deprivation?

For the past 2 years, the community musician/researcher has been working in collaboration with government, local authorities and community agencies, in an effort to establish an annual carnival/festival type celebration that would feature local music, dance, drama and food. During this time, there has been a concerted effort to build partnerships and strengthen community infrastructure. From the beginning, it has always been clear that the arts must be a vital component in this regeneration project. Music in this area is rich, vibrant and dynamic. It constitutes a strong sense of identity for many of its inhabitants. As an event held during a national summer holiday, the carnival/festival aims to provide the community with a stronger sense of identity and self-worth. Alongside an ethnographic analysis of the experience, the carnival/festival is a presentation of research outcomes demonstrating a clear relation between researcher and participants, a commitment towards local cultural and political issues, a useful and sustainable provision and the start of a different type of dialogue that stands to examine not only how things currently are but also how things might be otherwise.

4. How might a music programme enhance the lives of those serving long-term prison sentences?

Through invitation, the community musician/researcher designs a course to complement other curriculum subjects being offered at a maximum-security prison. The course is flexible enough to enable input and direction from those that will take part. In other words, the participants will guide the music content. Possible directions the course might take are discussed at the initial meetings. The participants are keen to make something that their families and friends can hear. They are candid with their comments about how life is in the prison and they talk openly about the importance of music both before they were incarcerated and since

The community musician/researcher is able to garner data that is rich and insightful. However, it is not until the inmates begin making and presenting their music, through performance poetry, raps and songs, that the significance of music in their lives becomes apparent. In order to provide both a creative outlet and an artefact that can be heard beyond the walls of the prison, the community musician/researcher teaches the participants how to use a hard disc recorder. Through the technology the inmates record each other's musical endeavours, cutting a final disc entitled 'Free to be Musical'. This CD, that is uploaded to a music streaming site, articulates an answer to the question in ways that a traditional paper cannot.

It is exciting that a culture of inquiry has the capacity to influence the core values of what practitioners believe to be the distinctive traits of the practice. We may also see practical projects being developed informed by current research. Rather than searching for 'proof', community musicians ask questions in order to probe the work they are involved with. Frequently the results are deeper and better questions, rather than irrefutable answers. Project questions are set and are refined and reconceptualised through this process.

We would like to suggest that as a grassroots practice, those involved can, to a certain extent, control the scholarly trajectory. Community music has historically carved a path through resistance rather than compliance and following this pathway those involved would do well to seek appropriate research strategies and methods through which to respond to important questions. We emphasise that one does not have to be in an academic programme or in a professorial role to be part of a culture of inquiry. If community musicians can feel part of a larger network, one that reflects the tenants of the practice, then trust and understanding can be built between those working in the Academy, those in the field, and increasingly those that occupy both spaces. From this position, collaboration and sharing take flight, creating an environment that ensures enhancement and growth in the field, both in breadth and depth.

Questions and Topics for Discussion

1 Discuss the research strategies and methods you see being used in community music research.

2 Focusing on one or two examples, discuss how effective you think they have been in responding to the questions they set out to answer.

3   Is it important for community music to develop a clear research agenda? If so, why; if not, why not?

4   Is there a culture of inquiry amongst your professional community music colleagues? What might it take to deepen the relationship between research and practice amongst the community musicians you are currently involved in?

5   Brainstorm the current research topics that community musicians should be thinking about. Turn these topics into questions and discuss how you might go about answering them.

Notes

1   Saint-Exupéry (1943, p. 18).
2   Willingham (2001, p. 5)
3   International Journal of Community Music, www.intellectbooks.co.uk/journals/view-Journal,id=149/
4   Some of these studies, currently underway at the time of writing, will be published. Others may be available through the Laurier Centre for Community Music website. Authors may be contacted for details.
5   See www.naturalvoice.net/
6   See Clayton, Sager, & Will (2004) for concepts surrounding the notion of entertainment.
7   For the classic text on critical pedagogy see Freire (2002). See also Darder, Baltodano, & Torres (2009).
8   See www.artsandhealth.ie/case-studies/reflect-lab/
9   See Ratushinskaya (1989).
10 Eisner, Elliot (2002) What can education learn from the arts about the practice of education? John Dewey Lecture, Stanford University. www.infed.org/biblio/eisner_arts_and_the_practice_of_education.htm

References

Allsup, R. E. (2016). *Remixing the Classroom: Toward an Open Philosophy of Music.* Bloomington, IN: Indiana University Press.
Ansdell, G. (2014). *How music helps in music therapy and every day life.* Farnham: Ashgate.
Arévalo, K. M., Ljung, M., & Sriskandarajah, N. (2010). Learning through feedback in the field: Reflective learning in a NGO in the Peruvian amazon. *Action Research, 8*(1), 29–51.

Barrett, E. (2010). *Practice as research: Approaches to creative arts enquiry.* New York: I.B.Tauris.
Barrett, M. S., & Stauffer, S. L. (2009). *Narrative inquiry in music education: Troubling certainty.* Netherlands: Springer.
Barz, G., & Cohen, J. M. (Eds.). (2011). *The culture of AIDS of Africa: Hope and healing through music and the arts.* New York: Oxford University Press.
Biggs, M., & Karlsson, H. (Eds.). (2011). *The Routledge companion to research in the arts.* New York: Routledge.
Boyd, M. R. (2014). Community-based research: Understanding the principles, practices, challenges, and rationale. In P. Leavy (Ed.), *The Oxford handbook of qualitative research* (pp. 498–517). New York: Oxford University Press.
Brochner, A., & Ellis, C. (2016). *Evocative autoethnography: Writing lives and telling stories.* New York: Routledge.
Camlin, D. (2015). This is my truth, now tell me yours: Emphasizing dialogue within participatory music. *International Journal of Community Music, 8*(3), 233–57.
Chang, H. (2008). *Autoethnography as method.* Walnut Creek, CA: Left Coast Press.
Clayton, M., Sager, R., & Will, U. (2004). In time with the music: The concept of entrainment and its significance for ethnomusicology. *European Meetings in Ethnomusicology, 11*, 1–82. Retrieved from http://dro.dur.ac.uk/8713
Darder, A., Baltodano, M., & Torres, R. (Eds.). (2009). *The critical pedagogy reader.* New York: Routledge.
Davis, C. S., & Ellis, C. (2008). Emergent methods in autoethnographic research: Autoethnographic narrative and the multiethnographic turn. In S. N. Hesse-Biber & P. Leavy (Eds.), *Handbook of emergent methods* (pp. 283–302). New York: Guilford Press.
Eisner, E. (2002). *What can education learn from the arts about the practice of education?* John Dewey Lecture, Stanford University. Retrieved from www.infed.org/biblio/eisner_arts_and_the_practice_of_education.htm
Elliott, D. J., & Silverman, M. (2015). *Music matters: A philosophy of music education* (2nd ed.). New York: Oxford University Press.
Ellis, C., & Bochner, A. P. (Eds.). (1996). *Composing ethnography: Alternative forms of qualitative writing.* Walnut Creek, CA: AltaMira Press.
Finley, S. (2008). Arts-based research. In J. G. Knowles & A. L. Cole (Eds.), *Handbook of the arts in qualitative research* (pp. 71–82). London: Sage.
Freire, P. (2002). *Pedagogy of the oppressed.* New York: Continuum.
Horton, M., & Freire, P. (1990). *We make the road by walking: Conversations on education and social change.* Philadelphia, PA: Temple University Press.
Jorgensen, E. R. (2003). *Transforming music education.* Indiana, IN: Indiana University Press.
Leavy, P. (Ed.). (2015). *Method meets art: Arts based research practice* (2nd ed.). New York: Guilford Press.
McNiff, S. (2008). Art-based Research. In J. G. Knowles & A. L. Cole (Eds.), *Handbook of the arts in qualitative research* (pp. 29–40). London: Sage.

Nelson, R. (2013). *Practice as research in the arts: principles, protocols, pedagogies, resistances*. Hampshire: Palgrave MacMillan.

Pettan, S., & Titon, J. T. (Eds.). (2015). *The Oxford handbook of applied ethnomusicology*. New York: Oxford University Press.

Ratushinskaya, I. (1989). *Pencil letter*. New York: Alfred A. Knopf.

Schön, D. A. (1991). *The reflective practitioner*. London: Basic Books.

Smith, H., & Dean, R. T. (Eds.). (2009). *Practice-led research, research-led practice in the creative arts*. Edinburgh: Edinburgh University Press.

Stige, B., Ansdell, G., Elefant, C., & Pavlicevic, M. (2010). *Where music helps: Community music therapy in action and reflection*. Farnham: Ashgate.

Woodford, P. G. (2005). *Democracy and music education: Liberalism, ethics, and the politics of practice*. Bloomington, IN: Indiana University Press.

Chapter 8
Careers and Management

If businesspeople should take art more seriously, artists too should take business more seriously. Commerce is a central part of the human experience. More prosaically, it is what billions of people do all day.[1]

Everyone has a plan until they get punched in the face.

Mike Tyson[2]

In this chapter, case studies are presented where community music projects are developed and sustained, where partnerships are forged and strategies for engaging in entrepreneurial processes for success are discussed. People who find themselves in music and arts careers have answered what is often described as a 'calling', a response to a deep personal urge to follow a path that often does not guarantee material wealth, demands creative and innovative action and most of all continues on a journey of service and facilitation with others. Arts workers engage, then, in portfolio careers that require a wide range of skills that have little to do with the artistic processes themselves. Where are these skills learned and how can they be applied to the community music context?

Exploring Relationships Between Music and Business: How Are They Mutually Beneficial?

The business of art is an oft-neglected aspect of the creative process. In fact, business is frequently perceived by society as being so closely allied with consumerist and capital gains initiatives that the very concept of operating as a business is an anathema to artists and arts communities. 'Artists routinely deride businesspeople as money-obsessed bores and many businesspeople, for their part, assume that artists are a bunch of pretentious wastrels' (Schumpeter, 2011). Part of this disparity comes from how success is measured. Hard data such as numbers and statistics rule decisions and actions. One hears the sentiment, 'if you can't count it, it doesn't count'. However, it must be pointed out that many musicians have been superb entrepreneurs, and we can even reach back in history to learn of how the Mozarts and Mendelssohns (Desmerais, 2013) generated a reasonably decent income as independent business operators. In modern times, freelance or independent musicians continue to rely heavily on revenue generated by projects that are funded with strategic planning based on business models. Business models and their effectiveness will be dealt with shortly, but first let us stay with this idea that the arts and business can operate on some mutually valuable territory.

How can the arts and business learn from each other? Business often relies on marketing or messaging. Artists are storytellers and are expert communicators. Business schools teach more about production and positioning merchandise than how to infuse them with meaning. Music, as discussed in Chapter 1, is a meaning-making enterprise. Business can also learn that managing musicians and artists is a process of managing bright and creative people. Goffee and Jones of the London Business School point out that 'today's most productive companies are dominated by what they call "clevers", who are the devil to manage' (Schumpeter, 2011). It can be appreciated that the music and arts world has centuries of experience in managing, or not managing such independent, non-conformist thinkers. Perhaps the greatest concept that business can learn from the arts is to become innovative and creative. But, what can community music glean from the business sector?

Project Building

Much of community music work – whether it is in a village setting, an educational or faith-based institution or part of an established large performing organisation – is based on project building. Launching such an enterprise can be a hit-or-miss proposition. Traditional approaches would include the formulation of an idea or proposal, a pitch to funding sources, assembling a team and a strategy to begin moving the plan into action. This, of course, depends on an affirmative response to each of the parts of the process, including a well-received proposal, sufficient funding secured, a capable team and the suitable context in which to enact the plan. Another approach favours experimentation rather than elaborate planning, market feedback rather than intuition and a developing or iterative design over the pre-formed big upfront design. Known in some circles as the 'lean start-up' (Blank, 2013, p. 66), it is based on assumptions that rather than building and executing a business model it searches for one that is repeatable and scalable. It emphasises nimbleness and speed and relies on input from customers, or in community music parlance, participants, to revise plans, assumptions and redesign offerings. We turn to a model of a community music 'lean start-up' that is provided by a business professor who is also a passionate community musician.

Stephen Preece
Developing a Systematic Business Plan for a Start-Up Project

Stephen's interests in the culture-arts sector have created a variety of opportunities for him to balance his passion for music with his academic interests in business and economics. His formula is quite simple. Find out what people are craving and what gives them meaning. Develop the product or event, and create a means to fund and deliver it to the appropriate customer segment.

In this case study, the nuts and bolts of a 'start-up' idea are explored, and an example of a successful community music initiative is described. A model canvas for developing a business plan is provided[3] (see also Figure 8.9) and will assist in building strategies for decisions, assessing the plan and ensuring success.

Projects in community music are essentially 'start-ups' in business jargon. Once an opportunity or a need has been identified, there are tried and true processes that are employed in the business sector that address all of the various steps in the journey. First, the *customer segment* must be identified. Customer segment is a subgroup within a population that has a particular need or desire that can be fulfilled, in this instance, in a community music context. An entrepreneur would seek to identify, define and understand the customer segment, and find the nuances that set it apart from the general population.

Let us consider, for example, the ageing population (characteristics of older learners and music are addressed in Chapter 2). Here, in a growing segment of population and within a wide range of age and abilities, people are seeking community, aesthetic expression and in general, meaningful experiences to add value to life. The first step is to identify the niche that needs to be filled. Is it community sing-alongs or drumming circles, lessons or songwriting clubs? Whatever it is within that customer segment, the project is defined, and market research is undertaken. This is known as a *value proposition*, matching to the particular needs of that customer segment. At this stage, research is required to find out what people would commit to. Interviews are conducted. Informal and formal discussions are held. In some instances, surveys are useful. A hypothesis is formed focusing on age groups and the socio-economic and cultural characteristics of the age group and interests.

Experiments or trial balloons are floated; let's try this or that and repeat it. These are known as 'hypotheses'. A hypothesis is tested and assessed. What frequency should be repeated? Monthly? Bi-weekly? This process is paramount in building engagement and leveraging the potential energy and commitment of the participant. The entrepreneur must take these meticulous steps to fully understand the population that is intended for this project or experiences.

Once there is a solid connect between the value proposition and the customer segment, a business model can be developed, including all of the details of marketing, budgets, administration and so on. On the Business Model Plan canvas are a number of boxes. A project can be launched either by identifying the customer segment and building value propositions to connect to that population, or, the other way round, where a value proposition (existing or developing project) is seeking the right customer segment. Those two categories are usually the place where the ideas are developed, revised, reworked and constantly revisited. If the customer segment is clear and stable, the attention is on getting the project or event or product right. And, if the customer segment is fluid and ever-changing, this affects how the value proposition would be rolled out.

Partners are recruited and engaged. Key activities are designed and described. Resources, means of delivery, costs and revenue streams are analysed. The whole process is interconnected and interdependent, but Stephen reminds us that things will likely go wrong if the connection between the customer segment and the value proposition is not a solid one.

One of the greatest human challenges is to move from the idea stage to action. The ability to mobilise efforts, energy and ideas that are already out there is a key quality for a project leader. Stephen suggests that the less you do by yourself, the better. If possible, plug into a community in order to leverage other people's skills and resources. Rather than creating independently, you are working within a context where pieces, people, ideas and resources can be connected. The leader is a catalyst to bring these aspects of a project into action. Depending on the nature of the project, it is helpful to tap into neighbourhood groups that already exist, piggybacking on what is already available. One asks, 'What skills must I possess no matter what?'

and 'What other skills must I leverage or find from others?' In this personal inventory stage, it becomes very clear about what dimensions of the project entrepreneurship you have the capacity to develop and what you can acquire through other means.

The Grand River Jazz Society

Stephen is a business professor, true. But, he is also a jazz pianist, a singer in one of the finest chamber choirs in Canada, a church music director and has been a classical music critic for a prominent newspaper. For years, he has felt that his city needed a live music venue that would attract local regulars and draw the finest musicians in the world. The idea of a jazz club that would feature local musicians on Friday nights and international quality musicians on Saturday was burning in him. This was his start-up project, his value proposition, and in 2010, the idea was mobilised into action. How? Stephen reports that it was partly luck, some strategic timing and the coming together of a team who shared the vision.

The venue was discovered in a heritage hotel-brewery-restaurant enterprise that was very popular locally. There was an interesting room with an abundant amount of character and history that had been shuttered for years. It clicked that this was a real opportunity, perhaps the catalyst that would energise and move the dream forward. From that discovery a team was assembled, and critical to the project was a business professor colleague who was approaching retirement. At a party she asked, 'How much would it cost to put on a season

Figure 8.1 Stephen Preece – Jazz Room

of live jazz?' When the figure was revealed, she guaranteed to back the project for that amount. (It turns out that she never had to touch that money, but it was the guarantee that provided the impetus to launch.) Very little was needed to be done to the venue. A stage was built. A fine piano, sound system and lighting purchased, and a partnership was forged with the management so that food and beverage profits would remain in-house, and all music-related costs and revenues would go to the jazz society.

Stephen wrote grant applications to several foundations, arts and cultural councils, and government funding departments. This is where he realised that grant writing was a nightmare and he might need someone to handle the operational details of booking artists, managing websites and marketing and dealing with the general budget. This was the stage addressed earlier where he assessed what he could do effectively and where help from others was needed. He also determined that the artistic processes of the enterprise needed to be outsourced and a local jazz musician was contracted to handle the programming for the big stage shows. This was a huge job that Stephen felt lifted from his shoulders.

The value proposition was developing: a fine venue, a solid partner, the promise of excellent music and a dedicated team. What about the customer segment? Who would come? How could the project be sustainable beyond a few initial months of guaranteed funding? The 'trial balloon' that was floated was to issue passes that for an annual fee would grant admission to all of the jazz events. Within a short time, 100 passes were sold. A stable revenue stream had been established. The customer segment was now emerging with the only known common link among them being the commitment to live jazz music in a new venue. Ages, occupations and economic status of the new patrons were not available to the team.

Along with the venue partner, other corporate sponsors were sought, and these came forward because of the owner or CEO's passion for live music. The message here again is to develop that customer segment so strongly that the values and passions of the population are leveraged into revenue or some other tangible form of capital.

The Jazz Room is a huge success story. Some of the most admired players in the world now grace the stage. Everyone is 'over the moon' about performing at the Jazz Room, and that sentiment is attributed to a listening, attentive audience, a good piano and sound and lighting . . . top quality. Education and outreach initiatives have included artists' workshops for school-age musicians, hosting high school jazz events and partnerships with the local jazz festival.[4]

Stephen reminds himself and his team that they need to stay true to the vision of creating and sustaining a sizzling night club dedicated to the best in

Figure 8.2 Jazz Room

jazz music presentations. It has a dual mandate – to support exceptional musicians from our own community and to invite talent from elsewhere for local audiences to hear. The Jazz Room has quickly become one of the most important cultural resources in the community. This venue provides the street-level nightlife that is the hallmark of great cities all over the world. A first-rate music club is a tangible community resource the community can point to as a marker of a culturally vibrant and liveable city. It functions on the principles of a business plan that is driven by an artistic and community-based mandate.[5]

Stephen Preece's experience in balancing arts projects within his own scholarship as a business and economics professor illustrates the symbiotic potential of the two sectors. His work emphasises three basic premises: operate in an area you know, hypothesise a business model and seek customer validation. Your entrepreneurial ideas are based upon who you are, your interests, experience and passions; what you know, knowledge, skills and insights; who you know, network, partners and resources.[6]

Following is a very different case study that incorporates many of the principles of creativity and sustainability. This is about the work of an internationally prominent community musician, Pete Moser.

Pete Moser
More Music

Pete Moser is the artistic director of a community music charity based in the north of England. More Music is a community music and education charity based in the West End of Morecambe, working throughout local communities as well as nationally and internationally. Year-round programmes are provided covering a breadth of music-making activity that involves people of all ages and all backgrounds. More Music is one of the longest running and most highly regarded community music and educational organizations in the UK.

Figure 8.3 Pete Moser – More Music

More Music has an impressive history of developing national and international projects that demonstrate flexibility, belief, imagination, partnership and connection. Pete sums up his role as including the general strategic management of the organisation, in project development (short and long term, including some as long as 10 years) and in creating sustained change within the Morecambe community. Morecambe is a seaside resort town that is past its prime and is considered on a socio-economic scale to be high on the deprivation list. More Music has grown over the years, starting with one person and now employing upwards of 25 people.

Pete states that the artistic director must hold and project a vision, and must be able to clearly articulate the values that support and drive the vision. Creativity and inclusion come from a vision of a community that is more cohesive, connected and collaborative. The result is the emergence of a better society, and the leader must create a pattern of work that responds to that evolving and ongoing change. Values underpinning More Music's work are:

Access: To create opportunities for people from across the social spectrum, including people from diverse communities and those with different needs;
Imagination: To create new and innovative work of the highest quality that gives individuals an opportunity to discover and share their unique voices;

Community: To lead on work that transforms communities and develops practice that uses the arts to transform people's lives.

Finding creative solutions, experimentation, trial and error are all part of project development. Knowing how to run things in general is essential. Producer, money manager, networker with other sector organizations, with musicians and other individuals and knowledge of the practical things such as grants, contracts, venues and basic functions of systems are all part of the role. Ideas must be developed and mobilised. Constant examining of the process with questions such as 'What will make it interesting?', 'What's it called?' or 'Who could do it?' and 'What is the guiding thread?'

Pete also has a wide range of approaches to facilitation and workshop development with more than 30 years of experience. He explores examples of participants' learning. How did we learn something? He leads people taking theoretical thinking and turning these ideas into a creative process. Reflective practice is all about thinking how we do what we do, and serves as a starting point for moving forward.

Pete uses the context and 'need' as a starting point for a project to happen. He stresses that he must be highly prepared, in the zone and not rushed. Planning and preparation are fundamental and once he is there in the venue or community, he connects with the programme very deeply. He states,

Figure 8.4 More Music Hothouse

Careers and Management **153**

'my stuff is about making new work. In the end it is like an active meditation. I must be in the moment and the result is usually more energy. We are all invigorated!' But he reiterates, the key is to give one's self time to digest, plan and prepare.

An example of a songwriting workshop in a school setting with 8-year-olds might include some pre-composed material to kick things off, perhaps with a few instruments and singing voices. He might bring four songs and two or three poems that could be used to create a zone or space for concepts to develop. These lead to all sorts of different ways to get to important questions, turn the ideas into lyrics and then turn these into song. He admonishes the facilitator to make friends with participants first, then talk, explore and get them involved. If one can make these types of activities happen, the final outcome is usually a surprise. Participants who make something together that is new, creative, accessible and part of their own story have a deeper and more enjoyable experience.

Pete exudes passion for this work, and he feels deeply that one's practice must develop out of one's passions. If repertoire is being taught, then be sure you like the songs! Include your own past and personal story; make sure that what you do connects with you as a person. Then, it is honest.

Pete's advice for those aspiring to do this work is to go and watch other people do stuff. Find some really good people to team up with. Work with

Figure 8.5 More Music Lantern Festival

154 Careers and Management

others as much as possible. Be inspired by learning from those with expertise and experience.

At More Music, it is held that the power of music and culture can transform people's lives for the better. Work is produced that is truthful and has a powerful artistic aesthetic. Events are beautiful and joyful. Many art forms are incorporated, with a focus on music. The work is dynamic and fluid, and changes with the times.

Pete is deeply interested in creating new art works, and developing a sense of place by working with and in communities. Pete concludes, 'I'm interested in telling the truth about things. You need to do what you do for a reason. Say things through what you do.' On the other hand, he describes his work as play: 'It's all about play . . . my workplace is a playful place. I like taking people to a playful place where play is in every sense part of the process.'

It is interesting to note how many common principles of strategic practice emerge from Pete's initiatives. As in the lean start-up methodology, Pete emphasises becoming familiar personally with your strategies and context, being reflexive and nimble, knowing your community or market segment and listening and learning from others.

Partnerships are key in building successful projects. As Stephen Preece admonished earlier to leverage the resources and skills of others, the following case study outlines very powerful and growing community music initiatives in Munich, Germany.

Alicia de Banffy-Hall
Strategic Development of Community Music in Munich

After completing her BA in community music in Liverpool, UK, Alicia served for more than 10 years as a community music practitioner in schools, community centres, kindergartens and other places. She now resides in Munich, Germany, where she grew up, and has engaged in strategically building a community music presence with a number of partners and arts agencies.

In Liverpool, Alicia founded her own business, a 'limited company' that provided fiscal credibility for her work and qualified her for various funding opportunities that would enable her to engage other artists and other partners in her practice. By registering as a company, her work could more easily be recognised by agencies and groups, rather than working merely as an individual.

Alicia is a strategic planner with an entrepreneurial spirit.[7] She is passionate about community music, and the principles of openness, inclusivity and democracy she embraced as a practitioner in England she now applies in dealing with key people who have leadership roles and handle funding for projects in Munich.

In exploring the activities of community music in Munich, it was clear that the prevalent modern Eurocentric vision of art-making dominates German music education. By 'modern', she refers to the focus on the artist and the pre-created works, the aesthetic, cultural idealism and formal education that has emanated from the traditional conservatoire programmes in Europe and North America. Alicia is a change-maker and, in that role, began to engage in a process of network building in the interest of moving towards a postmodern educational approach that emphasized people, process, community, participation and informal-non-formal pedagogies (de Banffy-Hall, 2016).

Soon after arriving in Munich, Alicia founded the Munich Community Music Action Research Group (MCMARG) as a result of a pilot research initiative where existing community music practice, organisations and practitioners in Munich were explored. The aim of this pilot was to build an understanding of the field, to build relationships, to learn about the practice of music in the community and to hear thoughts in general about the various activities in Munich. She also conducted semi-structured interviews with Munich-based practitioners, researchers, policymakers and organisations who had intersections with community music: 'What's going on in Munich? What needs change? What is missing? What is working? What is not?' MCMARG initially consisted of eight policymakers, practitioners and academics and worked for over 2 years to develop community music presence. Resulting from this work was an international conference that attracted participants from virtually every continent and an edition of the *International Journal of Community Music* that focused on community music as it is developing in Germany.

Through the research, reoccurring themes emerged: community music practitioners worked in isolation; they knew little about each other's practice; and they expressed a wish to have more opportunities to exchange ideas and challenges they face. Alicia also discovered that in the views of some, music was the most underrepresented art form in the field of arts education, and access and resources to music-making activities for socially disadvantaged groups were severely limited. As a strategist, Alicia developed an understanding between funders and policy as the meaning of what community music in the Munich context was.

People seriously listened to each other and ideas began to mobilise. For example, the Munich Philharmonic Orchestra has engaged in school and community music partnerships where their world-class players work along with school classes, refugee children and community music groups. A cellist from the philharmonic worked on reimagining the story of the Pied Piper of Hamlin with children aged 7–8. The children wrote songs and created their own scenes. In another instance, a community orchestra member who came from Georgia taught the other members of the orchestra folk songs from her country. These activities represent a shift in the usual western classical music paradigm employed in music education. Interestingly, Alicia noted that all of the participants were experiencing new creative processes; the professional orchestral players were anxious about their ability to create music with others, the children were composing new songs and the teachers were engaged in a different pedagogical practice.

Alicia attributes her success in large part to her ability to communicate. In dealing with musicians, managers, policymakers, funders and practitioners, it is essential to tune in to who they are and to speak their language. These various constituents represent very different worlds and to bring them together requires a facilitative approach – a creative, inclusive and positive approach that helps to determine an outcome with those qualities. An authoritarian style in leadership in these processes would not translate to the next level and would not yield desired outcomes. Alicia listens to people's needs, is passionate, supportive and, above all, reliable. There were those who doubted that community music could work in a network such as this.

Figure 8.6 Munich Philharmonic Community Music, Photo by Andrea Huber

Professional musicians were terrified that they would make a fool of themselves so they embarked on a journey of trust, and ultimately their growth and development within these creative processes fed back into their own personal musicianship.

From a strategic perspective, Alicia works with a 'bottom-up' democratic approach. By talking to a wide range of people, needs are assessed. What are the current key discourses and debates? Arm yourself with all the information possible. Musicians, head teachers, academics, policy people and directors of key music institutions collectively helped Alicia to gain an understanding of the complex and diverse contexts in which they practiced. To further deepen her knowledge of the values and challenges in community music in Munich, Alicia attended all the conferences and key events that had to do with music, community, policy and education. Her relentless search for understanding and discovering what was going on resulted in gaining a real sense of where the city stood culturally and socially.

Alicia has developed a role as a freelance community musician, consultant and community arts development worker, which has garnered funding through contracts, projects and other various revenue streams. It is hard work at times, and she admonishes not to shy away from getting your hands dirty! This work brings about change, and she is beginning to observe such change in schools, community groups and government agencies, even if tiny and incremental at

Figure 8.7 Munich Philharmonic Community Music, Photo by Andrea Huber

the start. Seek creative partnerships. Identify with the class or group. Find out what they are dealing with and adapt. Understand the field and the people who are working in it. When asked if she mentors others, Alicia's immediate reply was, 'I feel like the one who is being mentored!' The dream that was born in her initial work in Liverpool with her limited company business, her years of facilitating community music with children and youth, her study and research is now being realised in a changing and growing practice of inclusive music activities in a vibrant, culturally active city.

The power of music to change a community and to add social and cultural value is further illustrated in the following case study that describes a not-for-profit organisation in England.

Nikki-Kate Heyes
SoundLINCS

Nikki-Kate Heyes MBE has worked in community music for over 25 years and has been at the helm of soundLINCS,[8] a music education charity, since its creation in 1998. Nikki-Kate is an accomplished cellist, conductor and composer and in 2013 was awarded an MBE in the Queen's Birthday Honours as the founder of soundLINCS and services to music. In 2016, the organisation she directs will celebrate its 18th birthday. Nikki-Kate began the company as a sole trader operating from her home whilst she was a part-time freelance community musician. The remit given to her was to develop music across the fourth largest county in England, Lincolnshire. Today soundLINCS is an established not-for-profit organisation, with an office base in Lincoln, working across the whole of the East Midlands. Since its inception, it has made a major contribution to the transformation of the musical landscape of Lincolnshire, and East Midlands by initiating, managing and developing music programmes and projects across a wide range of genres. Whilst many of these programmes have been aimed at young people and those who work with young people, soundLINCS does not style itself as just an organisation for young people but rather a community music development agency whose remit encompasses work with all age ranges and social backgrounds. In the year 2011/12, for example, the company managed and delivered its first strategic programme for people aged 50 plus – 'soundGENERATION' 2016 will see the development of 'New Tricks', a music service for older adults. A major outcome of soundLINCS' work has been the development of a network of independent music facilitators based across the county of Lincolnshire, whose work on programmes and projects has enabled them to develop skills and expertise in facilitating, leading and designing music-making activities.

Partnerships Are Key

One of the key operating principles since its inception has been cultivating good, sustainable partnerships. Throughout its history, Nikki-Kate and her colleagues have gained skills and expertise in establishing and developing partnerships with organizations locally, regionally and nationally. These include: Arts Council England,[9] Youth Music,[10] Sing Up,[11] Lincolnshire County Council[12] and the seven district councils of Lincolnshire. Having previously enjoyed Regularly Funded Organisation[13] and National Portfolio Organisation, soundLINCS is now a Youth Music key strategic organisation and works directly with the 7 Music Education Hubs across the East Midlands.[14]

The company has an enviable track record for generating significant levels of funding for its work. From establishing Lincolnshire as a Youth Music Action Zone in 2000, the company has created and delivered numerous long-term projects and strategic programmes, thereby attracting development funding from Youth Music, a national charity that supports music making in the UK, and subsequently raised substantial amounts of match funding from Lincolnshire-based organizations and local authorities. SoundLINCS have also

Figure 8.8 Insert Group Star, soundLINCS

made successful bids for lottery funding and other national funding as well as securing funding and help in kind from a wide range of local, county-based organizations. Over the years, soundLINCS has developed significant expertise and acclaim for designing, delivering and developing in various areas such as working with young people in challenging circumstance, and with children alongside parents, carers and child-minders.[15]

Through the work with young children, soundLINCS has also become known for their accessible resource packs: for example, First Notes, Early Ears, Root Notes and PECS songbook. The resource packs incorporate a wider agenda beyond music, such as the Foundation Stage goals. They usually avoid the use of music notation and this area of work has grown steadily from the needs of the participants. 2016 saw the launch of the Company's inaugural digital resource, the 'First Notes App'. Additionally, the company has developed a reputation in producing large-scale and ambitious live events and community-based singing initiatives; a significant development in 2011/12 was the delivery of the Company's first international project at the Mercedes Benz International School in Pune, India.

In order to achieve the types of large-scale projects noted above, soundLINCS has developed and built a robust track record in workforce development both within the community music sector and across those organizations that support its activities. All this directly leads to the essential core of soundLINCS work, which is the capacity to problem-solve through strategic development.

When asked about the types of skills needed to develop community music projects, Nikki-Kate says that she strongly believes that a music leader needs to have the belief that anything is possible and everything is achievable. This is a conceptual idea suggesting the creation of situations where both parties stand to benefit, what some might call a win-win. She goes on to explain that in order to achieve this, community musicians need to 'break down' complexity into relatively simple starting points. Solutions arise from the excitement, enthusiasm and interest to ask the right questions rather than repeat the wrong answers. For that reason, Nikki-Kate has a strong commitment to open-ended enquiry in discussion with others.

> Where possible, I reach for my virtual reality headset to provide panoramic vision and a 360-degree awareness of my situation. This really does stem from workshop facilitation and the skill of ensuring good awareness of all participants. By ensuring as much awareness of a situation and the people that surround it – a crystal ball would also be ideal at this point, although very rarely an option! – one is able to employ skill sets in an informed way.

Other key dispositions would be: negotiating/compromising, conceptualizing, setting priorities, time management, getting the best out of a team, building capacities, partnership building, networking/collaboration, fund raising and financial planning. One of the vital things needed to create a sustainable company such as soundLINCS is investment in its staff. Cultivating effective internal leadership enables growth and development. On reflection, Nikki-Kate says that it has been exciting to develop soundLINCS into a learning organisation:

> My journey with the Company has been built upon the Board of Trustees allowing me to learn and develop myself. It seems to me to be common sense to enable and encourage others to grow themselves and I am grateful for the opportunities that the soundLINCS Board have offered me. I am still learning and we learn from each other. We learn through enabling each other and our peers to develop, to have a go, and to support staff to explore their strengths and challenges.

As with most things, developing leadership is achieved through a range of approaches both formal and informal. The company has formal processes such as Performance Development Reviews and a staff structure that encourages core members to seek development opportunities. Developmental schemes exist also for their 50 or so freelance community music workers, such as shadowing other facilitators' practice. The company regularly runs training days for staff and board, which are facilitated either by Nikki-Kate, or by guest practitioners. Moreover, each year there is the annual soundLINCS conference for staff, facilitators, board and partners. Within the company, there is an acute sensitivity towards running an organisation in the way you might run a community music workshop.

Conclusion

Those who pursue careers in community music and the arts more widely contribute greatly to the fabric of society. While often resisting terms such as social innovation, cultural capital building and entrepreneurship, in fact, musicians and artists are engaged in exactly those processes as they facilitate music making with segments of the population. In ancient times, the village musician was considered to be the one who held the power, the magic if you will, and it was this person who had the respect and contributed priceless value to the population (Summers, 2013). Community musicians embody much of those qualities and carry with them responsibilities that enhance

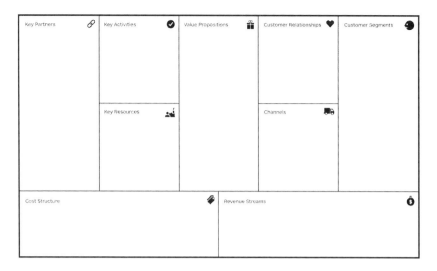

Figure 8.9 Business Model Canvas

the cultural value of the lives with which they practice their music making. In the practical arena of project building, designing successful initiatives that are sustainable and worthwhile, and in finding profound ways to touch and transform lives, the incorporating of some basic business strategies can accelerate the mobilization of great ideas into action.

Questions and Topics for Discussion

1 In your local setting, discuss the relationship between the arts and business sectors. Are they collaborative? In what ways do they share/not share a common vision?

2 Identify and discuss arts-music-based start-up projects in your community where the business aspects succeeded/did not succeed.

3 Using the Business Model Canvas (Figure 8.9), create a project based upon value proposition, customer segment and the various components to guarantee delivery.

4 Careers in music are often considered to be based upon creative and innovative action. Discuss how incorporating business intelligence in the music sector can be imaginative and creative.

5   In the career you are in or are planning to be in, how are you developing the essential skills to be able to follow your calling to its potential?

Notes

1   The art of management, *The Economist*, 17 February 2011.
2   www.quora.com/%E2%80%9CEverybody-has-a-plan-until-they-get-punched-in-the-face-%E2%80%9D-meaning
3   The Business Model Plan canvas is found at Strategyzer.com and is licensed as creative commons. The canvas is free for use, to share or to remix, as long as the source is credited.
4   www.kwjazzroom.com/
5   See Preece (2014, 2015a, 2015b, 2015c).
6   http://businessmodelgeneration.com/canvas/bmc?_ga=1.141194738.1115777936.1462569408
7   The term 'entrepreneurial' is usually defined as someone who manages and takes risks in the interest of making profit for a business. The term is currently widely used in the culture sector as someone who undertakes tasks with initiative, or one who brings various sectors together to create social capital (www.dictionary.com). See also Beckman (2011).
8   www.soundlincs.org/
9   www.artscouncil.org.uk/
10 www.youthmusic.org.uk/Sing Up
11 www.singup.org/
12 www.lincolnshire.gov.uk/
13 www.creativescotland.com/funding/latest-information/funded-organisations/regularly-funded-organisations-2015-18
14 www.musiceducationuk.com/music-hubs/
15 SoundLINCS mixes delivery to the 0–5 years with training for the adults in the children's lives. The company has developed several programmes, which address the varying needs of very young children providing approached that explore a range of learning styles.

References

Beckman, G. (2011). *Disciplining the arts: Teaching entrepreneurship in context*. Lanham, MD: Rowman and Littlefield.
Blank, S. (2013). Why the lean start-up changes everything. *Harvard Business Review*, 91(5), 63–72.
de Banffy-Hall, A. (2016). Developing community music in Germany: The journey to this journal issue. *International Journal of Community Music*, 9(1), 99–113.

Desmerais, C. (2013). 6 Things Mozart can Teach Entrepreneurs. Retrieved from http://www.inc.com/christina-desmarais/6-things-mozart-can-teach-you-about-business.html

Preece, S. (2014). Social bricolage in arts entrepreneurship: Building a jazz society from scratch. *Artivate: A Journal of Entrepreneurship in the Arts*, 3(1), 23–34.

Preece, S. (2015a). Acquiring start-up funding for new arts organizations. *Nonprofit Management and Leadership*, 25(4), 463–74.

Preece, S. (2015b). Applying lean startup methodology to cultural entrepreneurship. In O. Kuhlke, A. Schramme, & R. Kooyman (Eds.), *Creating cultural capital: Cultural entrepreneurship in theory, pedagogy, and practice* (pp. 312–21).

Preece, S. (2015c). Reimagining jazz music presentation: From for-profit club to not-for-profit society. *The American Journal of Arts Management*, 1–16.

Schumpeter. (2011). The art of management: Business has much to learn from the arts *The Economist*. Retrieved from http://www.economist.com/node/18175675

Summers, D., & O'Rourke Jones, R. (Eds.). (2013). *Music, the Definitive Visual History*. New York: Dorling Kindersley Press.

Chapter 9
Ways Forward

Music can change the world because it can change people.

Bono[1]

Engaging in Community Music: Locating Place and Purpose

Through the process of identifying and defining the foundational principles of community music, this book has explored a number of perspectives and practices within the field, building on the expertise and experience that collectively and globally may be considered *Engaging in Community Music*. The chapter headings are designed to assist the readers in locating their own place within the engagement of participatory music making, whether it be in developing a theoretical framework to inform their practice, or to further discover and enhance effective facilitation strategies.

Contextual Chapter Summaries

By way of brief summary, the opening chapter, 'Music and meaning in community contexts', provides an overview of music's place from a cultural perspective with particular attention to the social meanings of identifying a musical society, authenticity, identity, perception and mediation processes of music in a global context of cross-cultural practices.

In the second chapter, 'Negotiated curriculum, non-formal and informal learning', diverse pedagogical approaches are described and illustrated with applications to intergenerational settings where aspects of learning for life are explored. Considerable attention is given to learning music with older people based upon the case studies of practitioners who are effectively using music to fulfil a variety of social, health and activist roles. It is here that the spectrum of formal, non-formal and informal learning practices, including structured facilitated workshop models to non-structured self-taught practices are explored.

Central to community music values is the concept that participatory music making is built upon an 'open-door' policy, and the third chapter, 'Community music, inclusive, empathetic perspectives', reflected the importance of making space for others and explored music work from a position of inclusivity and hospitality.

At the core of community music engagement is active leadership and the fourth chapter, 'Strategic leadership and facilitation', presents the 'nuts and bolts' of community music practice where the case studies introduce key strategies used by contemporary practitioners. A variety of specific topics are addressed, including essential qualities for effective facilitation, devising, managing the workshop space, working inclusively, group dynamics and empowering people through music.

In the fifth chapter, 'Mindfulness, activism and justice', the dual roles of contemplative practice and activism in community music are explored. Community music, historically grounded in socio-political activism and embracing dimensions, such as symbolic values, inter-institutional relations, conflict and negotiation, is situated within the edges or boundaries of our society where tensions, risks and benefits of civic engagement are discussed. Case studies illustrate examples of those who have these ideals front and centre of their work.

The sixth chapter, 'Wholeness and well-being', opens up a discussion on the growing interest in music and health, community music therapy, and care in and through music. Holistic approaches to music making that address the nurturing of body, mind and spirit are introduced and illustrated through the practice of those whose focus is on the whole health of the individual in various community settings.

The seventh chapter, 'Culture of inquiry', acknowledges that community music can now be known as a field of study because of its emergent scholarly arm. As well as some examples of current research practices, hypothetical vignettes are included to engage the research community in imagining additional appropriate strategies and methods that will advance critical inquiry.

Finally, Chapter 8, 'Careers and management', places music project management within contemporary professional community music life. Partnerships, value propositions and customer segments are identified as planning strategies to further the effectiveness of community music projects. Examples of community music models are provided through a range of case studies.

Our case studies have illustrated a variety of practices and models of engagement ranging from Patricia Shehan Campbell's musicking with Native American song and dance in Fresno California, Gillian Howell's facilitative approaches with recently arrived children and teenagers in Australia, Phoene Cave's work with the British Lung Foundation, Debbie Lou Ludolph's hospitable music making with her community choir, Inshallah in Canada, through to Nikki-Kate Hayes's tips on directing a community music charity in the UK. Although diverse in their context, our collection of case studies presents strong thematic links that bind the practice and give it a distinctive nature. Our contributors' voices underline the central tenants that community music is occupied with people, places, participation, inclusivity and diversity. There are, however, amplifications of these ideas, which can be teased out in the following ways and are diagrammatically represented in Figure 9.1.

Community musicians honour *culturally diverse* environments, including race, gender, religion and socio-economic status. It is concerned with how music lives locally and across the globe. Sensitivity towards these issues creates a field that is interested in and prioritises issues of social justice.

Community musicians employ *flexible musical processes* when working with participants. Aiming to be adaptable to the circumstances of the group, community musicians seek to be open to an ever-changing environment. Working across the continuum of formal and non-formal education, including the promotion of informal learning, those who work in this field seek to be *inclusive* through *collaboration*. Collaboration also opens up the potential to build external partnerships that are often vital for sustainable projects.

Drawing upon a broad 'toolkit' of skills and activities, community musicians aim to respond to complex situations as they arise. With an eye towards making new work, they seek the participants' musical input by consciously generating accessible spaces through a diverse array of musical genres and styles. There is an inherent understanding that the most important voice in any session is that of the participants, not of the music leaders themselves whose role is to provide a space that enables individual input and ownership. Throughout our interviews there was a common belief that human beings are fundamentally musical and, by enabling positive musical agency, transformation can occur. The concept of transformation appears paramount to many of our contributors and we take this to mean that by engaging in *authentic* and *purposeful music-making activities* people are made to feel strong, positive and valued in their lives. The transformative music

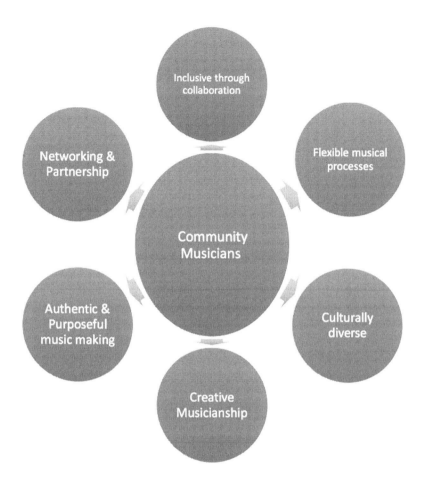

Figure 9.1 Networking and Partnerships

experience may result in a deepening of individual and group identity that in turn evokes positive changes, validates participant experiences and contributions and as a consequence builds resistance, resilience and confidence.

In terms of the key skills necessary to carry out this work, there are a number of general cornerstones such as being a confident *creative musician*, who has a knowledge of other art forms, and the ability to listen carefully and to explain concepts simply and straightforwardly to people who may not be trained in music. Preparation is certainly deemed to be an important factor to effectively transverse and negotiate complex group situations. Therefore, having a keen sense of how to structure a session, group of sessions or a project becomes critical to ensure that there is a good chance to fully engage the group in musical doing. It is evident that community musicians generate work based on *networking* and *partnership* building where the ability to make positive and long-lasting connections is key in building sustainable projects and careers. Having an informed business sense and practice, or at least an eye for the current economic situations both in the cultural sector and beyond, opens up channels of possibilities for the musician and those they work with, making available the resources needed to execute the work, and importantly, therefore, impacting the lives of those they are working with.

Qualities of Community Music Facilitators

What sort of personal dispositions are required to work in this way? The common features appear to be first and foremost a *passion* and *commitment* for the work one undertakes. These qualities are a driving force against a background that does not expect large economic awards. Reflective dialogue

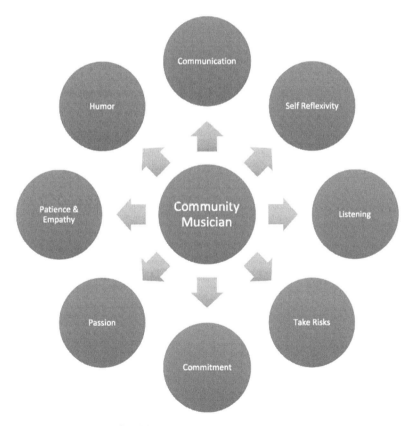

Figure 9.2 Facilitator Qualities

underlines the importance of *communication*, a key word used by many of those we interviewed. The ability to respond to a wide range of communicative expressions and to adapt and vary ways through which ideas are transferred from one person to another becomes vital when working with community groups. *Patience, empathy* and *humour* also seem to be vital traits. Community music work demands that the musicians have a well-developed sense of group dynamics and can manage diverse situations while keeping a sense of their own authenticity and vulnerability. *Self-reflexivity* is critical here for discerning what is currently taking place and informing next steps while *listening* carefully ensures both musical and group work excellence. Finally, community musicians must diminish the fear of failure for their participants and have the courage and confidence to *take risks* in the interest of facilitating profound and authentic musical experience. These qualities are diagrammatically shown in Figure 9.2.

Intersection and Future Pathways

What does this tell us? Figure 9.3 is an illustration of how the field of community music offers fruitful opportunities to open up interdisciplinary pathways and potential to enrich each other's professional lives and to develop close allies through which ideas, theories and practice may be shared. Through the process of interviewing such a diverse group of practitioners, we observe that there is considerable common ground in their perspectives of how music and people intersect and interplay, and if not completely in sync on the details of strategies and structure are at least, in a colloquial sense, moving down the same expressway.

There will be many ways to consider the intersections of work and we encourage the reader to think through how these might manifest within your own professional practice. We offer one possibility that has helped us understand the intersections that have affected the work we have been engaged in. Figure 9.3 is a diagrammatic representation of musical discourse that has synergy with the types of community music we have been doing. This simple Venn diagram points towards possible connections, meeting points and differences in order to invigorate future conversations and simulate the development of meaningful networks, working practices and research.
In this representation are four musical domains, each intersecting with various subsets that are deemed to have a close proximity to each other, reflecting the five keywords that have helped orientate this book: people, places, participation, inclusivity and diversity. The three intersecting fields, applied ethnomusicology, cultural diversity in music education and community music

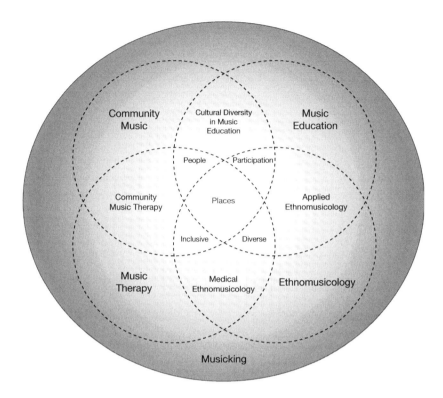

Figure 9.3 Intersections

therapy, have been previously introduced in Chapters, 1, 4 and 6 respectively. Along with our case illustrations, these fields represent approaches to music making that enable a deeper understanding of community music. We offer some summary statements here to underline their intrinsic connections.

From a perspective of school music education, a number of writers have argued for curriculum to include *musics* rather than music (Elliott, 1995; Jorgensen, 2003; Schippers, 2010; Westerlund, 1998). Cultural diversity in music education has been one expression of this and has helped those committed in finding a place for music in the lives of students to think through and to understand the shared need for art-making generally and music specifically. As an empowerment strategy and through transformative educational goals, cultural diversity in music education can serve as an effective vehicle for social change and emancipation. As a way of seeing the world and one's place in it, cultural diversity in music education helps enable students to develop skills and insights needed 'to question some of the latent assumptions and values within the mainstream society, to think critically about the gap between the nation's ideals and realities, and to develop a commitment to act to help create a just human society' (Banks, 1992). One might conclude that cultural diversity in music education promotes a general shift from teaching to learning and consequently from teacher to learner. This represents a change of focus to how one engages students in content and consequently informs ways of learning.[2] These approaches resonate strongly with community music ideals whilst practically community musicians often draw from musics of other cultures to provide frameworks and content for musical doing.

Over 40 years ago, John Blacking (1973, p. 4) predicted that '[e]thnomusicology has the power to create a revolution in the world of music and music education'. This prediction has come to pass and is now realised in the broader conceptualization of music that finds its way into academic courses and applied performance experiences for students of all levels of instruction, and through the questions, frameworks and processes of research that straddles the fields. The works of culturally diverse music educators and ethnomusicologists are augmented by the practice of the community musician who is committed to facilitating active music making with which a community identifies and that which engages learners in expressing themselves musically (Campbell & Higgins 2015). Overlapping the fields there appears to be a definitive commitment to embrace an ethnomusicological sense of people and place, to honouring the local and to understanding that music is situated within the lives of those who choose to make it.

Like community music, community music therapy (CoMT) seeks to reduce hierarchy and authority through an inherently participatory, performative, resource-oriented and actively reflective practice. Community music and CoMT originate from a common belief in 'musicking' as a means of working with people, each approach seeking to reclaim music for everyday life as a central force in human culture. By working more frequently with those within the community or at well-being stages, rather than with those who fall into the acute illness/crisis and rehabilitation stages of the healthcare continuum, there are considerable signs of similarity between the respected approaches. In 2002, there was a call for dialogue between the two areas of practice (Ansdell, 2002) and through the growth of scholarship within the two areas, this is finally happening, evidenced by a panel session organised for the British Association of Music Therapy conference in 2014 plus the writings of Gary Ansdell amongst others (Ansdell, 2014). Sitting between applied ethnomusicology and CoMT is medical ethnomusicology, another accent that seeks to deepen enquiry into the musician as a holistic being, reflecting new models that are rooted in physics, philosophy, psychology, sociology, cognitive science, linguistics, medical anthropology and music.

Two edited volumes point towards a multitude of approaches and offer plenty of evidence of the overlap and disciplinary consonance we are advocating (Barz & Cohen, 2011; Koen, 2008).[3]

In contemplating community music's immediate constellation and setting it within a wider universe of musicking provides the potential for understanding music, education and culture through fresh lenses. It is at this juncture where music education, ethnomusicology, music therapy and community music find themselves with robust intersections that new knowledge may be developed. From the pure to the practical, this crossroads of specialisations may be critical to future insights in each of these distinctive fields, revealing facets of their shared interests in music, learning and education.

Community Characteristics of Belonging

As indicated in the Introduction, community music began as a grassroots human practice and has evolved into a full-blown field of study with a far-reaching global impact. As the practices of experienced 'expert' facilitators are highlighted, it is also important to be cognizant that community music is at a crossroads. Schools of higher education are undergoing curriculum renewal and the principles and practices of community music are bearing some influence on decisions.[4] There is a palpable sense that now is the season to move forward, to develop, create, adapt and share best practices. In earlier research, Willingham (2001) described characteristics that point to a sense of community and belonging:

a   People are drawn to belong to a community because of a shared desire to participate in a common activity or experience;
b   People come in contact with, and establish relationships with other individuals with whom they have little or nothing in common, other than the activity or experience that drew them to the group;
c   People engage in activities within the safety of a like-minded community, that they otherwise would not attempt;
d   Given the right conditions, diverse individuals become supportive of each other's learning and growth within the domain of the community's focus;
e   In order for the community to function at its best, the individuals must be open, vulnerable, and in a centered place as far as the common activity is concerned (pp 163–4).

The 'community' in community music is premised on these characteristics. As people choose to participate in activities that really matter, that sustain quality life and most of all enhance the cultural and social capital of their communities, the vision of community music must embrace the opening up of pathways of interdisciplinarity and flexible purposing – all based upon the fundamental premise that everyone has the right to a full and meaningful musical dimension in their lives.

Questions and Topics for Discussion

1 We showed how the fields of music education, music therapy and ethnomusicology intersected with community music. Explore other fields that you feel intersect with community music. What would these look like as a diagrammatic model?

2 Our figures and diagrams respond to what those we interviewed expressed. What is missing from your perspective? Can you further enhance the models we have made? Is there a better way to represent the community musician?

3 Think about a community you belong to. How do the characteristics of belonging apply to your own contexts?

Notes

1 9 March 2010. www.examiner.com/article/music-can-change-the-world-because-it-can-change-people
2 As Göran Folkestad (2005) stresses, the most important issue is how the music is approached: there is an emphasis towards an artistic and musical framing rather than a pedagogical one. This perspective pushes against the didactic approaches educational institutions generally favour (Wiggins, 2005). With an emphasis on practice and musical doing, cultural diversity in music education has, as Huib Schippers notes, 'deep implications for thinking, designing, and realizing music education across the board' (2010, p. 167).
3 See also Jones (2014).
4 For example, Wilfrid Laurier University in Waterloo, Ontario, Canada, has created an undergraduate concentration in community music where the flexible programming will provide opportunities for students to become multi-instrumentalists, songwriters and arrangers, digital music creators while building a core of courses in other disciplines, such as business, communication studies, kinesiology and more.

References

Ansdell, G. (2002). Community music therapy & the winds of change. *Voices: A World Forum for Music Therapy.* Retrieved from www.voices.no/main issues/Voices2(2)ansdell.html

Ansdell, G. (2014). *How music helps in music therapy and every day life.* Farnham: Ashgate.

Banks, J. A. (1992). Multicultural education: Approaches, developments and dimensions. In J. Lynch, C. Modgil, & S. Modgil (Eds.), *Cultural diversity and the school: Education for cultural diversity convergence and divergence* (pp. 83–94). London: The Falmer Press.

Barz, G., & Cohen, J. M. (Eds.). (2011). *The culture of AIDS of Africa: Hope and healing through music and the arts.* New York: Oxford University Press.

Blacking, J. (1973). *How musical is man?* London: Faber and Faber.

Campbell, P. S., & Higgins, L. (2015). Intersections between ethnomusicology, music education, and community music. In S. Pettan & J. T. Titon (Eds.), *The Oxford handbook of applied ethnomusicology* (pp. 638–67). New York: Oxford University Press.

Elliott, D. J. (1995). *Music matters: A new philosophy of music education.* Oxford: Oxford University Press.

Folkestad, G. (2005). The local and the global in musical learning: Considering the interaction between formal and informal settings. In P. S. Campbell, J. Drummond, P. Dunbar-Hall, K. Howard, H. Schippers, & T. Wiggins (Eds.), *Cultural diversity in music education: Directions and challenges for the 21st century* (pp. 23–28). Brisbane: Australian Academic Press.

Jones, J. A. (2014). Health musicking in skiffle steel orchestra: Thoughts on collaboration between community music therapy and medical ethnomusicology. *International Journal of Community Music,* 7(1), 129–44.

Jorgensen, E. R. (2003). *Transforming music education.* Indiana, IN: Indiana University Press.

Koen, B. D. (Ed.) (2008). *The Oxford handbook of medical ethnomusicology.* New York: Oxford University Press.

Schippers, H. (2010). *Facing the music: Shaping music education from a global perspective.* New York: Oxford University Press.

Westerlund, H. (1998, July 12–17). *Reflective multicultural practice and music education (Summary).* Paper presented at the ISME: Many Music- One Circle, Durban: South Africa.

Wiggins, T. (2005). Cultivating shadows in field: Challenges for traditions in institutional contexts. In P. S. Campbell, J. Drummond, P. Dunbar-Hall, K. Howard, H. Schippers, & T. Wiggins (Eds.), *Cultural diversity in music education: Directions and challenges for the 21st century* (pp. 13–22). Brisbane: Australian Academic Press.

Willingham, L. (2001). *A community of voices: A qualitative study of the effects of being a member of the Bell'Arte Singers.* (EdD). Toronto: University of Toronto.

Contributor Biographies

Chris Bartram is Senior Lecturer in Music at York St John University, UK, where his roles include running a community music programme, and directing the community choir 'Communitas', part of Converge, an arts for mental health service users. Chris taught for many years in music education, in early years, primary, secondary and adult sectors. Following an MA in Music in the Community, he worked on numerous local and national arts projects, including with the National Centre for Early Music, Opera North, Manchester Royal Exchange Theatre and Accessible Arts & Media. Recent work for York Archaeological Trust saw Chris facilitating mental health service users in devising recorded soundscapes; current projects for the charity Jessie's Fund include supporting the development of music at a school for young people with learning disabilities.

Carol Beynon, PhD, is currently Associate Vice Provost of the School of Graduate & Postdoctoral Studies, former Acting Dean, Faculty of Education and Associate Professor in Music Education at the University of Western Ontario. She is the founding artistic director of the award-winning Amabile Boys & Men's Choirs of London, Canada. Carol's research focuses are varied and range from teacher development and identity to gender issues in singing and intergenerational singing. She has two published books: *Learning to Teach* (2001) and *Critical Perspectives in Canadian Music Education* (2012); she also has numerous scholarly articles in peer-reviewed journals. Carol is currently a co-investigator on two SSHRC-funded projects. She has received awards for outstanding teaching, and was recently named the Woman of Excellence in Arts, Culture and Heritage in London, Ontario. In 2010, Carol was inducted into the Wall of Fame at the Don Wright Faculty of Music.

Patricia Shehan Campbell is Donald E. Peterson Professor of Music at the University of Washington, where she teaches courses at the interface of education and ethnomusicology. She has lectured on the pedagogy of world music and children's musical cultures throughout the United States, in much of Europe and Asia, in Australia, New Zealand, South America and eastern and southern Africa. She is the author of *Lessons from the World* (1991), *Music in Cultural Context* (1996), *Songs in Their Heads* (1998, 2010), *Teaching Music Globally* (2004), *Musician and Teacher* (2008); co-author of *Music in Childhood* (2013, fourth edition); co-editor of the *Global Music Series* and the *Oxford Handbook on Children's Musical Cultures* (2013). Campbell was designated the Senior Researcher in Music Education (American-national) in 2002, and 2012 recipient of the Taiji Award for the preservation of traditional music. She is chair of the Advisory Board of Smithsonian Folkways and consultant in repatriation efforts for the recordings of Alan Lomax to communities in the American South.

Dave Camlin, PhD, is a singer/songwriter/educator/researcher whose professional work spans performance, composition, teaching, management, research and the development of creative human capital. His research interests include transforming the 'tacit' knowledge of the creative economy into praxis, through the critical engagement of individuals; the benefits of group singing; musician training; and community music. He is currently Head of Higher Education and Research at Sage Gateshead, where he leads the delivery of the undergraduate music programmes, as well as lecturing on Trinity-Laban's postgraduate course and Durham University's BA (Hons) Music. He performs solo, with vocal groups Mouthful and Human Music and with acoustic collective The Coast Road. He was the founding Creative Director of Cumbrian music organisation, SoundWave, from 2005 to 2010, and one of the organisers of Solfest music festival in Cumbria from 2004 to 2015.

Phoene Cave has been a jazz and pop singer and worked 'behind the scenes' in the theatrical, television and record industries. She has a BMus Hons degree from University of London, Goldsmiths College, and a PG Dip in Music Therapy from University of Roehampton teaching jazz singing, Improvisation and Access to Music courses within adult education settings and was head of the vocal team at Richmond Music Trust. She was a vocal trainer for Sing Up and mentor for a Trinity Guildhall CPD programme; trained as a vocal coach with the Estill-based Vocal Process team; was the consultant on the Rockschool vocal syllabus; and taught vocals at the Institute of Contemporary Music Performance in North West London. Phoene has facilitated singing groups with all ages from pre-school to pensioner, working in collaboration with the

Southbank Centre in London and has led children's choirs at the Albert Hall. She ran the original 'Singing for Breathing' project at the Royal Brompton hospital and produced a Singing for Breathing CD available from rb&hArts. Phoene delivers a training programme for the British Lung Foundation and continues to present on 'Singing & Health' nationally. She was Head of Music Services, London, at the music charity Nordoff Robbins until 2013 where she managed a team of over 20 music therapists. She delivered music therapy at HMP & YOI Bronzefield, a high security prison until September 2015. She delivered sessions with individuals with severe mental health or substance abuse issues as well as running groups on the mother and baby and healthcare units. She then returned to Royal Brompton and Harefield Hospitals in 2015 to review the 'Singing for Breathing' programme where she set up new work with inpatients on the transplant wing.

Don D. Coffman, Professor of Music Education, chairs the Department of Music Education and Music Therapy at the University of Miami's Frost School of Music and is Professor Emeritus at the University of Iowa. He has served on the Executive Committee of the Society for Research in Music Education and chaired MENC's Adult and Community Music Education SRIG and ISME's Community Music Activity Commission. He currently serves on the editorial boards of the *Journal of Research in Music Education* and the *International Journal of Community Music*. His passion is making music with 'chronologically gifted' adults in wind bands. He is the founding director of the Iowa City Iowa New Horizons Band, which has provided an opportunity for senior adults to learn or reacquaint themselves with wind and percussion instrumental music since 1995. In 2006 he was honoured for his work with this New Horizons Band with three awards: The University of Iowa President's Award for State Outreach and Public Engagement, the State of Iowa Governor's Volunteer Award and the Outstanding Continuing Educator Award from the Johnson County chapter of AARP. Coffman received a PhD from the University of Kansas, an M.M.E. from Wichita State University and a B.M.E. from the University of Kansas.

Mary L. Cohen, PhD, is an Associate Professor and Area Head of Music Education at the University of Iowa. She researches music making and wellness with respect to prison contexts, writing and songwriting and collaborative communities. Since 2009, she has led the Oakdale Prison Community Choir, comprised of male inmates and women and men from the community. She facilitates songwriting with choir members with over 90 original songs soon to be available via a choir website. Her research is published in the *International Journal of Research in Choral Singing*, *Journal* of *Research in Music Education*, *Australian Journal of Music Education*, *Journal of Historical Research in Music Education*, *Journal of Correctional Education*, *International Journal of Community Music* and *International Journal of Music Education*. A certified InterPlay leader, Dr. Cohen incorporates musical improvisation into her InterPlay sessions, prison choir rehearsals and university courses.

Andrea Creech was Reader in Education at UCL Institute of Education until September 2016, when she was awarded a Canada Research Chair in Music in Community at Université Laval, Canada. Following an international career in music performance and teaching, Andrea was awarded a PhD in Psychology in Education. Since then, she has led extensive funded research and published widely on topics concerned with musical learning and participation across the lifespan. She is a Senior Fellow of the Higher Education Academy and Graduate Member of the British Psychological Association. Andrea is co-author of *Active Ageing with Music* and co-editor of *Music Education in the twenty-first Century in the UK*.

Donald DeVito, PhD, is a music and special education teacher at the Sidney Lanier Center School in Gainesville, Florida, for students with disabilities. The school is linked in person and on Skype with International Society for Music Education (ISME) members from around the world focusing on adaptive curriculum development. He has published on networking universities, schools and community-based music programmes for the benefit of children with special needs throughout the world. He is a board member of ISME and a facilitator in the online Masters in Music Education programme at Boston University. DeVito assisted in promoting collaborative initiatives among ISME members in the Middle East, Low and Medium HDI countries and Asian Pacific regions. He recently assisted with music education development in the West Bank to help establish programmes in 2,500 Palestinian public schools, and is currently developing a music and special education programme at the Notre Maison Orphanage in Haiti. In 2011, DeVito was the Council for Exceptional Children national teacher of the year for special education.

Douglas Friesen is a music educator and advisor to the Toronto Public School Board and teaches courses at the Ontario Institute for Studies in Education and at Wilfrid Laurier University. In these areas and in workshops with students, educators and musicians, he has searched out and explored democratic and creative teaching models where teacher and tradition are guests, not starting points. He has been an assistant to composer R. Murray Schafer and leads improvisation, soundscape and creativity workshops to educators internationally. As a professional musician, Doug has played with Dave Bidini (Rheostatics), John K Samson (Weakerthans) and Ron Sexsmith.

Rebecca Gross is a music practitioner with extensive experience in working with children with special educational needs and disabilities. She holds an MA in Education, a PCGE and has more than 15 years' experience as a music practitioner. She also practices and works as a professional musician, and has high standards and aspiration for the children and young people she works with.

Alicia de Banffy-Hall worked as a community musician for 10 years in Liverpool, UK, before returning to Munich, her hometown, where she is now completing her PhD, as well as developing the first community music programme for the Munich Philharmonic Orchestra. Other projects include working for the Department of Arts Education of the City of Munich on building a professional development programme for community artists. Alicia has also worked on many different arts projects across Europe and has lectured in a number of universities. She partnered with the University of Applied Sciences Munich and co-edited the first German book on community music titled *Community Music – Beiträge zur Theorie und Praxis aus internationaler und deutscher* (Waxman, 2017).

Nikki-Kate Heyes MBE, is the CEO of soundLINCS, a not-for-profit community music organisation operating across the East Midlands and based in Lincoln, UK. As a cellist, conductor, composer and a champion for community music for over 25 years, Nikki-Kate began her musical studies at Leeds College of Music, before gaining her Leeds University degree in Music and Inter-Arts at Bretton Hall. From a cello & double bass peripatetic teacher in Wakefield, she became Music Development Officer/Outreach Worker at the Trinity Arts Centre in Gainsborough, West Lindsey. On completion of the contract she enjoyed a successful freelance career as a community musician while adding founder of the Heyes Ensemble.

Over the years, Nikki-Kate has served as an Executive Board member and Chair of Sound Sense, a national organisation for community music, and Regional Council member for the Arts Council England – East Midlands. In June 2013, Nikki-Kate was awarded an MBE in the Queen's Birthday Honours for CEO and Founder of soundLINCS and services to music.

Gillian Howell is a PhD researcher at Queensland Conservatorium Griffith University and lecturer in Community Music Leadership at Melbourne Polytechnic. Her research investigates participatory music initiatives in post-conflict countries, and diverse aspects of intercultural community music leadership and participation. She has worked as a music leader, trainer and consultant researcher in post-conflict settings in Europe, South Asia and South-East Asia, most recently as a 2016 Endeavour Research Fellow in Sri Lanka.

Kelly Laurila is of Sáami Indigenous and Settler Irish heritages. She is song keeper of an urban Indigenous community youth and women's drum circle. The drum has helped Kelly reclaim her Indigenous identity and a sense of belonging. Kelly holds these insights and teachings of the drum close to her and is inspired to help Indigenous and Settler peoples find balance, strength and positive relationships with themselves and others. Kelly is currently (2017) completing a PhD in Social Work, focusing on song as a bridge-builder.

Betsy Little has been an active leader in the London, Ontario non-profit community for over 20 years. Betsy joined the Alzheimer Society London and Middlesex (ASLM) in 2006 as CEO. Under her leadership, ASLM initiated Ontario's first *First Link(tm)* programme for the First Nations Community. As well, the organisation has also expanded its support programmes and services with the launch of the innovative social recreation and intergenerational programmes including the ASLM choir, cooking programme, art programme and a gardening programme.

Betsy has succeeded in increasing the level of funding support for dementia and has helped to effectively raise awareness of the Alzheimer Society within the London and Middlesex community. Betsy has also grown the ASLM team to now include 16 employees and 12 facilitators. Betsy sits as a Director for the Centre for Addiction and Mental Health (CAMH) since 2008 and a member of the Ontario Dementia Network. She is a recipient of the Queen Elizabeth II Diamond Jubilee Medal. Betsy has a Bachelor of Arts and a Bachelor of Education from the University of Western Ontario.

Debbie Lou Ludolph is Dean of Keffer Chapel at Waterloo Lutheran Seminary, Director of Worship Ministries for the Eastern Synod, and teaches voice at Wilfrid Laurier University. In addition, she is Director of both the Kanata Centre for Worship and Global Song and the Centre's global song community choir – the *Inshallah* Choir. The Kanata Centre links the public expression of faith to our deep connection with all of creation, and we hope to fulfil our mission by keeping forefront in our hearts and minds the goal of working towards the common good. Debbie Lou was named Companion of the Worship Arts in 2006 by the Evangelical Lutheran Church in Canada. She has led worship and music on four trips to Palestine-Israel with WLS, and also creates opportunities for public conversations about worship practice and community events where musicians and artists work together towards the common good.

Kathy McNaughton is a graduate of the University of Western Ontario, Faculty of Music and Education. She started her teaching career in the Peel Board of Education (Greater Toronto Area) before returning to London. Kathy teaches Senior Vocal Pedagogy and Curriculum Development at Western University, Faculty of Education. She is the Music Department Head at Medway High School in Arva. Kathy teaches vocal, instrumental and developmental music education and is continuing the traditions of choral excellence established at the school over the last 60 years. She is also conductor of the Amabile Treble Training Choir and the Intergenerational Choir of London.

Dana Monteiro is a proud New York City public school teacher with 13 years of experience, 12 spent at the Frederick Douglass Academy. Dana has a DMA in music education from Boston University. Originally a classical trumpet player, his interest in Brazilian music began on a trip to Rio de Janeiro, where he was brought by local musicians to the Vila Isabel Samba School. Since that first visit, Monteiro has made 16 study-related trips to Brazil and made visits to samba schools and community music ensembles in London, Tokyo, Chicago, Philadelphia, Las Vegas, Uruguay, Argentina and the Cape Verde Islands to study local musical practices and more importantly, the various methods for how music is taught. Monteiro was a panel discussant on alternative practices in music education at the 7th International Symposium of the Sociology of Music Education, a presenter in the Education Section at the annual meeting of the Society for Ethnomusicology in 2013 and presented a workshop in samba percussion at the 2015 Teaching World Musics Symposium at Northern Illinois University.

Phil Mullen has worked for over 30 years developing music with people who are socially excluded, including homeless people, offenders and seniors. Phil specialises in working with excluded children and young people at risk. He spent 8 years working in Northern Ireland using music as a tool for peace and reconciliation. Phil is a former board member of the International Society for Music Education (ISME) and former chair of the ISME commission on Community Music Activity. He has run workshops and seminars on community music and creativity in 25 countries across Europe, North America and Asia and in Brazil, South Africa, Australia and New Zealand. Publications include co-editing *Reaching Out: Music Education with 'Hard to Reach'*

Children and Young People (2013). He has an MA in Community Music from York University and is studying for a PhD at Winchester University.

Kathy McNaughton is a graduate of the University of Western Ontario, Faculty of Music and Education. She started her teaching career in the Peel Board of Education (Greater Toronto Area) before returning to London. Kathy teaches Senior Vocal Pedagogy and Curriculum Development at Western University, Faculty of Education. She is the Music Department Head at Medway High School in Arva. Kathy teaches vocal, instrumental and developmental music education and is continuing the traditions of choral excellence established at the school over the last 60 years. She is also conductor of the Amabile Treble Training Choir and the Intergenerational Choir of London.

Peter Moser is a composer, performer, producer, consultant and facilitator and is the founder and Artistic Director of More Music, one of the foremost community music organizations in the UK. He has written scores for theatre, opera and dance projects as well as songs for occasions and large-scale choral and orchestral pieces. Peter is a multi-instrumentalist and teaches percussion, voice, brass and songwriting as well as the art of running workshops.

He co-edited *Community Music: A Handbook* (2005), a book that covers a range of music and music workshop topics and is aimed at inspiring and empowering music leaders.

Stephen Preece, PhD, has taught Strategic Management and International Strategy at the Lazaridis School of Business & Economics, Wilfrid Laurier University since 1993. His research focuses on cultural industries, in particular the management of performing arts organizations (dance, music, theatre, opera). Dr. Preece's research projects have focused on sponsorships, audience patterns, partnerships, governance and new media. He does consulting in the area of strategic planning and analysis within the culture sector. Dr. Preece has published a number of articles in journals such as *Journal of Business Venturing, Long Range Planning, Journal of Small Business Management, International Executive, Canadian Public Administration* and *International Journal of Arts Management*. Stephen is Academic Director at the Schlegel Centre for Entrepreneurship and Social Innovation. His is also Founder and current President of the Grand River Jazz Society.

Brent Rowan is a performer, director, composer and educator of music. As a Guelph, Ontario, Canada-based saxophonist, who also plays flute, clarinet and other woodwind instrument, Brent performs in a wide variety of musical collaborations; including 2009 and 2015 Juno Nominated *Eccodek*,

Big Bands, small jazz combos, classical chamber groups and creative music ensembles. Brent has performed and recorded all across Canada, the UK and Germany, at music festivals in Vancouver, Calgary, Toronto and London, England, to name a few. He has released three recordings of his own compositions: *It's About Time* in 2006, *IZ* in 2012 and *Where is Local* in 2016. Brent composes and arranges music for the Guelph Youth Jazz Ensemble as well as for his small improvisation groups. Brent is the founding director of the Guelph Youth Jazz Ensemble and the New Horizons Band for Guelph. He is also the conductor of the Cambridge Concert band. Brent teaches woodwind and jazz improvisation techniques at his private music studio. He is also a clinician and adjudicator at music camps and festivals throughout southern Ontario, specializing in saxophone and improvisation concepts.

He holds a Master of Arts in Community Music, from Wilfrid Laurier University.

Nick Rowe, PhD, is Associate Professor working in the Faculty of Arts and the Faculty of Health and Life Sciences at York St John University, UK. He has a background in psychiatric nursing and dramatherapy. Nick was Project Coordinator of Skills for People working alongside people with learning disabilities. He is a performing member of Playback Theatre, York. Nick is the co-founder and Director of Converge, an organisation offering courses in the arts to people who use mental health services. He is the author of *Playing the Other: Dramatizing Personal Narratives in Playback Theatre* (2007).

Gerard Yun, DMA, trained concurrently in Western classical music and traditional cultural forms. He holds a doctorate of music arts degree in choral-orchestral conducting and literature from the University of Colorado at Boulder. While attending undergraduate and graduate school he studied with traditional masters in Japanese Zen Buddhist Shakuhachi, Native American flute, West African drumming, Tibetan harmonic overtone singing and Australian didgeridoo. He was Director of Choral Studies at Georgetown University in Washington, DC. He currently teaches at Wilfrid Laurier University and York University in Ontario, Canada. He has been commissioned to compose for choirs, soloists and instrumental and dance ensembles in the United States and Canada. His research interests include cross-cultural music ethics, cross-cultural improvisation and global community music.

Index

ability 11, 23, 45, 86
Aboriginal 13, 61, 66n6
access 4, 38, 41, 48, 50–1, 56, 69–70, 100, 110, 122–3, 152, 154, 156, 168
activism 1, 6, 7, 92, 94–104, 167
advocacy 91
aesthetic 11, 12, 85, 91, 121, 147, 155–6
ageing 37, 45n6
agency 32, 134–5, 168
anthropology 20, 174
Alzheimer's 119–122, 126n22
Ansdell, Gary 112, 117, 174
anxiety 49, 52, 57, 108, 123, 133
Applied Ethnomusicology 17, 21, 137, 172, 174
Asperger's Syndrome 73
assessment 26, 32, 42, 44
asthma 113
asylum seekers 28, 83
audience 2, 13, 36, 49, 76, 94–5, 134, 150–1, 185
autism 50, 56, 73
authority 7, 61, 118, 133, 173

band 34, 41–4, 49, 58, 77–9, 131–2
Bartel, Lee 49
Bartram, Chris 73

behaviour 57–8, 120
Beynon, Carol 118–19
Blacking, John 9, 173
boundary walker 65
British Association of Music Therapy 173
British Lung Foundation 114–15, 168
Bronchial Boogie 113
business 110, 130, 145–9, 151, 155, 159, 163, 169

Cameron, Linda 49
Camlin, Dave 131–2
Campbell, Patricia Shehan 17–18, 21, 168
carnival 140; *see* festivals
Cave, Pheone 113–14, 124, 168
charity 88n3, 151, 159, 160, 168
children 28, 34, 37, 40, 50–3, 56–8, 84, 92–3, 113, 157–9, 161, 164n15, 168
choir 14, 34, 41, 49, 58, 69, 70–1, 94, 97–9, 113, 149, 168
Cliff, Stephen 109
Coffman, Don 41
Cohen, Mary 101–2
collaboration 3, 14, 40, 55–6, 66, 103–4, 110, 140–1, 162, 168;

see also international 58; *see also* institutional 124
Communitas 74–5, 110–11; *see also* in every care home 109, 125n12; *see also* Intergenerational 38, 119–24; *see also* Natural Voice, 132–3; *see also* Oakdale Prison 102–4
community arts: drama 140, 158; engagement 22, 101; community music, career in 69, 74, 88n3, 117, 132, 145, 162–4; definition of 3; ensemble 37; facilitator 68, 170; field of 6, 52, 112, 129, 137, 156, 170; networks 1; orchestra 157; programme 37, 45, 54, 97; scholarship 137; skills 19, 28, 30–3, 39, 52, 68–9, 73–4, 113, 134–5, 138, 148, 160–1, 169; therapy 112, 167, 172–3
Community Music Activities Commission 1
composition 31, 53, 82, 84, 110, 139
constructivism 10, 33
contemplation 6, 96–7, 100
Converge 110–12, 124
Csikszentmihalyi, Mihaly 10
creativity 15, 65, 76, 87, 113, 151
Creech, Andrea 37
cultural diversity 18, 20, 80–1, 172–3, 175n2
cultural pluralism 81, 88n12
culturally responsive leadership 54
curriculum 28, 31, 51, 91, 140, 172, 174; *see also* adapted 56; *see also* multi-cultural 78; *see also* negotiated 1, 40–1, 166
Currie, Ruth 137
customer segment 147–50, 167

dance 18–19, 59, 62, 114, 117, 140, 168
de Banffy-Hall, Alicia 155
dementia 39, 119, 122–3
democracy 80–1; *see also* cultural 1, 3
Devito, Don 56, 58

dialogic 132, 134
disabilities 50, 56–8, 73, 108, 134, 178
diversity 4, 54–5, 65–6, 81, 85, 92, 121, 168, 172
drumming 14, 59, 61–4, 147

economics 51, 147, 151
education: adults 38; formal 27–8, 37, 50, 53, 156; informal 32; non-formal 1, 3, 4, 34, 36, 45, 50, 168
Eisner, Elliot 41, 136
emancipation 87, 173
empathy 6, 31, 50, 54, 59, 65, 74, 76, 113, 115, 124, 131–2, 169; *see also* musical 15
employment 74, 110
empowerment 1, 33, 55, 87, 109,112, 118, 173
English Language Schools 28, 83, 86
enterprise 104, 146, 149–50
entrepreneurial 145, 151, 156, 164n7
ethics 1, 11, 39, 131
ethnomusicology 17, 20, 172; *see also* applied ethnomusicology 17, 21, 23, 137, 172, 174; *see also* medical 22, 173
equality 70, 80
evaluation 31–2, 86, 95, 116
excellence 49, 73, 115, 169, 178
expert 26–7, 79, 117–18, 146, 174

facilitation 31, 68, 72, 171
family 32, 42, 63
festivals 20, 32, 49, 70–1, 93–4 140, 150, 154
Folkestad, Göran 175n2
freedom 77, 99, 113
Freire, Paulo 27
friendship 139
Friesen, Doug 81
funding 41, 51, 54, 58, 71, 86, 116–17, 123, 146, 150, 155–8, 160–1
gender 18, 63, 130–1, 168
Gibson, Joanne 137

Grand River Jazz Society 149
group work 53, 83, 169
Gross, Rebecca 69

Hayes, Nikki-Kate 168
healing 14, 22, 61, 63, 99, 113, 131
heritage 60-1, 149
heutagogy 44
hierarchy 98, 173
holistic 11, 19, 22, 86, 113–5, 167, 173
Howell, Gillian 28, 83, 168
hospitality 6, 31, 44, 48, 54, 59, 65, 95, 98, 167
humour 29, 35, 113, 122, 133, 169

identity 12, 36, 40, 61, 63, 65, 76, 86, 109, 135, 139–40, 166, 169; *see also* self- 9, 11, 91, 101, 105
imagination 65, 76, 96, 105, 152
immigration 92
inclusivity 54–5, 65, 69, 83, 131, 156, 167–8, 172
indigenous 61, 63, 94
individualism 96, 105
Industrial Revolution 97
inequalities 123
instruments 19, 30, 34, 36, 39, 40, 51, 53, 58, 74, 77, 83–5, 131, 154
interdisciplinary 22, 81, 94, 112, 124, 170
intergenerational 34, 36–9, 119–25, 166
intervention 3, 21, 32, 44, 59, 83, 109, 112, 117–18
investment 104, 121–2, 162

Jazz Room 149–51
justice 7, 91, 93–104, 130, 167; *see also* social 1, 6, 14, 80, 92, 168

Keil, Charlie 19, 21
Kierkegaard, Søren 11
Laurila, Kelly 60
leadership 10, 15, 27, 35, 38, 42, 50–5, 61, 64, 68, 73, 79, 83, 94, 131–5, 156–7, 162, 167; *see also* shared 96, 99, 103
learning: adult 43; informal 3, 26, 32–3, 42, 45, 166–8; life long 36
listening 10, 13, 15, 17, 32, 35, 43, 58, 75, 79, 81–6, 103, 122, 150, 169
Liverpool Philharmonic Orchestra 37
loneliness 39, 108
Ludolph, Debbie Lou 97, 168

McNaughton, Kathy 120-1
management 6, 18, 109, 118, 145, 150, 152, 162, 167; *see also* behaviour 52; *see also* breath 117; *see also* self- 33
Marginalization 59, 96
Mattern, Mark 92
Medical model 112, 117–18
mental health 57–8, 74, 110–12, 118, 124
mentoring 53, 75, 115, 117, 134
Monteiro, Dana 77–8
Mok, Annie On Nei 33
More Music 151–5
Moser, Pete 151
mindfulness 6, 91, 97, 167
Mullen, Phil 17, 27, 50
multigenerational 123
Munich Philharmonic Orchestra 156
museum 18, 139
music: aural 19, 30, 34, 98, 133; classical 12, 16, 22, 37, 72, 131, 149, 157; conducting 79, 120; conservatoire 2, 96, 156; folk 9, 13; improvisation 34–5, 53, 95, 139; melody 19, 20, 52; notation 12, 31, 79, 103, 133, 161; pentatonic 16; pitch 15, 82, 103; popular 122, 131; rock 38–9, 58, 131; technology 51, 74; therapy 2, 22, 112–13, 117, 124, 137, 172, 174
Music for Life 37–8
musicianship 7, 10, 18, 50, 52, 79, 95, 99, 130, 133, 158

musician/researcher 139–41
musicking 15, 54, 58, 86, 96, 103–4, 117–18, 124–5, 133, 168, 172–4; see also health 113

negotiation 3, 96, 167
networking 162, 169–70
neurological 109, 118
North Yorkshire Music Action Zone 71

open-door 48, 167
Opera North 73
ownership 53, 71, 74–6, 87, 122, 168

parents 51, 61, 69, 84, 161; see also grand 38
Parker, Palmer 48, 100
participation 4, 31, 37–9, 59, 85, 87, 91, 95–8, 101, 108, 124, 130–1; see also audience 134; see also group 29; see also intergenerational 34
partnerships 22, 58, 102, 140, 145, 150, 152, 155, 157, 159–60, 167–70
Paulston, Rolland 27
peace 1, 7, 92–5, 99
pedagogy 33, 54, 83, 103; see also critical 27, 134
personhood 36, 49, 65, 101
PhD 18, 60, 102, 137–8
physiotherapy 116
Piaget, Jean 26
play 15, 32, 98–9, 133, 155
political 2, 22, 91–3, 97, 104, 113, 140; see also socio- 96, 167
power 11, 27, 48, 64, 117, 133; see also of music 92–3, 114, 119, 130, 155, 159
Preece, Steve 147, 151, 155
prison 101–4, 135, 140–1
Procter, Simon 118
professionalism 39, 74
recording 13, 19, 30, 32, 43, 103, 131, 133

reflexivity 35, 39, 52, 109, 138, 169
refugees 28, 83
Reimer, Bennett 10
religion 18, 94, 168
research: autoethnography 139; see also ethnographic 11, 21, 130, 140; see also narrative inquiry 59, 136, 139; see also practice as 139
resilience 74, 76, 86, 169
resistance 92, 100, 141, 169
responsibility 21, 44, 68, 72, 74–5, 79, 97, 135, 137
revolution 93, 173
rhythm 18–16, 36, 39, 43, 57, 78–9, 83
Rousseau, Jean-Jacques 11–12
Rowan, Brent 34
Rowe, Nick 110–11

safe space 59
Sage Gateshead 38, 131–2
samba 13, 38, 76–80
Schafer, Murray 81–2
Schippers, Huib 80, 176n2
scholarship 1, 2, 6, 21–2, 95, 102, 124, 136–8, 151, 174
Schön, Donald 130
science 11, 69, 97, 100, 136, 174
self-reflexivity 109, 169
singing 15, 19, 29, 30, 32, 61–3, 70, 77, 85, 95, 99, 103, 113–17, 132, 154, 161; see also choral 103, 119–24; see also communal 61, 93, 109; see also gospel 38; see also revolution 93; see also rote 98
Sing Fires of Justice 93–5, 104
Silver Program 38
Small, Christopher 9, 103, 117–18, 125
society 11–12, 20, 27, 38, 45, 48, 54, 59, 65, 81, 92, 96, 97, 104, 112, 123, 145, 152, 162, 167, 173; see also musical 9; see also jazz 149–50
socio-economic 148, 152
solfege 103

songwriting 32, 39, 110, 118, 130, 132, 147, 154
soundLINCS 159–62
spiritual 13, 15, 31, 49, 61–3, 94, 99
Stige, Brynjulf 112
storytelling 59

Tallinn Song Festival 93
teaching 15, 17, 33, 36, 43–4, 50, 57–8, 61–4, 75, 77–9, 99, 113, 117, 132, 134, 173; *see also* peer 20
teenagers 28, 36, 119–21, 130, 168
therapeutic 112, 118–19
Titon, Jeff Todd 21
toolkit 30, 73–5, 168
training 2, 16, 38, 58, 75, 99, 113, 115, 117, 125n20, 132, 162, 164n15
transformation 3, 17, 22, 53–4, 131, 159, 168
trauma 29, 49, 51, 59, 61, 63, 130

ukulele 19, 131

value proposition 148–50, 163, 167
Van Buren, Kathleen 22
volunteer 16, 30, 36, 49, 85, 95, 98, 102, 119
vulnerability 81, 169
Vygotsky, Lev 26

welcome 31, 34, 48, 62–3, 68, 81, 87, 94, 97, 118, 120
wellbeing 28, 109, 123
World Health Organization 109
worship 20, 97, 98, 131

yoga 117
young people 18, 28, 37, 50–1, 71, 73, 78, 88n3, 101, 132, 159, 161
Yun, Gerard 14

Taylor & Francis eBooks

Helping you to choose the right eBooks for your Library

Add Routledge titles to your library's digital collection today. Taylor and Francis ebooks contains over 50,000 titles in the Humanities, Social Sciences, Behavioural Sciences, Built Environment and Law.

Choose from a range of subject packages or create your own!

Benefits for you
- Free MARC records
- COUNTER-compliant usage statistics
- Flexible purchase and pricing options
- All titles DRM-free.

Benefits for your user
- Off-site, anytime access via Athens or referring URL
- Print or copy pages or chapters
- Full content search
- Bookmark, highlight and annotate text
- Access to thousands of pages of quality research at the click of a button.

REQUEST YOUR FREE INSTITUTIONAL TRIAL TODAY — Free Trials Available. We offer free trials to qualifying academic, corporate and government customers.

eCollections – Choose from over 30 subject eCollections, including:

Archaeology	Language Learning
Architecture	Law
Asian Studies	Literature
Business & Management	Media & Communication
Classical Studies	Middle East Studies
Construction	Music
Creative & Media Arts	Philosophy
Criminology & Criminal Justice	Planning
Economics	Politics
Education	Psychology & Mental Health
Energy	Religion
Engineering	Security
English Language & Linguistics	Social Work
Environment & Sustainability	Sociology
Geography	Sport
Health Studies	Theatre & Performance
History	Tourism, Hospitality & Events

For more information, pricing enquiries or to order a free trial, please contact your local sales team:
www.tandfebooks.com/page/sales

 Routledge
Taylor & Francis Group

The home of Routledge books

www.tandfebooks.com